ARCHAEOLOGY OF EAST ASIA

Social Differentiation among Non-Elites in China's Central Plains, 1735-1530 BCE

A household archaeology perspective on the Erlitou site

XIANG LI

BAR INTERNATIONAL SERIES 3242

VOLUME 14

I0086030

BAR
PUBLISHING

Published in 2025 by
BAR Publishing, Oxford, UK

BAR International Series 3242

Archaeology of East Asia, 14
Social Differentiation among Non-Elites in China's Central Plains, 1735-1530 BCE

ISBN 978 1 4073 6368 4   paperback
ISBN 978 1 4073 6369 1   e-format

DOI https://doi.org/10.30861/9781407363684

A catalogue record for this book is available from the British Library

COVER IMAGE: *A group of Erlitou pottery vessels. Courtesy of Professor XU Hong.*

BAR
PUBLISHING

BAR titles are available from:

BAR Publishing
122 Banbury Rd, Oxford, OX2 7BP, UK
info@barpublishing.com
www.barpublishing.com

ARCHAEOLOGY OF EAST ASIA

A specialist sub-series in the BAR Series

Sub-Series Editor: Anke Hein (University of Oxford)

This sub-series provides a platform for data-rich studies on a variety of topics and materials from all over East Asia as well as conference proceedings reflecting the newest research insights and trends. The sub-series takes a regional approach to East Asia, encouraging projects that cross national borders, even into adjoining regions and/or areas usually overlooked in mainstream research. This includes all parts of China, Japan, Korea, Mongolia, the Russian Far East, the Tibetan Plateau as a whole, and the northern reaches of Southeast Asia. Especially encouraged are submissions proposing and conducting new approaches and methods in all aspects of archaeology including scientific techniques, spatial analysis, various digital methods, but also theory and model-based or traditional chronology-focused studies.

If you would like to submit a proposal for the *Archaeology of East Asia* sub-series, please contact editor@barpublishing.com.

Titles in the Archaeology of East Asia Sub-Series

Tangut Tombs
Art, rites, and afterlife beliefs in the Great Kingdom of the White and Lofty (1038–1227)
Diane Zhang-Goldberg
BAR International Series **3174** | 2024   Volume 12

Handbook of Plant and Insect Impressions in Archaeological Ceramics
Case studies from prehistoric Japan
Hiroki Obata
BAR International Series **3190** | 2024   Volume 13

Social Differentiation among Non-Elites in China's Central Plains, 1735–1530 BCE
A household archaeology perspective on the Erlitou site
Xiang Li
BAR International Series **3242** | 2025   Volume 14

Of Related Interest

Contacts Between the Shang and the South c. 1300–1045 BC
Resemblance and Resistance
Celine Y. Y. Lai
BAR International Series **2915** | 2019

Investigating Consumption: The Archaeology of Social Practice
Papers in honour of Penelope Allison on the occasion of her retirement
Edited by Daniël P. van Helden and Victoria Szafara
BAR International Series **3230** | 2025

The Technology of Large-Scale Zinc Production in Chongqing in Ming and Qing China
Wenli Zhou
BAR International Series **2835** | 2016

Development of Social Complexity in the Liaoxi Area, Northeast China
Xinwei Li
BAR International Series **1821** | 2008

Ancient Society and Metallurgy
A comparative study of Bronze Age societies in Central Eurasia and North China
Liangren Zhang
BAR International Series **2328** | 2012

Pottery Production, Settlement Patterns and Development of Social Complexity in the Yuanqu Basin, North-Central China
Xiangming Dai
BAR International Series **1502** | 2006

Emergent Social Complexity in the Yangshao Culture
Analyses of settlement patterns and faunal remains from Lingbau Western Henan China (c. 4900-3000 BC)
Xiaolin Ma
BAR International Series **1453** | 2005

For more information, or to purchase these titles, please visit **www.barpublishing.com**

Dedicated to my parents and my grandparents,
and in memory of Prof. Robert D. Drennan

Acknowledgements

Studying ancient societies through archaeological records is never an easy endeavor. I have been fortunate to receive tremendous help and support, which made this research both possible and rewarding. First and foremost, I wish to express my sincere gratitude to my committee members, Professor Robert D. Drennan, Professor Marc Bermann, Professor Bryan K. Hanks, and Professor Christian E. Peterson, for their unwavering support during my time at the University of Pittsburgh.

I am particularly privileged to have Professor Robert D. Drennan as my advisor. His consistent support and readiness to offer guidance have been invaluable. His courses on chiefdoms, regional settlement patterns, and data analysis provided me with rigorous training in scientific thinking about social complexity and quantitative methods in the study of early complex societies. Professor Marc Bermann and Professor Bryan K. Hanks taught exceptional courses on household archaeology and cross-cultural comparisons of ancient civilizations; their insightful perspectives inspired me to embark on this research. Professor Christian E. Peterson patiently instructed me on lithic characteristics, as well as methods for collecting and analyzing lithic materials. I am deeply grateful for their encouragement, astute observations on my arguments, and constructive suggestions for refining my work.

I also extend my heartfelt appreciation to the members of the Erlitou archaeological team, whose support and assistance were indispensable during my stay at the Erlitou archaeological station. Special thanks go to Professor Hong Xu 许宏 and Professor Haitao Zhao 赵海涛 from the Institute of Archaeology, Chinese Academy of Social Sciences (IA CASS). Without their generous permission and support, it would have been impossible for me to study the invaluable archaeological collections from the Erlitou site, and to complete this book. I am also grateful to Dr. Hongfei Li 李宏飞 of IA CASS, who shared valuable insights and ideas about China's Bronze Age. Additionally, I wish to thank Hongzhang Wang 王宏章, Congmiao Wang 王丛苗, Zhaopeng Guo 郭朝鹏, Chengguang Guo 郭晨光, Xiaozhen Guo 郭晓真, and Buyun Wang 王步云 for their expert guidance on identifying Erlitou ceramics. Their professional expertise and warm hospitality alleviated many challenges during my laboratory work, making me feel at home at the Erlitou archaeological station during the summer of 2021.

I am thankful to my fellow graduate students and friends in the Department of Anthropology at the University of Pittsburgh: Chuenyan Ng 吴传仁, Peiyu Chen 陈佩瑜, Chi Zhang 张驰, Yan Cai 蔡彦, Weiyu Ran 冉炜煜, Chao Zhao 赵潮, Hsi-Wen Chen 陈玺文, Yijia Qiu 邱益嘉, John Walden, Ryan Smith, Gligor Dakovic, Amanda Suarez Calderon, Courtney Besaw, Peter Daniel Ellis, Emma Messinger, Jaehoon Bae, Jung Eun Kwon, and others. Their help and companionship made my graduate experience in Pittsburgh truly wonderful.

I would also like to acknowledge the Department of Anthropology and the Asian Studies Center at the University of Pittsburgh for providing financial support for my graduate studies and research.

I also want to extend my thanks to the editors at BAR Publishing. Dan Etches Jones and his colleagues have put so much dedicated effort into this book. Without them, this book would never have come into being.

Last but not least, I wish to express my deepest gratitude to my family. My parents and grandparents have offered me unwavering support and unconditional love throughout my academic journey. Their tolerance and encouragement enabled me to overcome countless difficulties along the way.

Contents

List of Figures

List of Tables

Introduction

1.1. The Erlitou State

Prior to the second millennium BC, the Longshan period (3000–2000 BC) in the Yellow River Valley was marked by intense competitive interactions. As Liu and Chen (2012) argue, a multitude of regional polities emerged as chiefdom-level early complex societies, engaging in violent competition, evidenced by the proliferation of walled settlements. By the first half of the second millennium BC, during the Erlitou period (1735–1530 BC) in the Central Plains, this landscape of warring factions vying for military and economic dominance began to decline. The lowland states of the late Longshan period (2400–1900 BC) ultimately collapsed (Jaang 2023), giving way to a much larger-scale polity centered at the Erlitou site in the Yiluo Basin, which reorganized the political map of northern China (Xu 2012). In stark contrast to the fortified political centers of the Longshan period, the Erlitou site functioned as an unfortified primary capital. Xu (2018) posits that this absence of fortifications stemmed from reduced competition, as the number of peer polities dwindled, while defensive systems in peripheral regions secured both the unfortified Erlitou core and its second-tier centers within the Yiluo Basin. The Erlitou polity is widely regarded as marking the onset of China's Bronze Age and is either identified as the first territorial state (Xu 2009, 2014, 2022; Lee 2004; Liu and Chen 2003, 2012) or as a society approaching statehood (Shelach-Lavi 2015; Shelach and Jaffe 2014).

Archaeological surveys indicate that two significant population surges occurred in the Luoyang Basin, leading to a notable concentration of inhabitants in the region (Liu, Chen, Lee, Wright, and Rosen 2004; Zhongguo 2005). The first population boom took place during the Yangshao period: according to Qiao's (2010) estimates, the population of the Yiluo Valley grew from 131 in the Peiligang period to 4,447 by the end of the Yangshao period. The second population surge occurred during the Erlitou period. Wang (2006) notes that the area corresponding to present-day western Henan, centered on the Luoyang Basin and along the western piedmont of the Songshan Mountains, saw a marked increase in both the number and size of settlements during this time. In contrast, the large-scale settlements that had thrived east of the Songshan Mountains during the Longshan period were nearly abandoned, with survey and excavation data confirming a significant decline in settlement activity in that region (Jaang 2023). Population estimates for the Yiluo Valley during the Erlitou period reach as high as 7,011 (Qiao 2010). Among the newly emerging sites, the Erlitou site expanded dramatically to 540 hectares

(Zhongguo 2005). Urbanization began in phase II and peaked in phase III, with population estimates ranging from 18,000 to 30,000 (Liu and Chen 2003).

Several archaeologists have argued that the Erlitou polity developed a complex four-tier settlement hierarchy (Liu, Chen, Lee, Wright, and Rosen 2004; Lee 2004; Zhongguo 2019; Zhongguo and Zhongaomei 2019). Secondary centers began to emerge east of the Songshan Mountains after phase II (Jaang 2023). Correlating these settlement patterns with political organization, Lee (2004) suggests that the Erlitou state established territorial control, as evidenced by its secondary and tertiary centers, which likely functioned to regulate the tribute economy. In summary, despite the absence of walled towns in the survey area during the preceding Longshan period, population became strongly concentrated in the Luoyang Basin during the Erlitou period.

Chang (1983) argues that power was initially rooted in a monopoly over access to the spiritual realm and ancestral sacrifice. To maintain exclusive control over ritual practices, apical elites began to seek dominion over valuable and exotic resources, such as metals and jade, which were crafted into specialized ritual paraphernalia (Chang 1983; Liu 2003; Liu and Chen 2012). Recent findings at Erlitou reveal that scapulae from cattle, sheep, pigs, and deer were commonly used in divination rituals (Zhongguo 2019), though some scholars contend that neither this practice nor the techniques of bone preparation originated at Erlitou (Shelach-Lavi 2015: 192). Bronze vessels employed in ancestral sacrifice were produced in a workshop located near the palatial enclosure; this proximity has led many scholars to suggest that the industry was controlled by the state or elite (Campbell 2014; Liu 2003). Primary deposits of ritual sacrificial remains, including pairs of ground-level circular altars and subterranean rectangular ritual structures, are exceptionally abundant within and to the north of the palatial enclosure (Zhongguo 2003, 2019). Collectively, these findings indicate that sacrificial and ritual activities were restricted to the elite.

Once aggrandizers had secured power and authority, they displayed their social status through the exclusive consumption and distribution of prestige and ritual goods. Since the late Neolithic period, jade artifacts have been used to communicate with the supernatural realm (Liu 2003). The Erlitou polity not only continued the use of jade artifacts but also expanded the assemblage of prestige and ritual goods to include bronze and pottery vessels. These prestige and ritual artifacts circulated among Erlitou's elites, serving as markers of identity, social status, and power (Chen 2008; Hao 2008; Li, Z. 2008). Elite individuals were also interred with certain prestige goods upon their death, and Zhipeng Li has proposed a four-tier burial hierarchy (2008; Zhongguo 2019). White pottery ritual vessels are regarded as secondary prestige goods, circulating among lesser regional elites. This circulation integrated these elites into the Erlitou polity and helped construct extensive power networks (Liu 2003; Nishie and Kuji 2006; Tokudome 2015), reflecting the political influence of the Erlitou state during the late Erlitou period. Liu and Chen (2012) suggest that elites pursued military expansion to guarantee access to copper, salt, and other resources necessary for maintaining authority and political connections. Li (2018) argues that the Erlitou political network was built upon the transportation, exchange, and consumption of valuable natural resources, as well as the ritual material culture dependent on such resources. While archaeologists concur that Erlitou was a large territorial state, there remains significant debate regarding the extent of its territory.

A walled enclosure containing an array of large-scale rammed-earth structures, dating to the Erlitou period, is unique to the Erlitou site. The wall encircled an area of 11 hectares within the city (Xu 2009, 2022). The energy cost of construction, as indicated by the scale and building techniques, has led to the claim that these structures were early palaces (Zhongguo 2003, 2019; Xu 2009, 2022; Liu and Chen 2012). Most of the palaces consisted of walls and corridors on four sides, a principal building, and a courtyard in front of the principal building. All the palaces were built on rammed-earth platforms. To date, 12 palatial structures have been identified inside the major enclosure, forming two complexes (Zhongguo 1999, 2014, 2019). Although these rammed-earth structures have been referred to as palaces, their functions and nature remain debated. Zou (1980) and Tu (1987) have argued that they served not only as residences for Erlitou rulers but also as ancestral temples, given the close relationship between luxury tombs, sacrificial remains, and the large-scale rammed-earth structures. Du proposes that Palace No. 1 was one of the ruler's administrative structures (Du 2005), Palace No. 2 was an ancestral temple (Du 2007a), and Palace No. 4 was a ritual/ceremonial structure (Du 2007b).

Workshops specializing in bone-tool making, bronze casting, and turquoise processing have been discovered at Erlitou (Zhongguo 2019). Two of these are interpreted as state/elite-controlled bone tool workshops producing personal ornaments (hairpins) and weapons (arrowheads); one is located within the palatial enclosure, and the other lies adjacent to the sacrificial area north of the palatial enclosure (Chen and Li 2016). South of the palatial enclosure, another walled area contains turquoise-processing and bronze-casting workshops. The bronze-casting workshop, covering an area of 1.5 to 2 hectares, is situated in the southern part of this enclosed workshop complex. Multiple traces of bronze casting have been identified, including pottery molds, copper slag, crucibles, and kilns for baking molds (Zhongguo 2003, 2019). In contrast to contemporaneous polities, the Erlitou polity

was the first to employ the piece-mold technique for casting bronze vessels. Craftsmen began using multiple types of alloys in bronze production, though they were still experimenting with optimal formulas (Zhongguo 2014). The turquoise-processing workshop is located north of the bronze foundry, where large quantities of raw turquoises, semi-finished artifacts, waste materials, and processing tools were uncovered. The inlay technique was already in use for turquoise processing at this site (Chen, F. 2006). Erlitou obtained copper ore and raw turquoise from various sources (Zhongguo 2019). Liu and Chen (2012) argue that Erlitou expanded westward and southward to secure supplies of valuable metals. Consequently, the workshop complex and the long-distance transportation of raw materials are regarded as a state/elite-sponsored industry (Xu 2009, 2022; Liu and Chen 2012; Zhongguo 2019).

1.2. Social Hierarchy in the Bronze Age of China

Clans, lineages, and families were important nodes in ancient Chinese polities during the Bronze Age (Chang 1983; Lu and Yan 2005). Numerous studies have revealed that the family-lineage system made significant contributions to the administration and governance of both the Shang and Western Zhou states (Zhu 2004; Li, F. 2008, 2013, 2022). Feng Li (2008, 2013, 2022) referred to the Western Zhou state as a "delegated kin-ordered settlement state," where regional delegates were either heads of the Western Zhou royal lineage or leaders from the lineages of royal marriage partners. The Western Zhou state was organized through the kinship structure of lineages, which underpinned political power (Li, F. 2008). The Shang state, by contrast, has been described as an aggregation of self-governing communities sharing a common cultural background (Li, F. 2008, 2013, 2022). Both the Shang royal families and local groups were organized according to the family-lineage system, with elites and non-elites alike bound by blood lineage and united in their hope of receiving blessings from their ancestors (Allan 1991; Reinhart 2015). Settlement studies at Yinxu, Anyang, have demonstrated that multiple families or lineages occupied the site during the Shang period. Residential and mortuary data from the vicinity of the palace-temple complexes at Yinxu suggest these groups likely formed family-based occupational neighborhoods (Zheng 1995; Tang 1998, 2004; Campbell 2018; Wang and Jing 2020).

Mortuary data from Yinxu also reveal social hierarchies within families and lineages: elites, regardless of their prominence, were likely the heads of lineages at various levels, while non-elites within each family or lineage exhibited differentiation across multiple dimensions (Zhu 2004). Thus, the internal social differentiation within lineages during the Shang and Western Zhou periods probably generated elites in the form of lineage heads at different levels and heads of lineage sub-branches. Non-elite families, which constituted the majority of each lineage, also displayed differentiation in various aspects. The family-lineage system and political power were deeply intertwined (Lu and Yan 2005; Zhu 2004; Li, F. 2008, 2013, 2022; Campbell 2018).

Research since 2006 has identified residential blocks that formed a "#" shaped urban plan at Erlitou, surrounding the palatial enclosure. These residential blocks, like the palatial and workshop enclosures, were bounded by walls. Zhao (2020) argues that these new findings on the settlement layout suggest each enclosed residential block at Erlitou was likely occupied by a single family or lineage.

Scholars have made numerous attempts to reconstruct the social structure of Erlitou, drawing on evidence ranging from mortuary practices to residential remains. These studies indicate that the Erlitou state featured multiple social strata. Based on burial goods and tomb sizes, Zhipeng Li (2008) identifies four tiers within the mortuary system, which he interprets as corresponding to middle and lower elites, non-elites, and human sacrifices. Meanwhile, other archaeologists (Xu 2009, 2022; Zhongguo 2019) have reconstructed the social structure using residential evidence, positing that groups of different social statuses inhabited distinct types of buildings. According to this framework, kings and their consorts occupied the large-scale rammed-earth structures within the palatial enclosure; middle and lower elites resided in medium-sized and small on-the-ground rammed-earth structures outside the palatial enclosure; and non-elites lived exclusively in semi-subterranean structures.

Non-elites, or commoners, constitute a large portion of society. Compared to the elaborate lifestyles of elites, archaeologists have often viewed non-elites as "impoverished," "unempowered," and "anonymous" (Lohse and Valdez 2004). Non-elites are also frequently perceived as a homogeneous group (Marcus 2004). Due to this "top-down" perspective, non-elites have received little attention. However, non-elites are of great significance. In complex societies, non-elites were the primary adapters to their social environment and the main producers of food and many other goods (Lohse and Valdez 2004). The operation and maintenance of complex societies depend on the fulfillment of social duties and the support of non-elites. After investigating pottery production at the central sites of Donguan 东关 and Nanguan 南关 in the Yuanqu Basin, north-central China, Dai (2006, 2010) argues that during the Longshan period and Erligang phase, specialized non-elite potters produced daily ceramic vessels for local elites, other residents, and possibly for long-distance exchange. Some of this production likely took place in household-based workshops. Non-elites also carried out most subsistence production, supporting the daily needs of prestigious and ritual elites. Ran (2022) found that rural non-elite households in the Hongshan core zone were more engaged in food production than other Hongshan communities, contributing to feeding the ritual-focused residents (possibly ritual elites) around the Niuheliang 牛河梁 ceremonial structures.

Meanwhile, social class is fluid, though it remains relatively stable and predefined for the most part. Class

also operates at multiple levels, shaped by a variety of social relations. As such, individuals can negotiate their identities within a society (Blackmore 2016). For instance, a royal court might consist of a king surrounded by courtiers, nobles, and individuals of lower rank (Inomata and Houston 2001). These low-ranking court members may acquire influence and access to privileges within administrative systems and political organizations. Non-elites are also heterogeneous. Examining the differentiation among non-elites sheds light on how they fit into complex social networks.

However, despite the recognition of complex social differentiation within the Erlitou state in numerous studies, most research remains focused on the elites, particularly the ruling class. These studies investigate and discuss the social, political, and economic lives of elites, depicting their luxurious and elaborate lifestyles as well as how they maintained and exercised political power (e.g., Liu 2003; Nishie and Kuji 2006; Chen 2008; Shelach-Lavi 2015; Tokudome 2015; Xu 2012, 2014, 2016a, 2016b). In contrast, our understanding of Erlitou's non-elites remains limited. There is much to explore regarding how non-elites lived within the state, the nature of their interactions with one another, and their contributions to the Erlitou community. This study focuses on social differentiation to assess the extent of heterogeneity among non-elite residents in the Erlitou state.

1.3. Dimensions of Social Differentiation

This study examines a sample of probable bottom-level household units, or non-elite households, from three locations, focusing on differentiation within this group across several distinct dimensions: wealth differentiation, prestige differentiation, ritual differentiation, and productive differentiation (Drennan and Peterson 2012). Archaeological evidence for such inter-household differentiation is derived from artifact assemblages recovered in association with different household units (Peterson, Drennan, and Bartel 2016).

Wealth differentiation refers to the varying accumulation of material wealth across different households (Drennan and Peterson 2012). High-value utilitarian craft items, personal adornments made from diverse materials, and non-utilitarian wealth items typically serve as reliable indicators of wealth. Additionally, the volume of stored goods can sometimes function as an indicator of wealth.

Prestige differentiation pertains to the distribution of respect within society (Drennan and Peterson 2012). While wealth accumulation and distinguished ritual status may contribute to prestige differentiation in some polities, this is not universally the case. Feasting often serves as a means to gain such respect, thereby enhancing one's prestige. A larger quantity of serving vessels (or other evidence of ceremonial feasting) is typically indicative of higher prestige. In Bronze Age China, individuals of greater prestige tended to possess more drinking vessels and high-quality serving vessels, which were made from pottery and occasionally from metals.

Ritual differentiation refers to disparities in access to the supernatural realm within human societies, as well as unequal access to ritual or ceremonial paraphernalia, objects used in religious activities that embody and signal such differentiation. Furthermore, proximity to sites of ritual activity may also play a role in shaping ritual differentiation.

Productive differentiation often emerges among households and differs significantly from elite-oriented workshops that produce luxury or specialized goods. It typically operates within the realm of the utilitarian economy, focusing on mundane goods for daily use. Such utilitarian economic activities encompass subsistence production, the crafting of tools from wood, bone, or stone, and the manufacturing of utilitarian items like ordinary pottery, basketry, and textiles. Productive differentiation involves variations in the balance of productive activities across households, which in turn leads to the exchange of distinct products and fosters interdependence among them (Drennan and Peterson 2012). Archaeological indicators of this type of productive differentiation include production debris, with lithic implements being a particularly notable example.

1.4. Delineating the Household Units that Compose the Household Sample

The household has emerged as a key topic in Chinese archaeology for understanding prehistoric societies in ancient China. Scholars have approached this theme from diverse angles: some investigate building materials and floor areas of houses to identify differences in social status (Underhill 1994); others estimate population size based on the number and dimensions of residential structures at a site to explore community adaptive strategies (Shelach 2006; Shelach et al. 2011); still others analyze household artifact assemblages to determine the economic activities practiced by households and, further, to unravel social differentiation within communities (Liu 2004; Peterson & Shelach 2010, 2012; Drennan et al. 2017; Underhill et al. 2021; Ran 2022). By categorizing wall construction materials into adobe, wattle-and-daub, mud-and-straw, and earth, Underhill (1994) argues that status differentiation, particularly in household wealth, became increasingly prevalent along the Yellow River during the Longshan period, as reflected in housing structures. Such differentiation in housing was more pronounced in major centers than in minor ones. After estimating the population size of Zhaobaogou 赵宝沟 by examining residential floor areas and analyzing household assemblages within structures, Shelach (2006) found that the average house size among the Zhaobaogou people was larger than that of the Yangshao people at Jiangzhai 姜寨. This difference likely stemmed from the fact that Zhaobaogou residents conducted household activities indoors, whereas Yangshao communities at Jiangzhai carried out such

activities outdoors. These indoor practices suggest that the Zhaobaogou people were more self-sufficient and less interdependent compared to the more communal orientation observed at Jiangzhai (Shelach 2006). Liu (2004) analyzed artifact quantities and potential gender-related associations in 19 well-preserved houses from Jiangzhai, Dahecun 大河村, Huanglianshu 黄楝树, Yuchisi 尉迟寺, and Yinjiacheng 尹家城. She argues that the increasing quantity of household material possessions throughout the Neolithic period indicates growing social complexity, accompanied by a more pronounced gender-based division of labor. Additionally, Liu (2004) discusses the role of ritual feasting in fostering cooperation within a household group at Kangjia 康家, which consisted of an extended family occupying 33 superimposed houses. Underhill and colleagues (2021) explored cooperation in tool production and lithic raw material acquisition among households at the Liangchengzhen 两城镇 site.

However, most previous research has focused on Neolithic communities. While Shelach and colleagues (2011) discuss the function of fortifications, as well as the integration and defense strategies of local populations at Sanzuodian during China's Bronze Age, with population estimates based on the number and size of dwellings, further work is still needed to understand the lives of non-elites and the role of non-elite households within local communities during China's early Bronze Age. Existing studies have explored non-elites and the development of social complexity through the lens of households along the Yellow River during China's Neolithic period. Yet, comparable efforts are required to examine non-elites through household analysis in the Yellow River region during China's Bronze Age, shedding light on how non-elites lived and contributed to communities within ancient states.

Jaang (2023) seeks to explore social networks among basic units within the Erlitou state through a residence-based analysis. She acknowledges that "it would be ideal to carry out a comparative analysis of household-level rituals between residential spaces and the mortuary realm" (Jaang 2023: 236) to understand the mechanisms underlying Erlitou's sociopolitical order. However, due to the difficulty of identifying household units, her analysis ultimately focuses on funerary data.

House structures, associated features, and artifact assemblages in household garbage all reflect the status and daily lives of residents, making them valuable evidence for studying social differentiation. This research examines a sample of household units at Erlitou, some with both structural and artifact evidence, and others with only artifact evidence. The overall objective of this study is to reconstruct the social differentiation within and among bottom-level groups, or non-elites, at Erlitou using this sample of households.

The data derive from excavations conducted at the Erlitou site during the 1999–2006 seasons by the Erlitou

Archaeological Team of the Institute of Archaeology, Chinese Academy of Social Sciences (Zhongguo 2014). A total of 8,963.89 square meters were excavated during this period, in addition to a full-scale systematic coring survey. Most excavations were concentrated within the palatial enclosure and the northern part of the workshop enclosure, with supplementary work carried out at the eastern end of the site (Figure 1.1). This study samples household data from these three locations, with the following coding system: household samples in or near the palatial enclosure are labeled "G"; those in or near the workshop enclosure are labeled "W"; and those from the eastern end of the site are labeled "D".

According to the published report *Erlitou: 1999-2006* (Zhongguo 2014), 21 small housing structures have been discovered. These structures date from the Erlitou period through to the Erligang period, a time when the Erlitou state was defeated and supplanted by the Erligang state (Zhongguo 2014, 2019). While poor preservation makes it difficult to discern the floorplans of these small houses, some can still be identified as either on-the-ground or semi-subterranean structures (Xu 2009, 2022; Zhongguo 2014, 2019). Of the 21 small houses, 11 were found within the palatial enclosure, 6 in the workshop enclosure, and 4 at the eastern end of the site.

Small housing structures include on-the-ground houses and semi-subterranean houses. Such housing forms have existed in the Yellow River valley since the Neolithic period. Some small on-the-ground houses may have rammed-earth footings, while others may be built directly on the ground (Yang 2008; Li 2007). Evidence from the Erlitou site indicates that this type of housing structure could feature wooden wall frameworks plastered with mud (Figure 1.2). Semi-subterranean housing structures consist of a pit with a rammed and baked living floor, and a roof covered with mud and straw (Yang 2008). Both round and square semi-subterranean housing structures have been found at the Erlitou site (Figure 1.3).

However, not all small houses discovered during the 1999–2006 excavations will be included in this study. Among the eleven small houses in the palatial enclosure, F4, F5, F13, F14, F16, and F17 are excluded. F5 is likely part of the No. 3 large-scale rammed-earth structure, while F13, F16, and F17 are possibly components of the No. 6 rammed-earth structure. F4 and F14 are omitted due to the absence of artifact assemblage data within the structures and the lack of adjacent contemporary ash or storage pits. Of the six small houses in the workshop enclosure, F8, F12, and F15 are excluded. F12 and F15 were damaged by each other, with no assemblage data from their

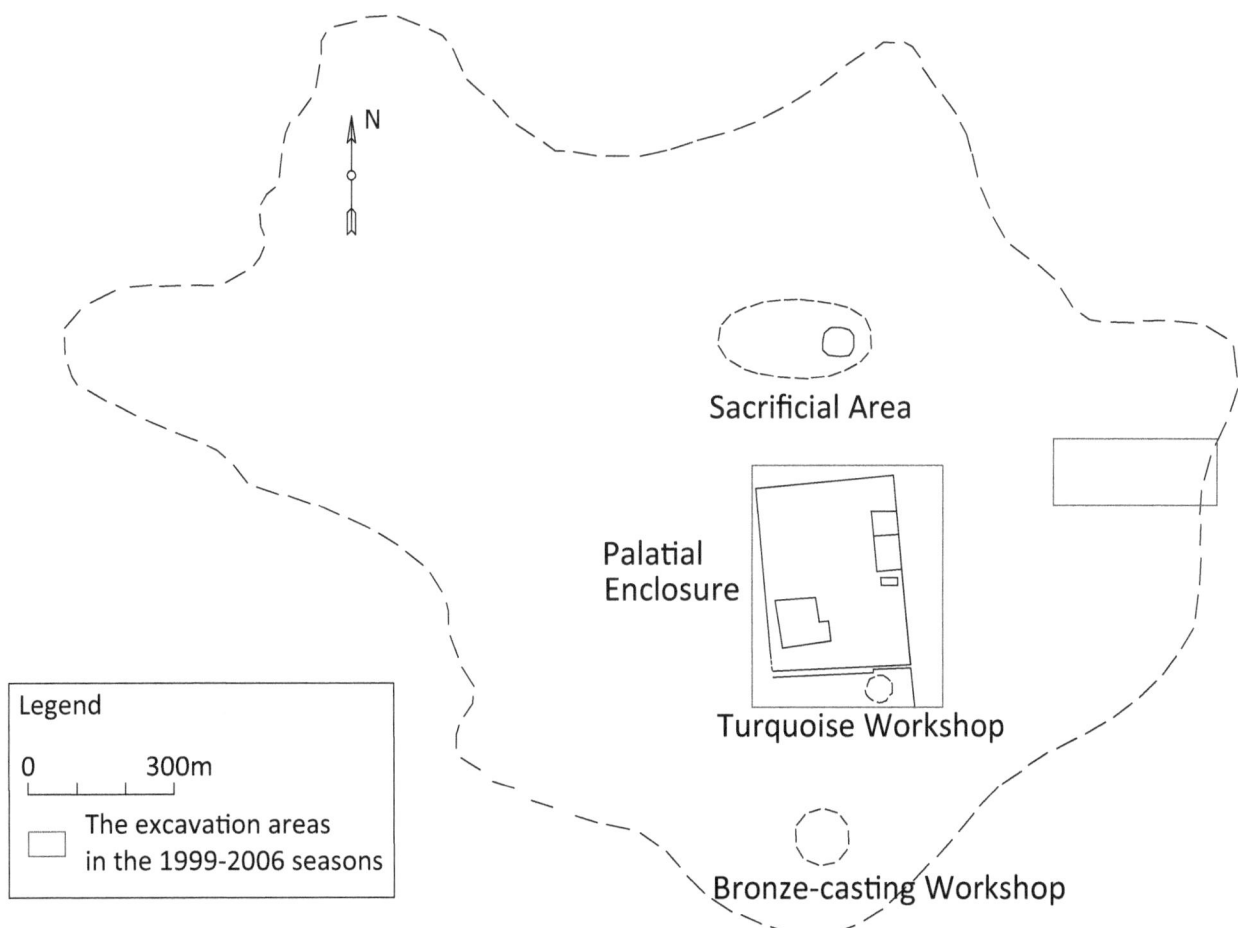

Figure 1.1. Plan of the Erlitou site and the excavation in the 1999-2006 seasons (redrawn from *Zhongguo* 2014, Figure 1-1-3-3, pp 7).

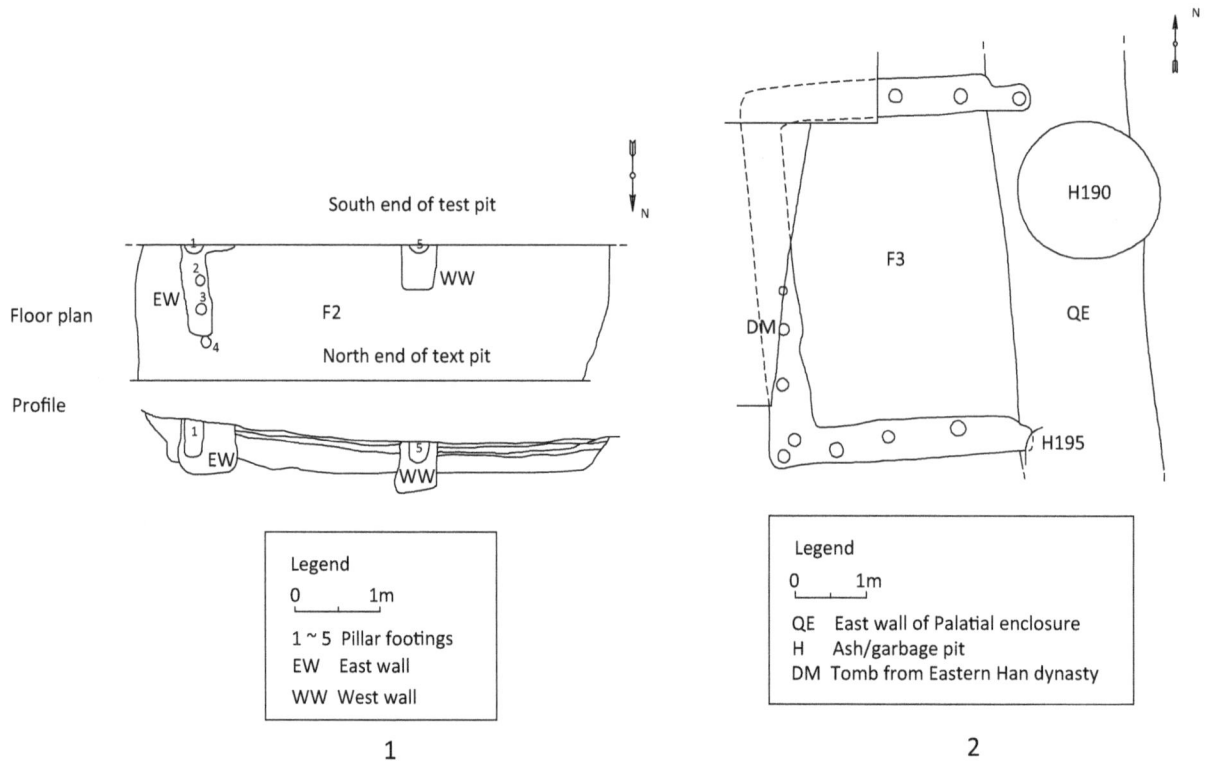

Figure 1.2. Examples of Erlitou small on-the-ground housing structures. (1. modified from *Zhongguo 2014*, Figure 6-4-1-2-1, pp 704; 2. modified from *Zhongguo 2014*, Figure 6-4-1-3-1, pp 706).

occupational period and no associated contemporary ash or storage pits. F8, despite yielding some practical tools, is also excluded from statistical analysis because no ceramic data from its occupational period were available, nor were there any surrounding contemporary ash pits. Regarding the four houses at the eastern end of the site, F1 and F3 are excluded due to the absence of adjacent contemporary ash pits and assemblage data. Thus, this study focuses on 10 household contexts with confirmed structural information from the published report (dating from Erlitou Phase II to the Late Erligang period). Among these, 5 are located within or in close proximity to the palatial enclosure, 3 in the workshop enclosure, and 2 at the eastern end of the site. Of these 10 household units: G1/F2 (Figure 1.2:1), G14/F10, G16/F3 (Figure 1.2:2), W3/F9, and D5/F4 are on-the-ground housing structures; G18/F1 (Figure 1.3:2) and W4/F11 (Figure 1.3:3) are semi-subterranean housing structures; and the remaining 3 (G9/F6, W1/F7, and D2/F2), though identified with housing structures, cannot be definitively classified by form due to the lack of distinguishing features.

A household encompasses not only a house structure but also associated surrounding ash or garbage pits. The household artifact assemblage consists of all artifacts recovered from a house structure and its associated pit features. For instance, Peterson and Shelach (2012) included artifacts from contemporaneous pit features located near residential structures. Winter (1976) argued that storage pits within 10 meters of one side of a house were associated with that house. More recently, a systematic survey in the Upper Daling region found that

Hongshan households occupied an area with a maximum length of 20 meters (Peterson, Lu, Drennan, and Zhu 2017). In this study, artifacts from trash pits within a roughly 10-meter radius around house structures at the Erlitou site are included. The 10 household units with housing structures examined here each have several associated ash or garbage pits.

This study also includes 24 household clusters represented solely by ash pits, storage pits, and their associated artifacts. Here, a cluster of ash or garbage pits within a roughly 10-meter radius is treated as a chain representing a single household unit. This sample of households, defined only by ash or garbage pits, consists of 17 clusters in or near the palatial enclosure, 4 in or near the workshop enclosure, and 3 at the eastern end of the site. Core-drilling surveys and excavations indicate the presence of a series of borrow pits that functioned as the eastern boundary (Zhongguo 2014; Xu et al. 2004). These borrow pits are thought to have later been repurposed as garbage pits by surrounding households.

Table 1.1 presents the floor sizes of the relatively well-preserved houses discovered at Erlitou to date. According to Shelach (2006), the residential density at the Zhaobaogou site in northeastern China was 6 m² per person. However, a slightly higher residential density of 4 m² per person appears more reasonable for central China (Peterson & Shelach 2012). Whether using 4 m² per person or 6 m² per person as a benchmark, the small housing structures at Erlitou likely housed nuclear families, similar to household units in Neolithic China.

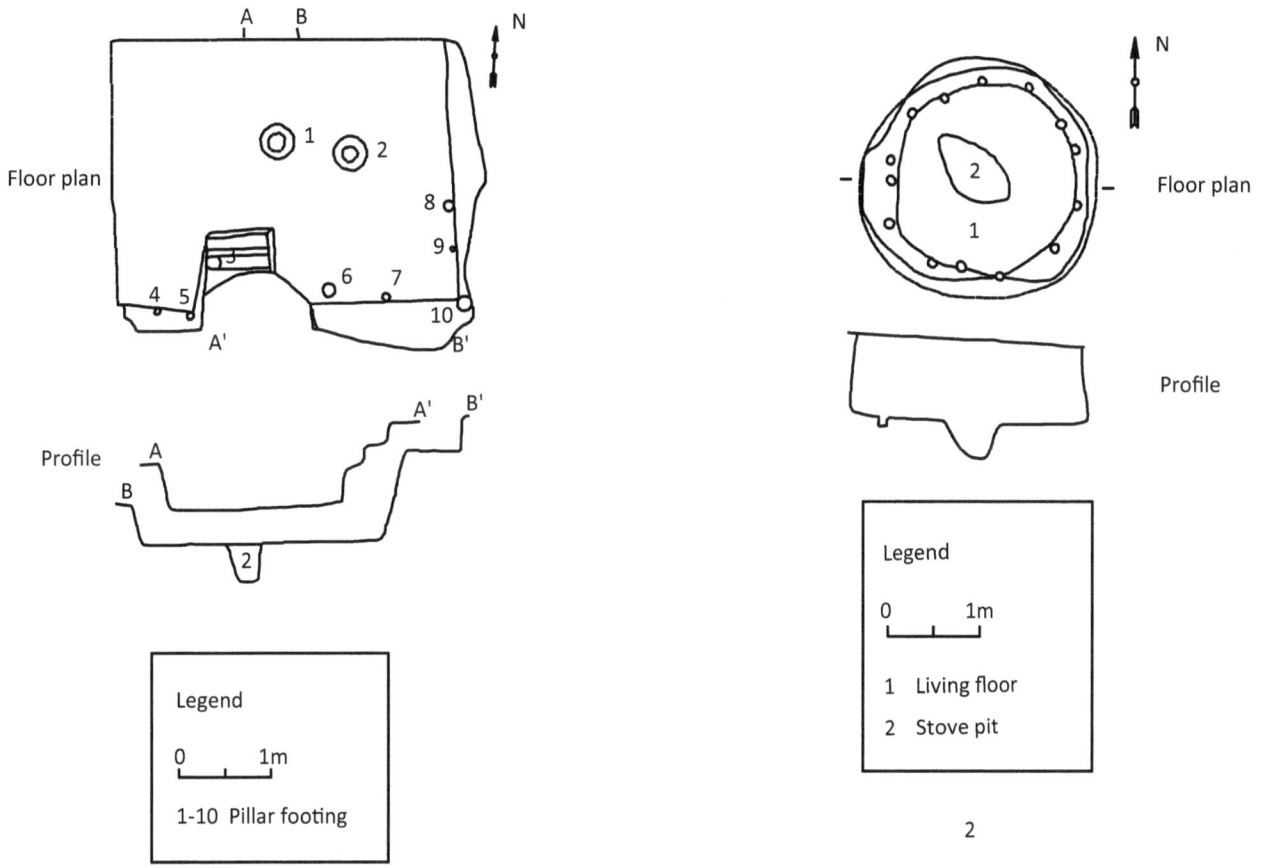

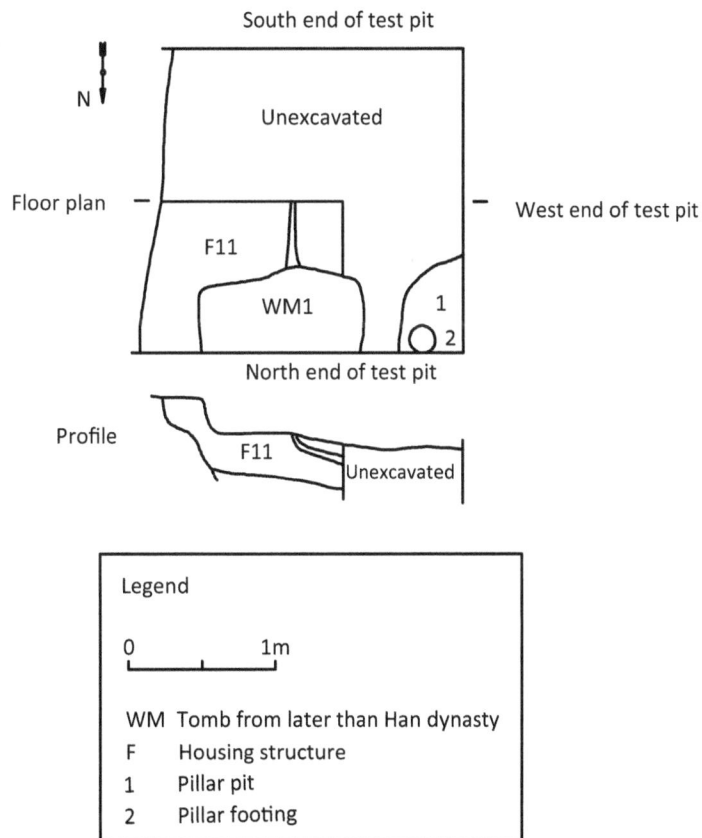

Figure 1.3. Examples of Erlitou semi-subterranean housing structures. (1. modified from *Zhongguo 1999*, Figure 41, pp 77; 2. modified from *Zhongguo 2014*, Figure 6-4-1-1-1, pp 702; 3. modified from *Zhongguo 2014*, Figure 5-4-2-4-1, pp 344).

Table 1.1. Relatively well-preserved small houses in the Erlitou site.

Code	Area (m²)	4 m² / person	6 m² / person	References
VIIIF1	9.9640	2.4910	1.6607	*Zhongguo 1999*, pp. 75
IVF1	8.9900	2.2475	1.4983	*Zhongguo 1999*, pp. 59
IIIF2[1]	39.7700	9.9425	6.6283	*Zhongguo 1999*, pp. 160–161
IIIF1	34.0000	8.5000	5.6667	*Zhongguo 1999*, pp. 162
80YLVIF1	6.2350	1.5588	1.0392	*Zhongguo 1983*
82秋YLIXF1[2]	Lower: 13.2000	3.3000	2.2000	*Zhongguo 1985*
	Upper: 11.9000	2.9750	1.9833	
2003IIIF4[3]	38.6750	9.6688	6.4458	*Zhongguo 2014*, vol. 1, pp. 213–215; vol. 5, pp. 56
2002VF1	4.9063	1.2266	0.8177	*Zhongguo 2014*, vol. 2, pp. 701–703; vol. 5, pp. 56
2003VF3	13.0000	3.2500	2.1667	*Zhongguo 2014*, vol. 2, pp. 705–707; vol. 5, pp. 56
2004VF4[4]	4.1527	1.0382	0.6921	*Zhongguo 2014*, vol. 2, pp. 707; vol. 5, pp. 56

*1. IIIF2 is coded for a two-roomed house although the western room is still separated by 1.4 m from the eastern room. The eastern room is damaged. The area listed in Table 1.1 is only for the western room.

2. 82秋YLIXF1 is coded for two housing structures, one of which is superimposed by the other. The lower one is a rectangular-shaped semi-subterranean structure, and the upper one is an on-the-ground structure built after filling and leveling up the lower one.

3. 2003IIIF4 was only exposed the eastern part during the 2003 excavation. The area is only the floor area exposed.

4. 2004VF4 is a round-shaped semi-subterranean structure only exposed the northern half during the excavation. The area is estimated by the bottom diameter.

Thus, this study will analyze artifacts from a sample of 34 nuclear-family households (5 in small on-the-ground structures, 2 in semi-subterranean structures, and 27 in structures of indeterminate type) to reveal social differentiation both within and among these households. This analysis aims to illuminate the daily lives of bottom-level groups or non-elites across the three locations represented by the sample during the Erlitou state period, as well as to investigate potential changes immediately following the defeat of the Erlitou state. The sampled household assemblages include ceramic sherds, productive tools and debris made of stone, bone, and other materials, and other artifacts such as decorative items and oracle bones (Table 1.2).

This sample of 34 household units is coded into three groups. Twenty-two household units (coded as "G1/F2 ~ G22") are located in or near the palatial enclosure (Figures 1.4–1.5): 21 are inside the enclosure, and 1 (G1/F2) is close to the outside of the enclosure's east wall. Seven household units (coded as "W1/F7 ~ W7") are in or near the workshop enclosure (Figure 1.6): 6 are inside the enclosure, and 1 (W7) is close to the outside of the enclosure's north wall. Five household units are situated at the eastern end of the site (coded as "D1 ~ D5/F4") (Figure 1.7).

1.5. Research Questions

This study broadly examines how a sample of 34 household units interacted within and contributed to the social network of Erlitou. Given that their household assemblages are less elaborate than those presumably belonging to elites, and that some occupied small houses (small on-the-ground structures and semi-subterranean structures), these households likely represented bottom-level social members from each of the three areas of the Erlitou site: the palatial enclosure, the workshop enclosure, and the eastern end. Is it accurate to consider them members of different classes? If they did belong to different classes, what specific classes were these? What forms of differentiation existed within and among household units from the three locations, and how pronounced was this differentiation? Alternatively, did they all belong to the same class—i.e., non-elites? If they were all non-elites, what types of differentiation existed among non-elites across the three locations, and how significant was it? To address these questions, this study investigates the following issues.

1) How much wealth differentiation is detectable among the households in this sample?

Wealth differentiation among the household units in this sample is evaluated based on resource storage, food preparation capacity, and possession of ceramics decorated with complex incised or stamped patterns, as well as personal ornaments. A wealthier household would possess more such correlated artifacts. Given that sample sizes vary significantly across different households for various reasons, proportions, rather than actual counts, of storage vessel sherds, decorated sherds, and personal decorative artifacts will be used. Assessing wealth

Table 1.2. Artifact assemblages from the 34 household units.

Household unit	Housing structures and garbage pits	sherds	Lithic artifacts	Bone artifacts	Antler artifacts	Tooth artifacts	Shell artifacts	Bronze artifacts	Turquoise artifacts	Non-vessel pottery artifacts	Oracle bone	Raw material - rock	Raw material - bone	Raw material - antler	Raw material - shell	copper ore and slags	Raw material - turquoise
G1/F2	VF2, VH197, VH202, VH213, VH214	243	3	1	-	-	3	-	-	-	-	5	1	2	-	-	-
G2	VH105, VH125	845	4	1	-	-	2	-	-	2	3	-	1	-	-	-	-
G3	VH182, VH183, VH188, VH192	1324	1	-	-	-	-	-	-	-	2	-	-	1	-	-	-
G4	VH127, VH129, VH133, VH134	420	-	1	-	-	-	-	-	-	-	-	-	-	-	-	-
G5	VH12, VH28, VH32, VH34, VH45, VH255	1910	2	3	-	1	2	-	-	-	3	-	1	1	3	-	-
G6	VH293, VH295, VH296	218	2	1	-	-	-	-	-	-	1	-	-	-	-	-	-
G7	VH62, VH67, VH99	1236	2	3	-	-	1	-	-	-	1	2	1	2	-	1	-
G8	VH13, VH14, VH18, VH19, VH22, VH26, VH27, VH36, VH40, VH41	2947	1	1	-	-	2	-	1	-	1	-	2	-	1	-	-
G9/F6	VF6, VH292, VH294, VH298, VH299	617	-	1	-	-	-	-	-	-	-	2	-	-	1	-	-
G10	VH35, VH37, VH38, VH110	1748	2	-	-	-	1	-	-	-	1	-	-	-	-	-	-
G11	VH258, VH277, VH327	252	1	2	-	-	-	-	-	-	-	-	-	-	-	-	-
G12	VH232, VH236, VH259, VH262, VH270	1082	1	2	-	-	-	-	-	1	-	1	4	-	-	-	-
G13	VH61, VH128, VH131, VH132, VH136, VH137, VH138, VH144, VH147, VH150, VH168, VH189	3581	9	12	2	1	3	3	-	2	3	1	16	3	1	6	10
G14/F10	VF10, VH397	76	-	-	-	-	-	-	-	-	-	-	-	-	-	-	-
G15	VH16, VH52, VH53, VH92	2686	5	10	-	-	3	-	-	-	3	5	5	-	1	-	-
G16/F3	VF3, VH139, VH218, VH219	544	2	3	1	-	-	-	-	-	-	-	-	-	-	-	-
G17	VH77, VH78, VH79, VH98, VH123	1869	6	2	-	-	3	-	-	5	1	2	1	-	-	-	-

(Continued)

9

Table 1.2. (*Continued*)

Household unit	Housing structures and garbage pits	sherds	Lithic artifacts	Bone artifacts	Antler artifacts	Tooth artifacts	Shell artifacts	Bronze artifacts	Turquoise artifacts	Non-vessel pottery artifacts	Oracle bone	Raw material - rock	Raw material - bone	Raw material - antler	Raw material - shell	copper ore and slags	Raw material - turquoise
G18/F1	VF1, VH141, VH142, VH190, VH193, VH195, VH205	1616	7	3	-	-	2	1	-	3	3	-	1	-	-	-	1
G19	VH11, VH47, VH48, VH50, VH65, VH66, VH100, VH122	3750	15	12	-	-	6	-	-	3	1	6	3	-	-	-	-
G20	VH126, VH154, VH155, VH160, VH162, VH165, VH167	1437	2	1	-	-	-	-	-	-	-	-	-	1	-	-	-
G21	VH3, VH4, VH5, VH17, VH21	1536	9	3	-	-	3	-	-	2	-	1	-	2	1	-	-
G22	VH20, VH23, VH25	1654	2	-	-	-	1	5	-	-	1	-	-	-	-	-	-
W1/F7	VF7, VH306, VH307, VH312, VH315, VH316, VH317, VH320, VH364, VH367, VH370, VH372	1632	5	4	-	-	1	-	-	1	1	3	4	-	1	-	-
W2	VH274, VH275, VH276, VH281	1136	4	-	-	2	7	-	-	-	-	-	-	1	1	-	1
W3/F9	VF9, VH332, VH337, VH344, VH358, VH360, VH362	1795	4	4	-	-	-	-	-	-	-	-	4	-	-	-	-
W4/F11	VF11	103	-	-	-	-	1	-	-	1	-	-	-	-	-	-	-
W5	VH252, VH278, VH282, VH283, VH284, VH290, VH300, VH301, VH302, VH303, VH304, VH323, VH330, VH333, VH341, VH342, VH343, VH345, VH346, VH347, VH348, VH354, VH355, VH356, VH357, VH369, VH373, VH374	8582	44	22	1	3	14	1	-	2	9	11	21	-	2	2	4084

Household unit	Housing structures and garbage pits	sherds	Lithic artifacts	Bone artifacts	Antler artifacts	Tooth artifacts	Shell artifacts	Bronze artifacts	Turquoise artifacts	Non-vessel pottery artifacts	Oracle bone	Raw material - rock	Raw material - bone	Raw material - antler	Raw material - shell	copper ore and slags	Raw material - turquoise
W6	VH265, VH266, VH258, VH271, VH297	1001	3	1	-	-	-	-	-	-	1	-	2	-	-	-	-
W7	VH269, VH402, VH403	394	1	2	-	1	-	-	-	-	-	-	2	-	-	-	-
D1	IIIH1, IIIH14, IIIH25, IIIH26, IIIH27	936	3	8	1	-	1	-	-	-	-	6	-	-	-	-	-
D2/ F2	IIIF2, IIIH9, IIIH28	437	4	4	-	-	-	-	-	-	-	-	-	-	-	-	-
D3	IIIH4, IIIH7 IIIH13, IIIH23, IIIH35	2128	12	8	-	-	3	-	-	1	-	15	-	-	-	-	-
D4	IIIH5, IIIH8, IIIH10, IIIH15, IIIH17, IIIH18, IIIH22	2711	16	1	-	1	3	-	-	2	1	12	4	-	-	-	1
D5/ F4	IIIF4	199	-	-	-	-	-	-	-	-	-	-	-	-	-	-	-

Note:

1. Roman numerals are the codes for the site sections. The Erlitou site is divided into 15 sections by the archaeologists according to the modern roads and village plans. The excavations at the eastern end of the site during 1999 – 2006 were in Section III, and the excavations in the Palatial enclosure and the northern part of the Workshop enclosure during 1999 – 2006 were in Section V. The same applies to similar cases below.

2. F refers to housing structure. The same applies to similar cases below.

3. H refers to garbage pit. The same applies to similar cases below.

differentiation allows me to determine whether families residing near the rammed-earth palaces were wealthier than those living farther from the palatial enclosure, and whether residents of the workshop enclosure held greater wealth associated with their involvement in production activities.

2) How much prestige differentiation is detectable among the households in this sample?

Feasting constitutes valuable archaeological evidence for the accumulation of prestige (Drennan and Peterson 2012). It has been interpreted as a means of creating and maintaining a stratified social order, negotiating social status, and enhancing group solidarity (Pollock 2003). Elaborate vessels would have been used to serve and display food and drink (Dietler 2001). Feasting requires serving and drinking vessels to facilitate the sharing of food and beverages, and prestigious families tend to possess a greater number of decorated ceramic vessels used for serving, sharing, and storing food and drink. While feasting is often viewed as a practice that distinguishes

elites from non-elites, on a smaller scale, it could also function as a means of establishing hierarchy within non-elite groups. During the Shang dynasty, Shang potters engaged in community-based and household feasts, which empowered their groups and enabled artisans to negotiate social power (Reinhart 2015). This study will assess the proportion of feasting utensils and vessels, as well as polished and/or fingernail-incised decorated ceramics, to evaluate prestige differentiation among the sampled households.

3) How much ritual differentiation is detectable among the households in this sample?

The diverse array of ritual paraphernalia from the Erlitou period indicates that a wide range of religious activities were conducted within the Erlitou state. The consumption of various types of ritual paraphernalia and the practice of divination using oracle bones serve as effective indicators of ritual differentiation. It has been hypothesized that power initially emerged from the monopoly of ritual activities (Chang 1983).

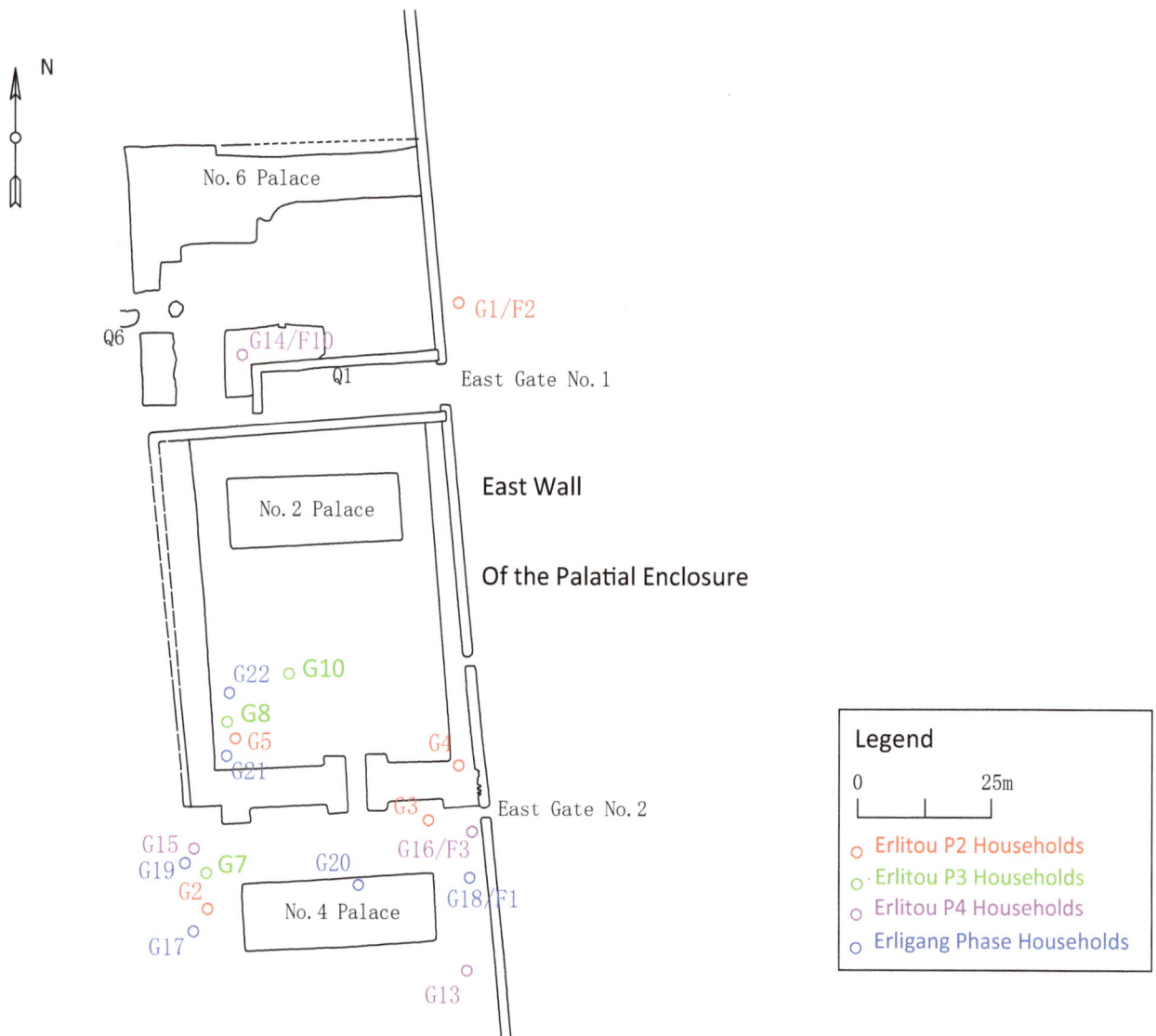

Figure 1.4. Household units in this sample in or near the east complex of the palatial enclosure (modified from *Zhongguo 2014*: Figure 5-0).

During China's Bronze Age, elites are thought to have monopolized communication with ancestors and deities, while non-elites and other members of political communities relied on elites as intermediary to contact supernatural beings (Chang 1989). Scapulimancy, divination using oracle bones, was a key ritual practice. Non-elites and craftsmen may have performed divination in their homes or workshops, possibly with the assistance of professional diviners (Chen and Li 2013). Thus, disparities in access to divination paraphernalia can reveal differences in ritual status.

4) *How much productive differentiation is detectable among the households in this sample?*

Specializations in turquoise and bronze crafts suggest that Erlitou may have been a society where people's daily needs were supplied by large-scale workshops of some kind. In such a scenario, only common, everyday activities would have taken place in most households. Liu (2006) examines diachronic changes in craft specialization at the

settlement level in Erlitou, based on the distribution of six types of productive tools. She proposes that there existed not only attached craft production but also independent craft production, and that the urban population could obtain certain goods from local communities. This study aims to investigate the operation of Erlitou's utilitarian economy. It will examine whether and to what extent productive activities were differentiated among households by comparing the proportions of different productive tools in household artifact assemblages. Farming tools such as sickles and shovels, hunting tools/ weapons like arrowheads, and sewing tools including awls and needles are frequently found in household artifact assemblages. Significant productive differentiation would indicate that goods were not solely supplied by large workshops, but rather that a vibrant bottom-up utilitarian economy may have existed. Conversely, if all households possessed highly similar productive artifacts, it would suggest that they primarily engaged in food production and preparation, while obtaining other necessities from large workshops.

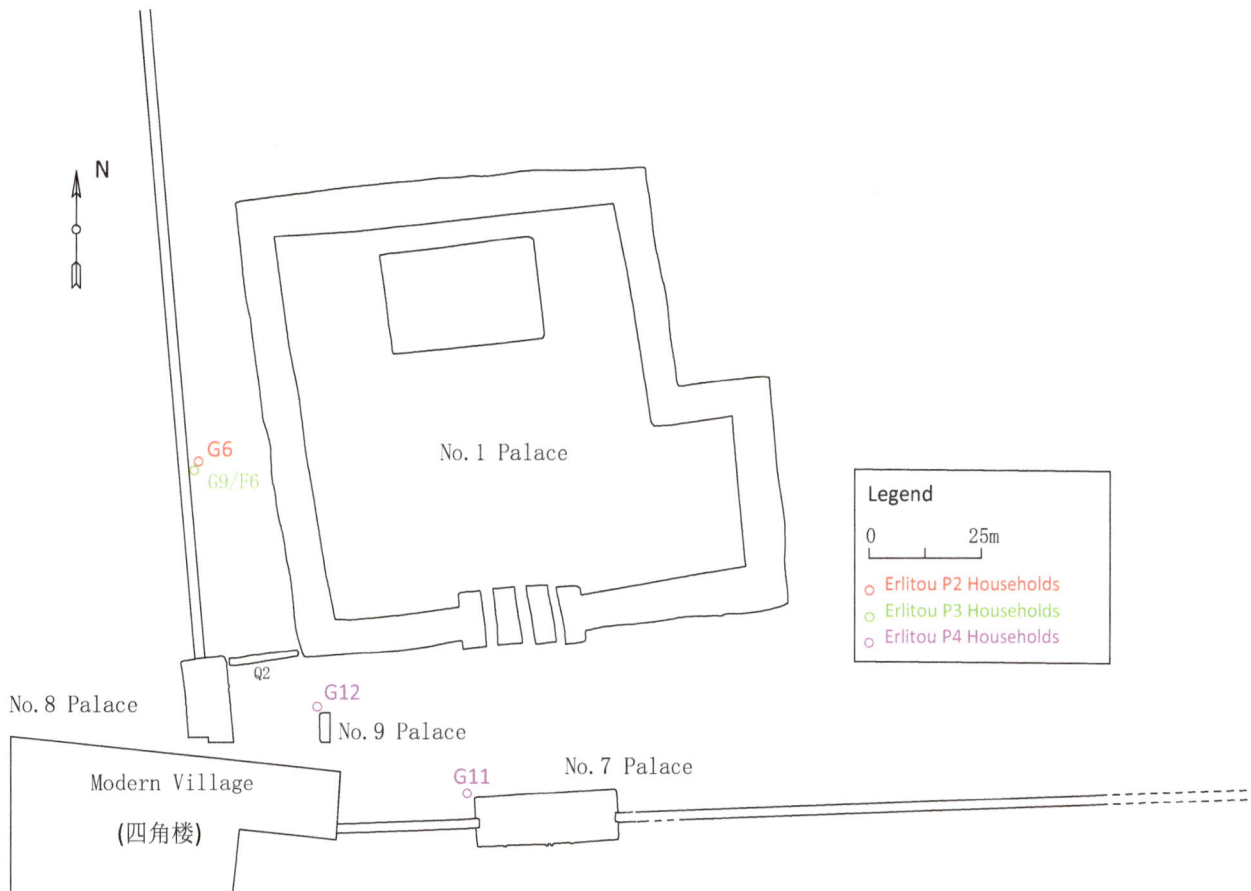

Figure 1.5. Household units in this sample around the west complex of the palatial enclosure (modified from *Zhongguo 2014*: Figure 5-0).

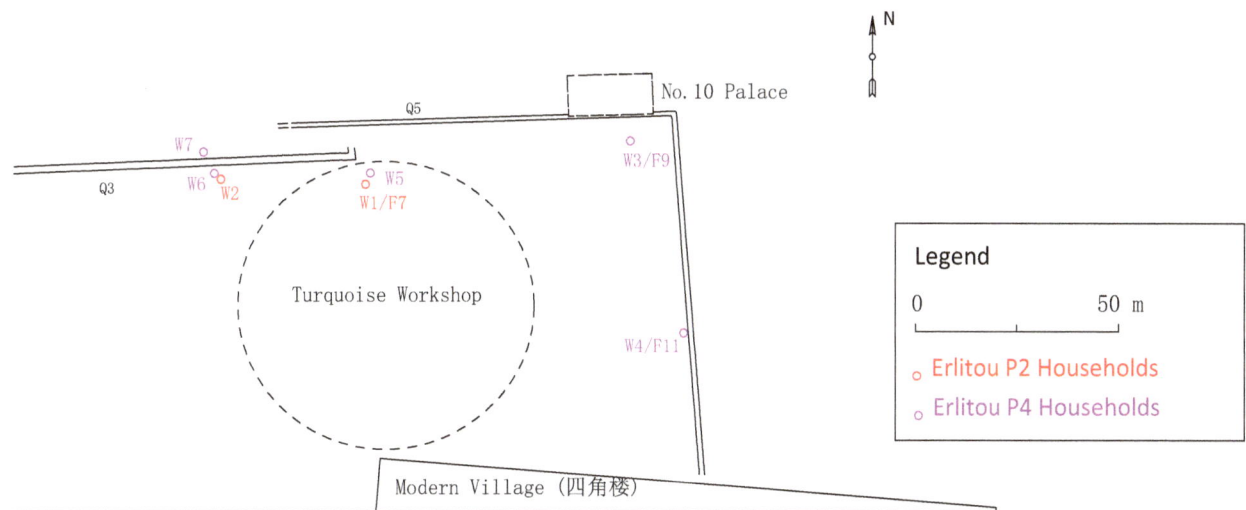

Figure 1.6. Household units in or near the workshop enclosure (modified from *Zhongguo 2014*: Figure 5-0).

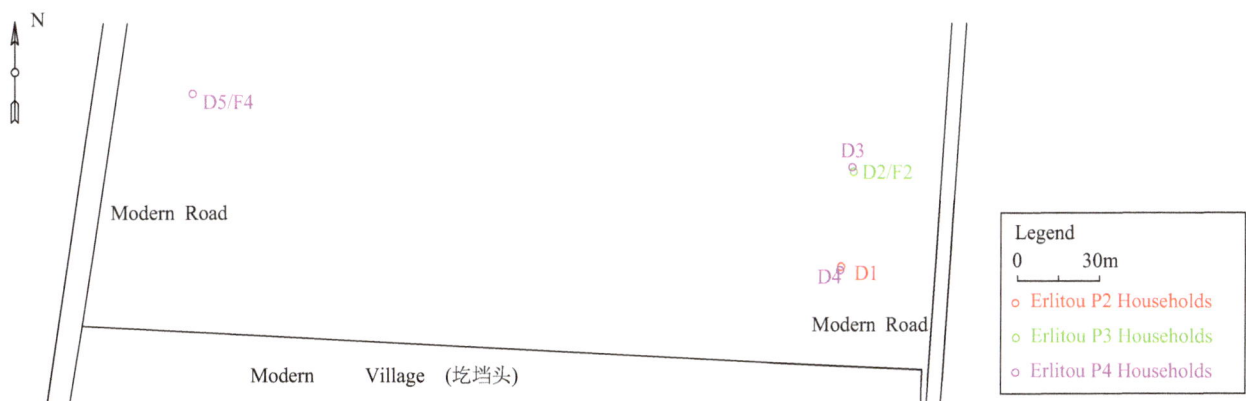

Figure 1.7. Household units in this sample at the eastern end of the site (modified from *Zhongguo 2014*, Figure 1-1-3-4, pp 8).

5) *Whatever differentiation is documented in answering the questions above, how much of it seems to differentiate households living in on-the-ground structures as a group from those living in semi-subterranean structures?*

Addressing this question helps us determine whether households residing in on-the-ground structures can be accurately characterized as members of a class distinctly separate from those living in semi-subterranean structures.

6) *Whatever differentiation is documented in answering the questions above, how much of it occurs among households living in on-the-ground structures and how much among those living in semi-subterranean structures?*

The answer to this question builds on the answer to the previous one by examining the differentiation that existed within each of the two groups.

Erlitou Household Artifact Assemblages
and Multidimensional Scaling

2.1. Multidimensional Scaling

To address the research questions, this project employs multidimensional scaling (MDS) to analyze the artifact assemblages of Erlitou households. Multidimensional scaling is widely regarded as "the simplest and most intuitive of the various approaches to multivariate analysis" (Drennan 2010), making it a suitable choice for examining the complex relationships within the dataset. Specifically, nonmetric multidimensional scaling (NMDS) possesses the capability to represent the underlying structure of a dataset, including the formation of clusters and the axes of scalar variation. This structure, in turn, serves as an indicator of the relationships between the individual cases within the dataset (Drennan et al. 2017). When the dataset consists of a group of household units from a local community, NMDS provides a valuable means to delve deeper into the social relationships within that community and to explore the emergence and development of complex societies (Drennan et al. 2017).

In the context of this study, nonmetric multidimensional scaling enables the visualization of similarities between the artifact assemblages of Erlitou households in the form of a graph. In this graph, each point corresponds to a household assemblage. A key characteristic of such a visualization is that assemblages with greater similarity are represented by points that are positioned closer to one another, while those with more significant differences are shown as points that are farther apart. The process of creating the configuration within the graph involves a trial-and-error iterative procedure. This procedure works to position the points in such a way that it maximizes the rank-order correlation between the matrix of interpoint distances in the graph and the measure of similarity between the artifact assemblages, which serves as the input to the procedure. The outcome of this process is that the graph effectively conveys large differences between household assemblages as large distances between their corresponding points, and small differences as small distances. Through the structure of points displayed in the graph's configuration, we can gain insights into the relationships between the household units in the Erlitou local community, thereby enhancing our understanding of the Erlitou complex society. It is important to note that multidimensional scaling is grounded in a codification of the relevant variability present in the artifact assemblages, which are then transformed into a defined set of variables.

For the purpose of obtaining meaningful and interpretable configurations through multidimensional scaling, one of the critical factors to consider is the number of variables used to measure the similarity scores and distances between cases. If the number of variables is excessively large, there is a substantial risk of identifying fallacious patterns, as the random noise within the data can distort the results. Conversely, if the number of variables is too small, there is a significant possibility of missing meaningful information, which can lead to the identification of patterns that are not representative and hinder accurate interpretation. As a general rule of thumb for multidimensional scaling, the number of variables should not exceed approximately half the number of cases (Drennan 2010). This guideline helps to strike a balance between capturing sufficient information and avoiding the pitfalls associated with an overabundance or scarcity of variables, ensuring that the results of the analysis are both reliable and interpretable.

2.2. The 19 Variables for Multidimensional Scaling

During the 1999–2006 excavation seasons, archaeologists uncovered a large array of remains at Erlitou. These remains include ceramic sherds, practical tools, ritual paraphernalia, and other types of artifacts. Based on the attributes of these household assemblages, this study conducts multidimensional scaling using a set of 19 variables (Table 2.1). The data for the 34 household units across these 19 variables are presented in Table 2.2.

Sherds constitute the largest proportion of the assemblages. A great number of pottery vessel forms have been identified at the Erlitou site, which are generally categorized into cooking vessels, water-drawing vessels, storage vessels, food preparation vessels, serving vessels, drinking vessels, and miscellaneous vessels (Zhongguo 1995, 2003). This study specifically focuses on and investigates storage vessels, drinking vessels, serving vessels, and food preparation vessels. On the other hand, some sherds have been selected from the general collection, pieced together, and published as specimens of specific forms in the report (Zhongguo 2014). This study also includes these published specimens, as well as the white pottery sherds from the associated household garbage pits published in the appendix tables of the archaeological report (Zhongguo 2014: Volume 5, Appendix Tables 9-5A and 9-5B, pp. 287–309), with each counted as one sherd under specific categories. According to the report, sherds collected from the footings or wall footings of some housing structures are likely not from the period when these structures were occupied, so they are excluded from this study. Of course, many sherds are too small to display the defining characteristics of any particular vessel form, and some remain unidentifiable in terms of function even after being pieced together; these have been counted as "indeterminate form." Storage vessels, serving vessels, drinking vessels, and food preparation vessels, along with cooking vessels,

Table 2.1. List of 19 variables.

Variable 1. Fingernail Incising	number of sherds with fingernail incising divided by total sherds for each household
Variable 2. Incising/Stamping in Complex Patterns	numbers of sherd with incising/stamping in complex patterns divided by total sherds for each household
Variable 3. Polishing	number of polished sherds divided by total sherds for each household
Variable 4. Feasting Utensils and Vessels	number of feasting utensils and vessels (*bi*, bowls, plates, cups, and pitchers) divided by total sherds of identifiable vessel forms for each household
Variable 5. Storage Vessels	number of storage vessels (jars, vats, and basins) divided by total sherds of identifiable vessel forms for each household
Variable 6. Food Preparation Artifacts	number of food preparation artifacts (grater-bottom bowls, pestles and mortars) divided by total sherds of identifiable vessel forms each household
Variable 7. Ornaments	number of ornaments (hairpins, beads, circles, and turquoise sheets for inlay) divided by total sherds of identifiable vessel forms for each household
Variable 8. Carpentry/Construction Tools	number of carpentry/construction tools (axes *fu*, adzes, spades, and saws) divided by total sherds of identifiable vessel forms for each household
Variable 9. Agricultural Tools	number of agricultural tools (knives, and sickles) divided by total sherds of identifiable vessel forms for each household
Variable 10. Textile Tools	number of textile tools (awls, needles, spindle whorls) divided by total sherds of identifiable vessel forms for each household
Variable 11. Weapons/Hunting Tools	number of weapon/hunting tools (axes - *yue*, and arrowheads) divided by total sherds of identifiable vessel forms for each household
Variable 12. Resharpening Tools	number of resharpening tools (whetstones) divided by total sherds of identifiable vessel forms for each household
Variable 13. Fishing Tools	number of fishing tools (darts and net sinkers) divided by total sherds of identifiable vessel forms for each household
Variable 14. Ritual Paraphernalia	number of ritual paraphernalia (oracle bones and hollow-bottomed vessels) divided by total sherds of identifiable vessel forms for each household
Variable 15. Lithic Production	number of lithic cores, flakes and blanks divided by total sherds of identifiable vessel forms for each household
Variable 16. Bone Production	number of bone cores, blanks and wastes divided by total sherds of identifiable vessel forms for each household
Variable 17. Antler Production	number of antler cores, blanks and wastes divided by total sherds of identifiable vessel forms for each household
Variable 18. Shell Production	number of shell blank/wastes divided by total sherds of identifiable vessel forms for each household
Variable 19. Bronze Working	number of copper ores (or ore shatters), and slags divided by total sherds of identifiable vessel forms for each household

water-drawing vessels, and miscellaneous vessels, all fall into the category of identifiable vessel forms. The total number of sherds across the 34 household units ranges from 76 to 8,582, while the number of sherds of identifiable vessel forms for each household unit ranges from 34 to 6,917.

Practical tools made of stone, bone, antler, shell, and bronze form another significant group of artifacts found in the collections from the 1999–2006 excavations and documented in the archaeological report (Zhongguo 2014). To investigate the specific economic activities in which these households were engaged, this study categorizes these practical tools into distinct functional groups: construction/carpentry tools, agricultural tools, textile tools, weapons/hunting tools, resharpening tools, and fishing tools. Notably, some lithic, bone, antler, shell, and bronze items, referred to in the report as *canjian* (残件, or "broken artifacts"), exhibit artificial modification but lack the defining characteristics necessary to classify them as specific tool or artifact forms. For the purposes of this study, these items are therefore categorized

as "indeterminate lithic items," "indeterminate bone items," "indeterminate antler items," "indeterminate shell items," and "indeterminate bronze items." Similarly, tooth artifacts (*yaqi* 牙器) display artificial features but no clear indicators of a specific tool or artifact function, leading this study to classify them as "indeterminate tooth items." Importantly, all these indeterminate items, regardless of their material, are excluded from the functional categories of practical tools. Beyond tools, other remains found in household contexts include raw materials such as stone, bone, antler, shell, and turquoise, all of which are also documented in the archaeological report (Zhongguo 2014). These raw materials may provide evidence of artifact or tool production occurring at the household level, offering insights into the domestic economies and craft activities of the Erlitou households.

Variable 1. Fingernail Incising

Numerous studies have indicated that pottery vessels with elaborate decorations likely served as an indicator that

Table 2.2. The data of the 34 household units under the 19 variables.

Household unit	N sherds	N sherds of identifiable vessel forms	Fingernail incising	Incising/stamping in complex patterns	Polishing	Storage vessels	Feasting utensils & vessels	Food preparation artifacts	Ornaments	Carpentry/construction tools	Agricultural tools	Textile tools	Weapon/hunting tools	Resharpening tools	Fishing tools	Ritual paraphernalia	Lithic production	Bone production	Antler production	Shell production	Bronze working
G1/F2	243	164	-	-	38	89	12	-	1	2	1	1	1	-	-	-	2	1	2	-	-
G2	845	601	-	-	28	234	30	8	-	-	1	-	-	1	1	3	-	1	-	-	-
G3	1324	1063	6	1	221	463	54	7	-	-	-	-	-	-	-	2	-	-	1	-	-
G4	420	317	1	1	57	150	18	2	1	-	-	-	-	-	-	-	-	-	-	-	-
G5	1910	1498	29	4	648	703	124	12	2	1	1	-	1	1	-	3	-	-	1	3	-
G6	218	150	3	-	29	66	7	4	-	1	1	1	-	-	-	1	-	-	-	-	-
G7	1236	927	6	2	197	462	49	7	1	-	2	1	1	-	-	1	1	1	2	-	1
G8	2947	2264	10	2	630	956	191	18	1	-	1	-	-	1	-	1	-	2	-	1	-
G9/F6	617	491	-	-	80	165	28	5	-	-	-	-	-	-	-	-	1	-	-	1	-
G10	1748	1331	6	1	303	558	67	29	-	1	-	1	-	-	1	-	1	-	-	-	-
W1/F7	1632	1239	12	1	267	336	45	4	2	-	1	2	-	4	-	1	1	3	-	1	-
W2	1136	945	-	-	340	422	69	3	-	-	3	-	-	1	-	-	-	-	1	1	-
D1	936	805	8	2	92	304	82	4	2	1	-	3	-	2	1	-	2	-	-	-	-
D2/F2	437	337	3	1	48	156	8	-	3	-	2	1	1	1	-	-	-	-	-	-	-
G11	252	182	-	1	35	67	10	1	-	-	-	-	2	1	-	-	-	-	-	-	-
G12	1082	877	1	-	89	259	13	3	-	1	-	1	1	-	1	-	-	4	-	-	-
G13	3581	2538	29	1	356	1087	81	5	5	4	3	2	8	1	-	3	1	15	2	1	6
G14/F10	76	34	-	-	5	18	1	-	-	-	-	-	-	-	-	-	-	-	-	-	-
G15	2686	2048	9	2	268	1005	136	50	9	1	1	-	1	-	-	3	3	5	-	1	-
G16/F3	544	344	5	-	44	149	19	1	-	-	1	-	3	1	-	-	-	-	-	-	-
W3/F9	1795	1022	5	2	173	487	35	10	2	3	-	-	2	1	-	-	1	-	-	-	-
W4/F11	103	52	1	-	35	31	3	1	-	-	-	-	-	-	1	-	-	-	-	-	-
W5	8582	6917	49	9	1087	2836	154	41	5	6	11	8	7	27	1	9	4	17	-	2	2
W6	1001	807	7	-	117	357	26	4	-	2	1	-	-	-	-	1	-	2	-	-	-
W7	394	336	3	-	37	114	14	1	1	-	1	-	-	-	-	-	-	2	-	-	-
D3	2128	1698	10	1	259	766	42	26	2	2	4	6	2	4	1	-	8	-	-	-	-
D4	2711	2276	16	4	418	910	131	14	1	4	2	-	-	6	-	1	5	4	-	-	-
D5/F4	199	65	-	2	11	35	4	1	-	-	-	-	-	-	-	-	-	-	-	-	-
G17	1869	1545	6	5	122	550	42	6	1	2	4	4	1	1	3	1	1	1	-	-	-
G18/F1	1616	998	12	1	204	441	47	8	4	1	3	-	4	-	-	3	-	1	-	-	-
G19	3750	2820	9	5	264	913	115	14	7	4	7	5	4	2	-	1	2	2	-	-	-
G20	1437	1062	6	2	116	475	34	12	-	1	1	-	-	-	-	-	-	-	1	-	-
G21	1536	1148	3	-	173	372	65	9	-	2	1	2	-	1	1	1	-	-	2	1	-
G22	1654	1129	31	-	413	599	173	2	-	1	1	-	1	-	-	1	-	-	-	-	-

their possessors held high social rank. Fingernail incising (*zhijia wen* 指甲纹) is commonly found on pitchers, jars, and vessel covers (*qigai* 器盖), and it can also be observed on bowls. Typically, this form of incising is applied to the shoulder of a vessel (Figure 2.1).

While there are no specific statistics on the proportion of sherds or vessels adorned with fingernail incising, some archaeologists have noted that among the reconstructed vessels unearthed during excavations from 1959 to 1978, those featuring various incised patterns accounted for only 2.6% in Erlitou Phase 1, 4.5% in Phase 2, 4.8% in

Phase 3, and 3.5% in Phase 4 (Zhongguo 1999). Given the rarity of fingernail incising on Erlitou pottery vessels and the fact that applying this decoration, particularly on storage vessels or drinking vessels, would have been time-consuming, it is reasonable to argue that such vessels are strongly associated with either wealth or prestige.

Variable 2. Incising/Stamping in Complex Patterns

Incising or stamping in complex patterns typically consists of deep incisions or stamped motifs featuring intricate spirals, other geometric designs, and a range of additional

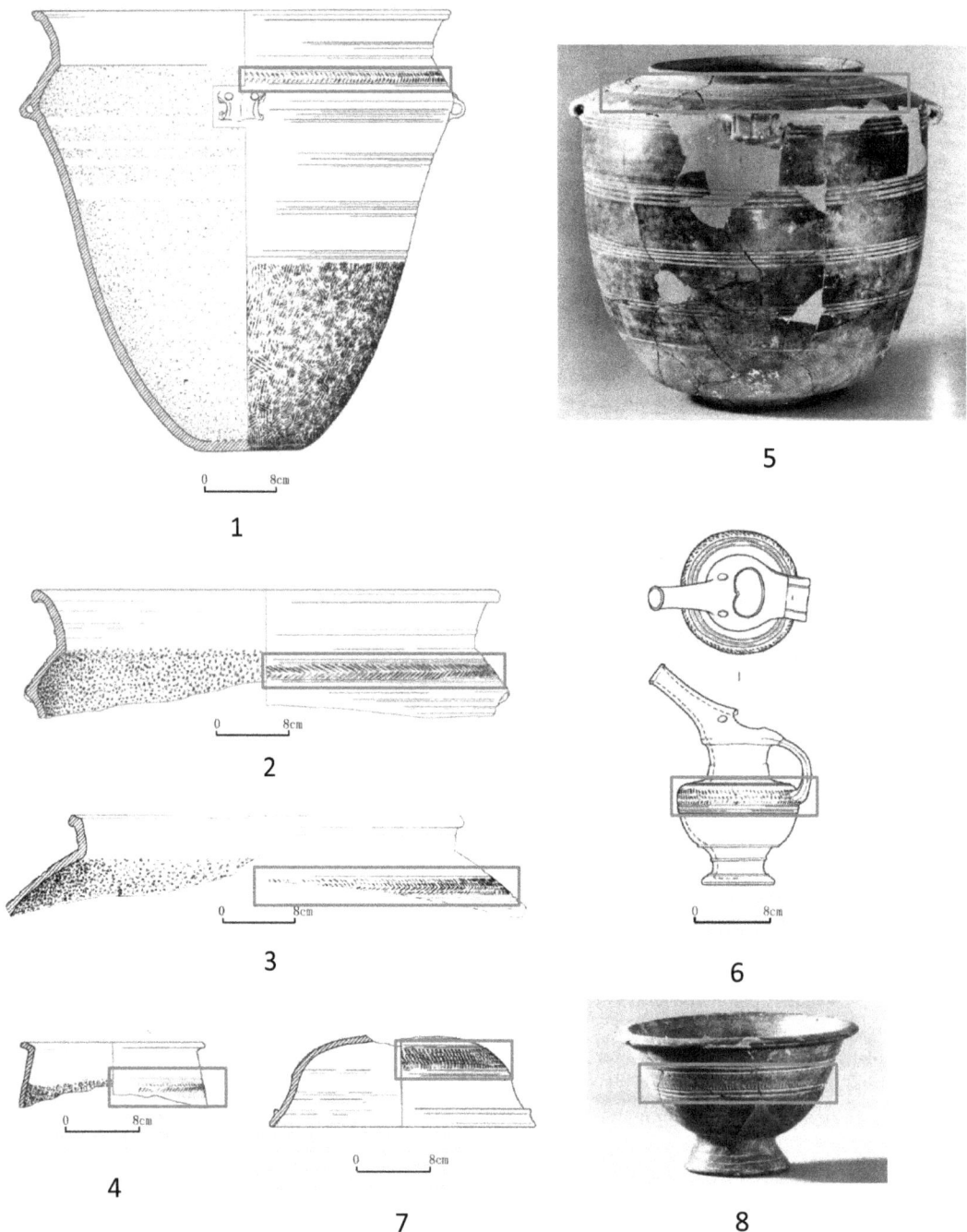

Figure 2.1. Examples of Variable 1. Fingernail Incising. 1. Jar *zun* 尊 (*Zhongguo 2014*, pp 245, figure 4-4-1-11-2E: ①10);
2. Jar *zun* 尊 (*Zhongguo 2014*, pp 272, figure 4-4-1-20-2F: 56); 3. Jar *weng* 瓮 (*Zhongguo 2014*, pp 276, figure 4-4-1-20-2J: 39);
4. Jar *guan* 罐 (*Zhongguo 2014*, pp 891, figure 6-4-2-59-2A: 17); 5. Jar *weng* 瓮 (*Zhongguo 1995*, plate 340); 6. Pitcher *he* 盉
(*Zhongguo 2014*, pp 791, figure 6-4-2-18-2B: 25); 7. Vessel cover *qigai* 器盖 (*Zhongguo 2014*, pp 221, figure 4-4-1-4-2A: 22);
8. Pedestal bowl *gui* 簋 (*Zhongguo 1995*, plate 288).

varied elements. These complex incised or stamped patterns (*hua wen* 花纹) are most commonly found on storage vessels, with jars being the primary form. Within the artifact collection from the 1999–2006 excavations, several sherds bearing this type of decoration have been documented under the designation *huawen taopian* 花纹陶片 (decorated pottery sherds) in the archaeological report (Zhongguo 2014).

Some archaeologists further categorize these decorations into stamped motifs and incised motifs, the latter encompassing fingernail incising (as defined in this study) as well as other relatively simple patterns. Their research reveals that among the reconstructed vessels unearthed

during excavations from 1959 to 1978, those adorned with either stamped or incised decorations accounted for only 4.1% in Erlitou Phase 1, 4.8% in both Phase 2 and Phase 3, and 4.4% in Phase 4 (Zhongguo 1999).

This type of decorative pattern is typically applied to the outer surface of a vessel, specifically on the shoulder or upper belly, and appears in a variety of distinct shapes (Zhongguo 1995, 1999; Figure 2.2). Moreover, such decorations are usually limited to one or two rows on a single vessel, a characteristic that would make them significantly rarer within large assemblages of sherds. Adding to their uniqueness, creating these complex patterns would have required considerably more time and

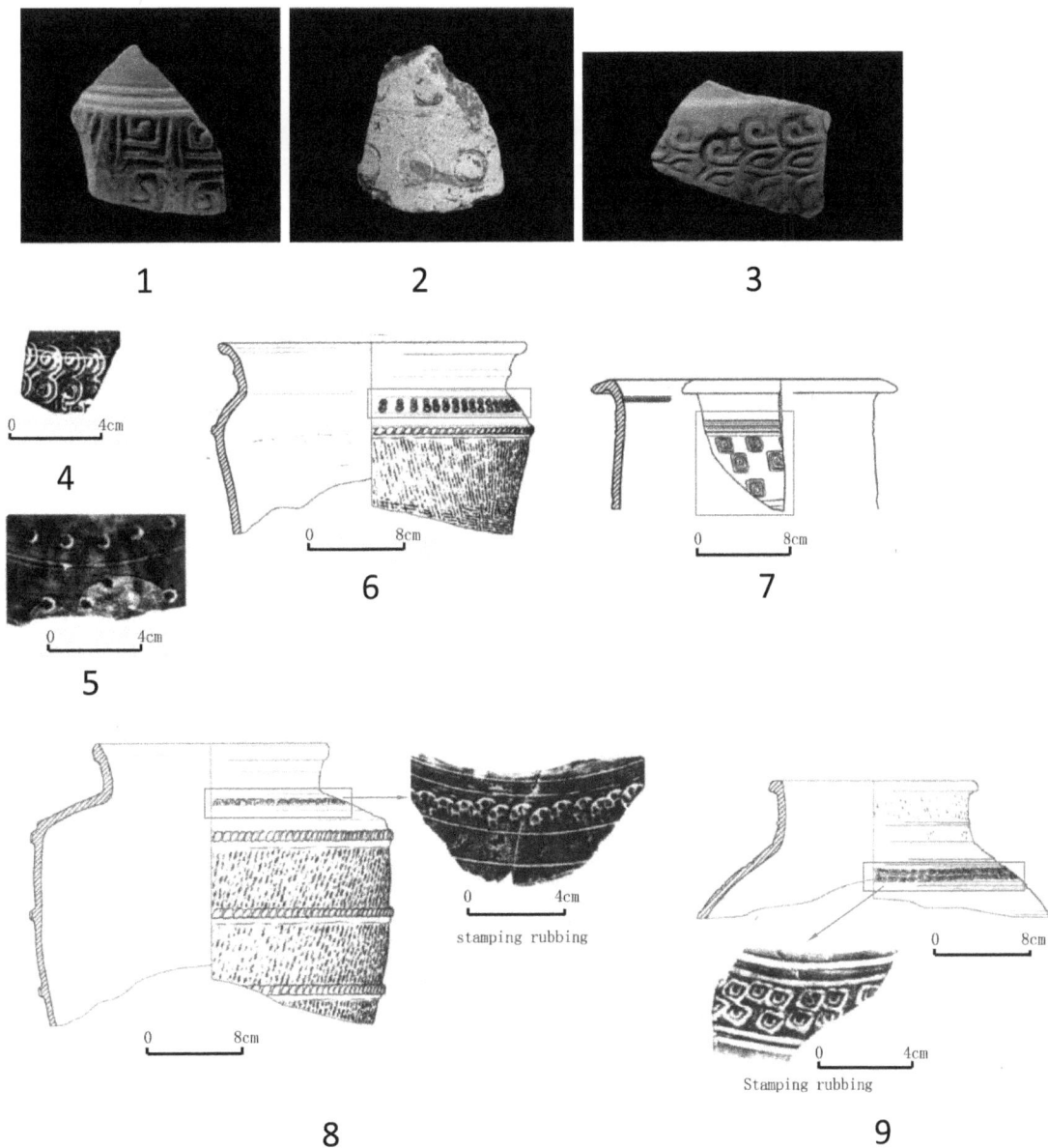

Figure 2.2. Examples of Variable 2. Incising/Stamping in Complex Patterns. 1. Sherd decorated with incising/stamping in complex patterns *huawen taopian* 花纹陶片 (*Zhongguo 2014*; colorful plate 254: 7); 2. White pottery in unknown form *tongxing baitaoqi* 筒形白陶器 (*Zhongguo 2014*, colorful plate 242: 3); 3. Sherd decorated with incising/stamping in complex patterns *huawen taopian* 花纹陶片 (*Zhongguo 2014*; colorful plate 248: 3); 4. Sherd decorated with incising/stamping in complex patterns *huawen taopian* 花纹陶片 (*Zhongguo 2014*, pp 392, figure 5-5-1-25-2A: 40); 5. Sherd decorated with incising/stamping in complex patterns *huawen taopian* 花纹陶片 (*Zhongguo 2014*, pp 392, figure 5-5-1-25-2A: 55); 6. Jar *zun* 尊 (*Zhongguo 2014*, pp 781, figure 6-4-2-15-2C: 5); 7. Basin *pen* 盆 (*Zhongguo 2014*, pp 972, figure 6-4-2-81-2A: 6); 8. Jar *zun* 尊 (*Zhongguo 2014*, pp 849, figure 6-4-2-46-2: 1); 9. Jar *guan* 罐(*Zhongguo 2014*, pp 957, figure 6-4-2-79-2B: 36).

effort compared to other, simpler forms of decoration. Given these intrinsic traits, their rarity, the labor-intensive nature of their production, and their association with specific vessel types, it is compelling to argue that complex incised or stamped patterns are strongly linked to either wealth or social prestige.

Variable 3. Polishing

Jars, basins, plates, bowls, cups, pitchers, and vessel covers can all be polished, either entirely or only on parts of their outer surfaces. Polishing was more common than fingernail incising (*zhijia wen* 指甲纹) and incising or stamping of complex patterns (*hua wen* 花纹), which are typically found only on specific parts

(such as the shoulders or upper bellies) of the vessels. Furthermore, it is not uncommon to see more than two types of decoration on a single vessel, even all three types of decorations discussed here. A polished sherd or vessel may also feature fingernail incisions or incised/ stamped complex patterns (see Figure 2.3). According to archaeological findings, among the reconstructed pottery vessels unearthed during excavations from 1959 to 1978, polished vessels accounted for 31.8% in Erlitou Phase 1, 31.2% in Erlitou Phase 2, 22.1% in Erlitou Phase 3, and 17.3% in Erlitou Phase 4 (Zhongguo 1999). Notably, polishing enhances the refinement of certain vessels. Given that polished vessels indicate a significant investment of time and energy in pottery production, they can be strongly associated with either wealth or prestige.

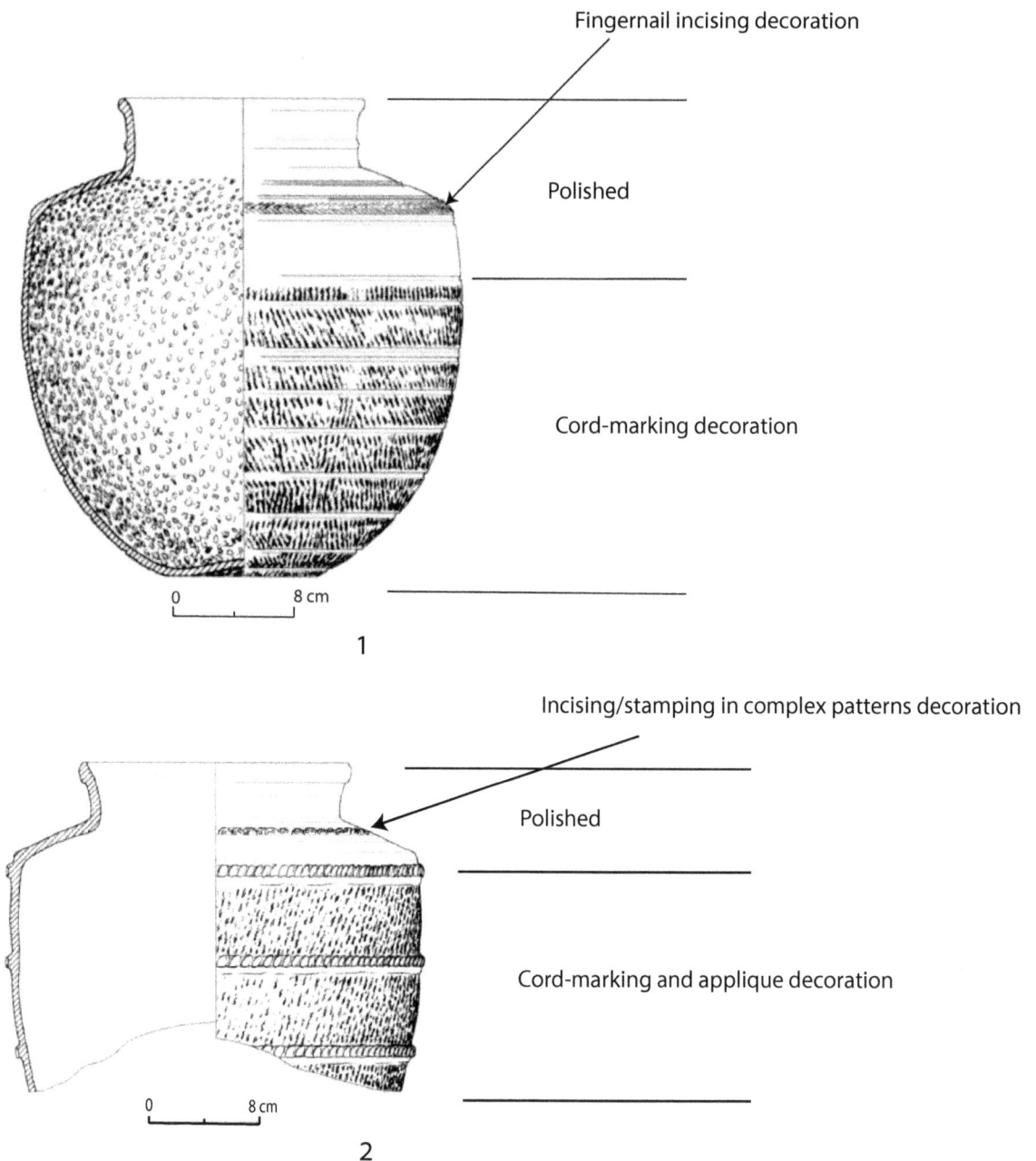

Figure 2.3. Examples of polished vessels with fingernail incising or incising/stamping in complex patterns. 1. jar *guan* 罐 (modified from *Zhongguo 2014*, pp 881, figure 6-4-2-56-2E: 62); 2. jar *zun* 尊 (modified *Zhongguo* 2014, pp 849, figure 6-4-2-46-2).

Variable 4. Feasting Utensils and Vessels

Feasting constitutes a crucial arena for aggrandizers to compete and sustain their prestige (Clark and Blake 1994; Spielmann 2002). The act of sharing food demands substantial consumption of serving and drinking utensils and vessels. Since feasting also functions as a display of competitive capacity and power, elaborate serving and drinking vessels would have been consumed in large quantities. During China's Bronze Age, food offerings and communal banquets played a vital role in political economies, operating as a sophisticated gift-based system that strengthened familial ties and even extended to the realm of political authority (Sterckx 2005; Cook 2005).

Feasting utensils and vessels identified at Erlitou include bone utensils, serving vessels, and drinking vessels (see Figure 2.4). Bone utensils (*gu bi* 骨匕) likely functioned like spoons for conveying food to the mouth (Wang 1990; Wang 2000). Serving vessels encompass stemmed plates (*dou* 豆), tripod plates (*sanzu pan* 三足盘), pedestal plates (*quanzu pan* 圈足盘), flat-bottomed bowls (*pingdi pen* 平底盆), and pedestal bowls (*gui* 簋). Drinking vessels consist of cups (*jue* 爵, *gu* 觚, and *bei* 杯) as well as pitchers (*he/gui* 盉 / 鬶).

Drinking vessels and serving vessels were frequently interred in elite tombs, with some archaeologists arguing that they signify prestigious identity and social status (Xu 2009, 2022). Pitchers functioned as vessels for heating or pouring wine, while cups served as drinking utensils (Zhongguo 1995; Xu 2009, 2022). Notably, certain pitchers were even crafted from kaolin paste, a much finer clay that requires a higher firing temperature, distinct from the material used for other pottery vessels. Plates and bowls are recognized as serving vessels, all of which were made from fine clay (Xu 2009, 2022; Hu 2020; Liu 2021). Most of these vessels were polished, and some serving vessels were further adorned with fingernail incisions.

Variable 5. Storage Vessels

Storage vessels encompass diverse forms such as jars (*Zun* 尊, *Weng* 瓮, *Guan* 罐, and *Hu* 壶), vats (*Gang* 缸), and basins (*Pen* 盆 / *Yu* 盂) (see Figure 2.5). The storage vessels unearthed from the Erlitou site were primarily functional for storing crops; however, some scholars have conjectured that certain specimens may have served dual roles as both fermenting implements and storage containers for beverages (Fang 1995; Zhongguo 2003; Xu 2009, 2022). Regardless of their specific functional variations, there is no doubt that they all fall categorically under the definition of storage vessels. From a socioeconomic perspective, the greater the number of storage vessels possessed by a household unit, the larger the volume of crops or beverages it could store and subsequently consume. In this context, the quantity of storage vessels can be strongly correlated with the wealth status of the household in question.

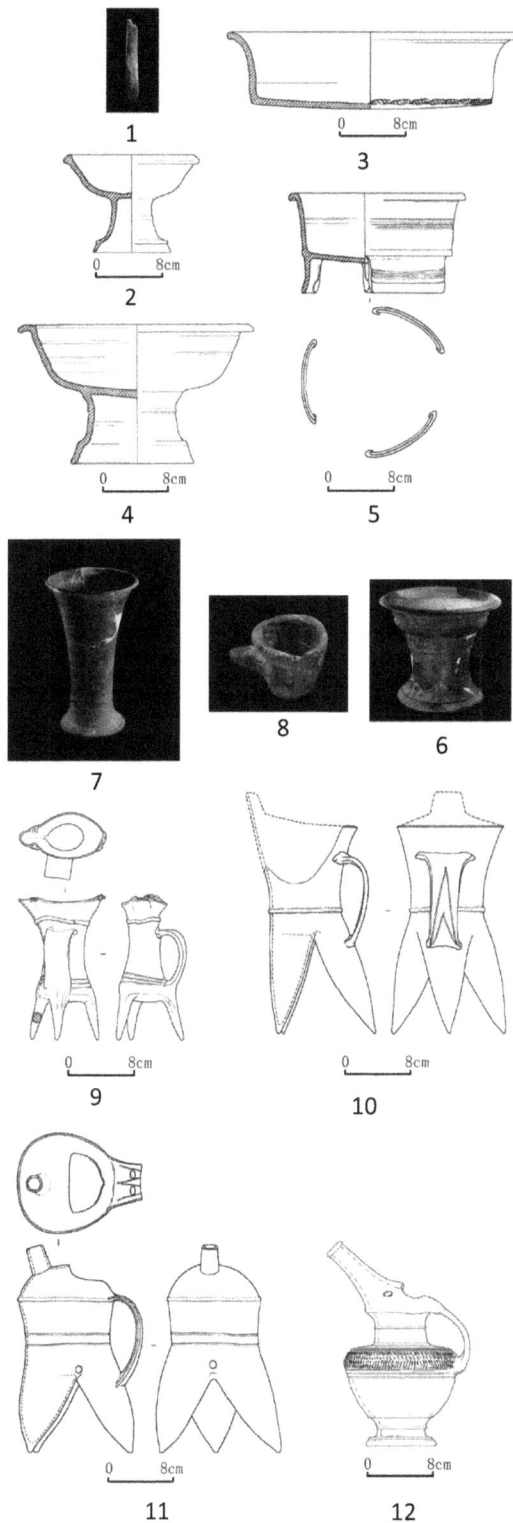

Figure 2.4. Examples of Variable 4. Feasting Utensils and Vessels. 1. Bone utensil *gu bi* 骨匕 (*Zhongguo* 2014, colorful plate 343: 7); **2. Plate** *dou* 豆 (*Zhongguo 2014*, pp 79, figure 3-2-1-11: AbIII); **3. Bowl** *pingdi pen* 平底盆 (*Zhongguo 2014*, pp 77, figure 3-2-1-9B: AbIII); **4. Bowl** *gui* 簋 (*Zhongguo 2014*, pp 81, figure 3-2-1-12: AII); **5. Plate** *sanzu pan* 三足盘 (*Zhongguo 2014*, pp 78, figure 3-2-1-10: AbI); **6. Plate** *quanzu pan* 圈足盘 (*Zhongguo 2014*, colorful plate 236: 3); **7. Cup** *gu* 觚 (*Zhongguo 2014*, colorful plate 231: 1); **8. Cup** *bei* 杯 (*Zhongguo 2014*, colorful plate 232: 6); **9 Cup** *jue* 爵 (*Zhongguo 2014*, pp 107, figure 3-2-1-25: AI); **10. Pitcher** *gui* 鬶 (*Zhongguo 2014*, pp 104, figure 3-2-1-23: AI); **11. Pitcher** *he* 盉 (*Zhongguo 2014*, pp 106, figure 3-2-3-24A: AbII); **12. Pitcher** *he* 盉 (*Zhongguo 2014*, pp 107, figure 3-2-1-24B: BII).

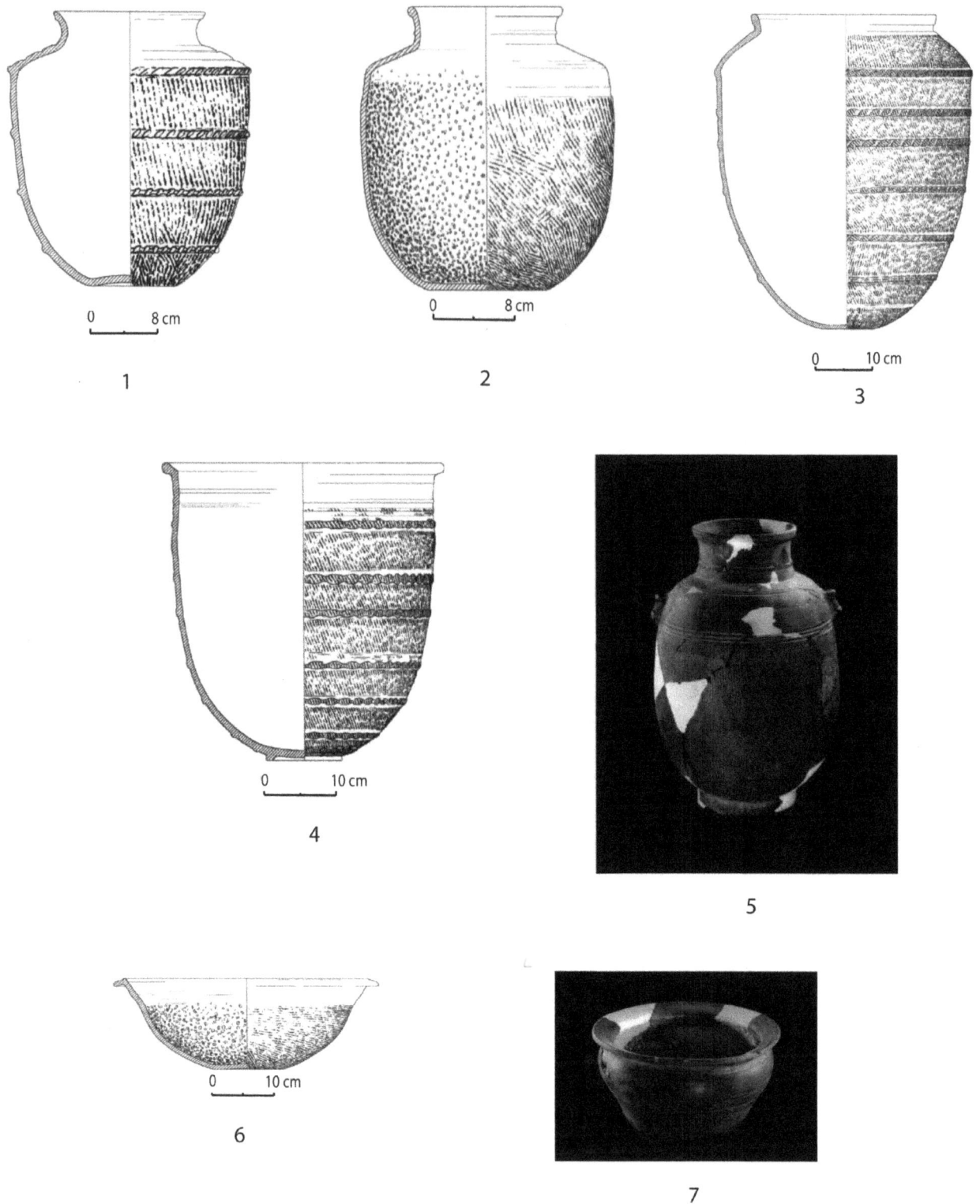

Figure 2.5. Examples of Variable 5. Storage Vessels. 1. Jar *zun* 尊 (*Zhongguo 2014*, pp 89, figure 3-2-1-16B: BbII); 2. Jar *guan* 罐 (*Zhongguo 2014*, pp 97, figure 3-2-1-15B: BI); 3. Jar *weng* 瓮 (*Zhongguo 2014*, pp 97, figure 3-2-1-21D); 4. Vat *gang* 缸 (*Zhongguo 2014*, pp 99, figure 3-2-1-22A: AIV); 5. Jar *hu* 壶 (*Zhongguo 2014*, colorful plate 224: 4); 6. Basin *pen* 盆 (*Zhongguo 2014*, pp 71, figure 3-2-1-7B: BaV); 7. Basin *yu* 盂 (*Zhongguo 2014*, colorful plate 235: 2).

Variable 6. Food Preparation Artifacts

Food preparation artifacts encompass a range of implements, including grater-bottom bowls (*kecao pen* 刻槽盆), lithic mortars (*jiu* 臼), pestles (*chu* 杵), and round-shaped lithics (*shibing* 石饼) (see Figure 2.6).

Within the sampled household units, the majority of food preparation artifacts are pottery grater-bottom basins, which are widely recognized as grinding tools in archaeological research. Recent starch grain analyses conducted on samples from the Lingjiatan 凌家滩 site in Anhui Province and the Diaolongbei 雕龙碑 site in Hubei

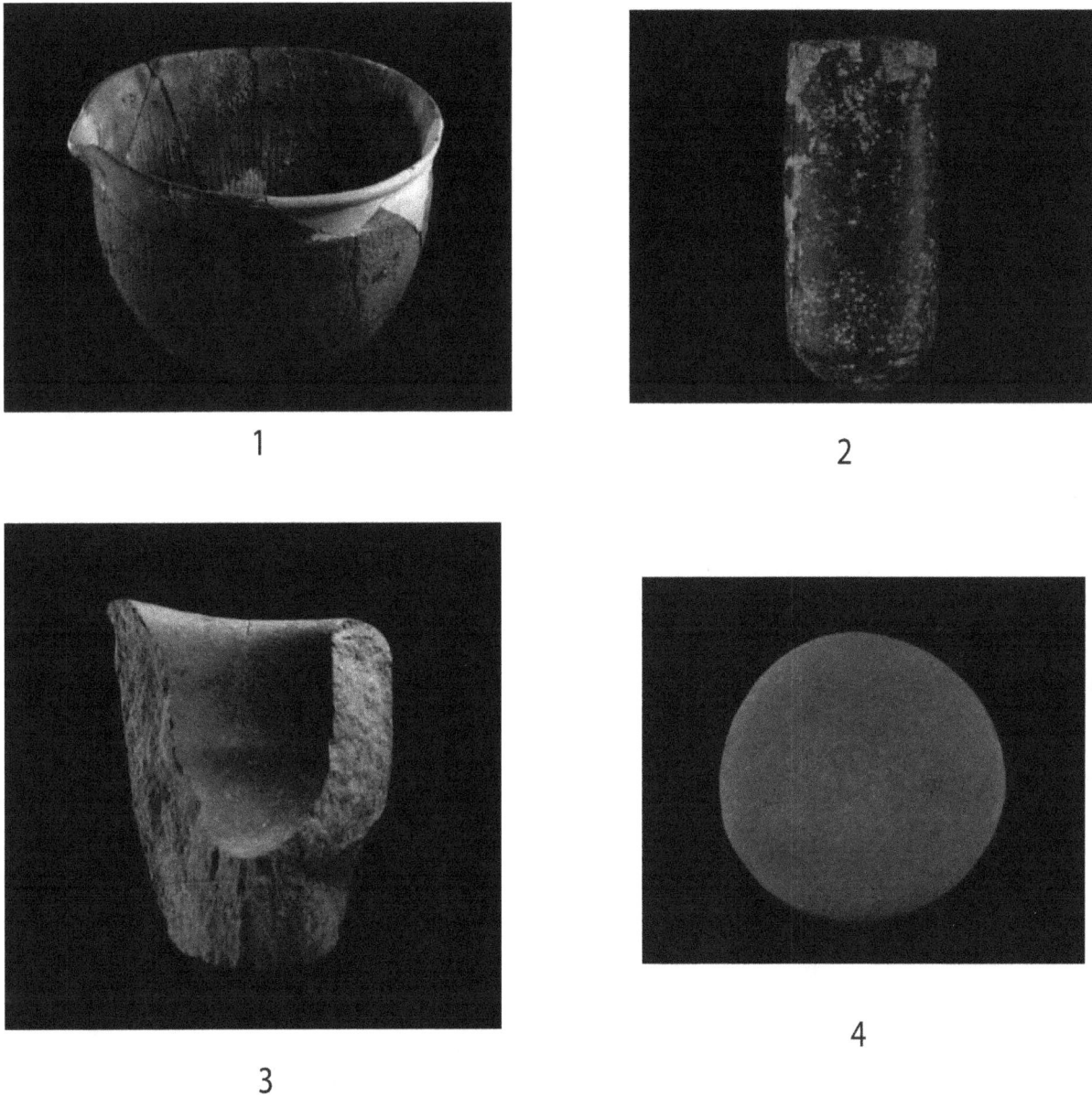

Figure 2.6. Examples of Variable 6. Food Preparation Artifacts. 1. Grater-bottom bowl *kecao pen* 刻槽盆 **(***Zhongguo 2014***, colorful plate 186: 3); 2. Lithic pestle** *chu* 杵 **(***Zhongguo 2014***, colorful plate 316: 7); 3. Lithic mortar** *jiu* 臼 **(***Zhongguo 2014***, colorful plate 317: 2); 4. Round lithics shibing** 石饼 **(***Zhongguo 2014***, colorful plate 323:3).**

Province have provided empirical evidence that these grater-bottom bowls were primarily used for grinding wild plants, specifically including species from the Poaceae and Triticeae families, as well as other root and tuber plants collected from the surrounding environment (An 1986; Ye 1989; Ding 2007; Tao et al. 2009; Sun et al. 2019). In addition to pottery implements, a smaller number of lithic food preparation artifacts have been identified in the sample. Specifically, one household unit (G2) was found with only a lithic pestle, two household units (G3 and D4) contained solely lithic mortars, and another household unit (G21) possessed a complete mortar-pestle pair. This distribution pattern suggests that mortars were not necessarily accompanied by lithic pestles, implying the probable use of pestles made from organic materials such as wood, which may have decomposed over time and left no archaeological trace. Archaeological research

has conjectured that mortar-pestle assemblages played a role in rice threshing processes (Song 1997; Xu 2017), a finding that aligns with broader discussions about rice consumption at Erlitou. It has been argued in scholarly literature that both the supply and consumption of rice at the Erlitou site likely depended on tribute-based importation from surrounding regions (Zhongguo 2014; Zhao & Liu 2019). Round-shaped lithics represent another category of potential lithic food preparation artifacts. The presence of pounding scars on their surfaces indicates that they may have been used for cracking nuts, further expanding the functional scope of lithic tools in food processing. Taken together, these findings suggest that the majority of food processing implements in the sample were likely oriented toward the processing of wild-collected food resources, reflecting the continued importance of foraged plants in the subsistence strategy of Erlitou households.

Palaeobotanical studies indicate that during the Erlitou period, the staple food economy at the site was primarily composed of millets (including *Setaria italica* and *Panicum miliaceum*) and rice (*Oryza sativa*), supplemented by consumption of wheat (*Triticum aestivum*) and soybeans (*Glycine max*) (Zhongguo 2014; Zhao & Liu 2019). Scholarly research further suggests that agricultural production, and in particular the food tribute economy, accounted for the largest proportion of food consumption at the Erlitou site (Zhongguo 2014). This form of centralized food supply would have alleviated the need for individual households to engage in full-scale food production and preliminary processing activities. It is plausible that specialized workers or communal groups were responsible for tasks such as millet or rice threshing, meaning that while households consumed these grains, they did not need to perform threshing on a household-by-household basis. However, households would still have required certain food preparation artifacts to process wild-collected food resources, thereby diversifying their dietary intake. Importantly, this pattern does not preclude the existence of other types of pestles and mortars in the archaeological record. For instance, archaeologists have documented semi-subterranean mortars dating to the Yangshao period (5000–3000 BCE) at sites such as Qingtai 青台 in Henan, Dadungzi 大墩子 in Jiangsu, and Honghuatao 红花套 in Sichuan. Similarly, wooden pestles have been unearthed at the Bashidang 八十垱 site (7000–6000 BCE) in Hunan and the Hemudu 河姆渡 site (5000–4000 BCE) in Zhejiang (Song 1997; Xu 2017). If such organic or semi-subterranean processing tools were also in use at Erlitou, it would imply that some degree of household-based food preparation persisted; however, the perishable nature of organic materials and the potential invisibility of semi-subterranean features would undoubtedly hinder the identification and quantification of these artifacts in the archaeological record. On another note, recent research has highlighted that rice consumption at Erlitou was predominantly concentrated among elite groups (Gao & Wu 2022). Non-elite households, while likely having limited access to rice, would therefore have had less demand for specialized food preparation artifacts dedicated to rice threshing. This socioeconomic differentiation helps explain why food preparation artifacts appear in relatively small proportions within individual household units. Nevertheless, the presence and quantity of such artifacts can still be reasonably associated with household wealth, reflecting disparities in access to processing technologies and dietary diversity across different social strata.

Variable 7. Ornaments

Ornaments recovered from the site encompass a diverse range of forms, including bone hairpins (*zan/chai* 簪/钗), beads made from bone, shell, and pottery (*gu zhu* 骨珠, *bang zhu* 蚌珠, and *tao zhu* 陶珠), pottery circles (*tao huan* 陶环), and turquoise sheets intended for inlay work (see Figure 2.7). Within the sampled household units, bone hairpins (*zan/chai* 簪/钗) constitute the most prevalent category of ornaments. Additionally, some households are associated with bone, shell, and pottery beads, as well as pottery circles. Scholarly investigations into beads and circular ornaments from contemporaneous or related archaeological sites have suggested that these artifacts likely served as decorative elements attached to garments, while pottery circles may have also functioned as rings

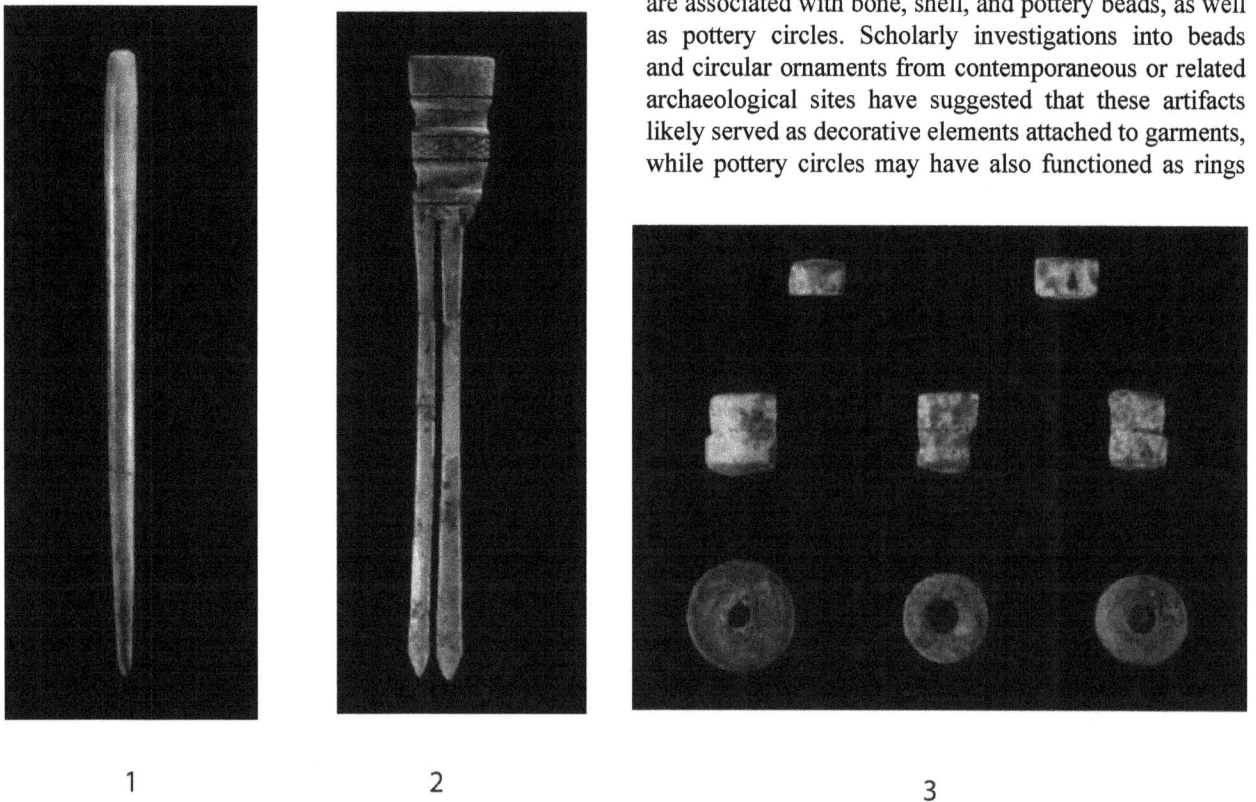

Figure 2.7. Examples of Variable 7. Ornaments. 1. Hairpin *zan* 簪 (*Zhongguo 2014*, colorful plate 353:8); 2. Hairpin *chai* 钗 (*Zhongguo 2014*, colorful plate 358:2); 3. Bone beads *gu zhu* 骨珠 (*Zhongguo 2014*, colorful plate 365:2).

or earrings (Li & Huo 1990; Zhang 2003). Although the personal ornaments found in household contexts are generally undecorated and appear relatively plain, lacking the opulence of jade ornaments and elaborate turquoise artifacts unearthed from elite burials at Erlitou, they nonetheless hold significance in socioeconomic analysis. These everyday ornamental items, despite their modest appearance, can be reasonably interpreted as indicators of wealth, reflecting disparities in access to craft products, personal adornment practices, and social status among different household units at the site. Their presence and variety within households offer valuable insights into the material expression of identity and economic differentiation in Erlitou society.

On the other hand, one household unit (G8) was found to possess a turquoise sheet prepared for inlay work, suggesting that this household may have had access to or the capability to own luxury items adorned with turquoise. To date, luxury goods and ritual paraphernalia featuring turquoise inlays have exclusively been documented in elite burials at Erlitou (Li, Z. 2008). Qin (2014) notes that turquoise sheets or pieces were typically inlaid through three primary methods: 1) on bronze artifacts (such as turquoise-inlaid bronze plaques, weapons, and circular ritual bronzes); 2) on organic material substrates; and 3) on jade objects. Thus, to a certain extent, turquoise sheets or pieces used for inlaying primarily served decorative functions, albeit they may also have carried ritual connotations and enhanced the ritual symbolism of

bronzes or jades. Scholarly research has argued that the Erlitou state procured turquoise from multiple sources through long-distance trade networks (Xian et al. 2021; Qin 2022). Given this context, such exotic ornamental materials can reasonably be interpreted as indicators of wealth and social status.

Variable 8. Carpentry/Construction Tools

Carpentry and construction tools identified at the site include lithic adzes (*beng/zao* 锛/凿), spades (*chan* 铲), axes (*fu* 斧), as well as bone spades (*chan* 铲) and saws (*ju* 锯) (see Figure 2.8). Scholarly research has established functional distinctions among these implements: axes are generally recognized as tools for felling trees and chopping wood, spades are conjectured to have been used for digging activities, while adzes and saws likely served purposes related to wood processing and carpentry (Yang 1982; Yin 1986; Xie 2008; Xiao 2020). Given their digging functionality, spades could potentially have been utilized in agricultural contexts as well. However, this study categorizes spades under carpentry and construction tools based on archaeological evidence: archaeologists have documented digging impressions on the walls of certain garbage pits that match the morphological attributes of the spades unearthed at the site (Zhongguo 1999). This classification does not entirely exclude the possibility of their secondary use in agricultural activities, but prioritizes the contextual evidence linking them to construction-related tasks.

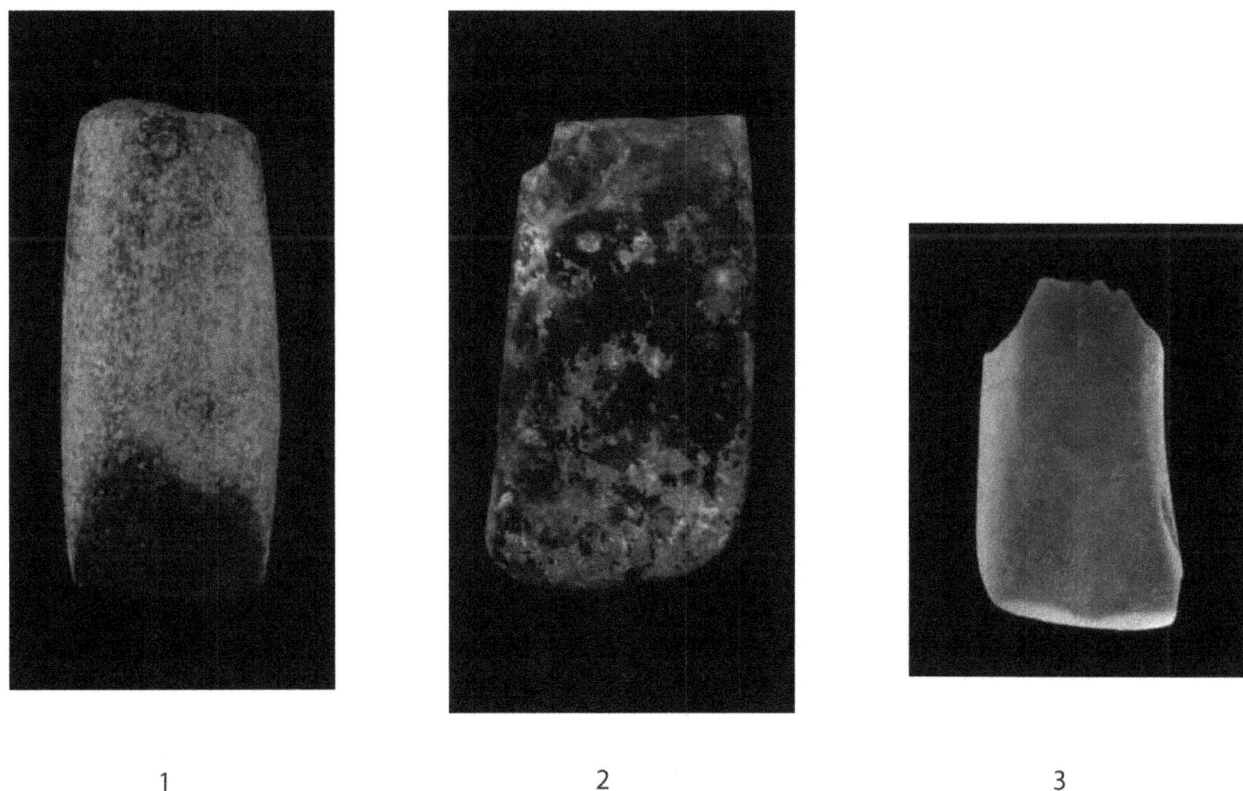

1   2   3

Figure 2.8. Examples of Variable 8. Carpentry/construction Tools. 1. Lithic axe *shi fu* 石斧 (*Zhongguo 2014*, colorful plate 313:5); 2. Lithic spade *shi chan* 石铲 (*Zhongguo 2014*, colorful plate 306:4); 3. Bone spade *gu chan* 骨铲 (*Zhongguo 2014*, colorful plate 342:7).

Variable 9. Agricultural Tools

Agricultural tools identified at the site include lithic knives (*shi dao* 石刀), lithic sickles (*shi lian* 石镰), bone knives (*gu dao* 骨刀), as well as shell knives (*bang dao* 蚌刀) and shell sickles (*bang lian* 蚌镰) (see Figure 2.9). Scholarly research has consistently categorized knives and sickles as specialized agricultural implements primarily used for harvesting activities, specifically for cutting mature grains and tubers such as millets, rice, beans, root crops, and other cultivated plants (Xie 2008; Liu et al. 2018; Peng 2019; Yang 2021). These tools played a critical role in the subsistence economy of the Erlitou period by facilitating the efficient collection of agricultural produce, directly supporting the site's food production system.

Variable 10. Textile Tools

Textile tools uncovered at the site include lithic spindle whorls (*shi fanglun* 石纺轮), bone needles (*gu zhen* 骨针), bone awls (*gu zhui* 骨锥), shell awls (*bang zhui* 蚌锥), and pottery spindle whorls (*tao fanglun* 陶纺轮) (see Figure 2.10). Based on archaeological functional analysis, spindle whorls are recognized as key implements for spinning fibers into thread, while needles would have served essential sewing functions in garment production.

Awls, meanwhile, are conjectured to have been utilized in weaving processes or for working with cloth and leather materials, such as piercing holes or adjusting fibers during textile manufacturing. These tools collectively reflect the technological complexity of textile production in the Erlitou period, underscoring the importance of cloth-making in both subsistence and craft economies.

Variable 11. Weapons/Hunting Tools

Weapons and hunting tools identified at the site include lithic axes (*shi yue* 石钺), as well as arrowheads made from various materials: lithic arrowheads (*shi zu* 石镞), bone arrowheads (*gu zu* 骨镞), antler arrowheads (*jiao zu* 角镞), shell arrowheads (*bang zu* 蚌镞), and bronze arrowheads (*tong zu* 铜镞) (see Figure 2.11). These implements collectively represent the technological diversity of tools used for both defensive/offensive purposes (weapons) and subsistence hunting activities during the Erlitou period, reflecting the integration of resource utilization and functional adaptation in ancient tool production.

Weapons and hunting tools identified from the 1959–1978 excavations indicate a gradual increase in such artifacts throughout the Erlitou period. This trend may be attributed to military expansion, driven by the need to

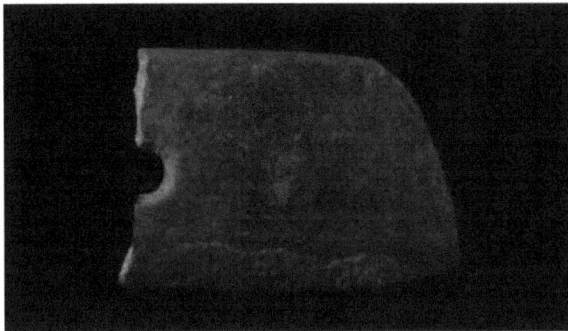

1

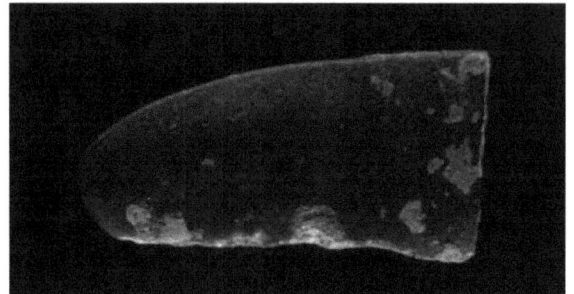

2

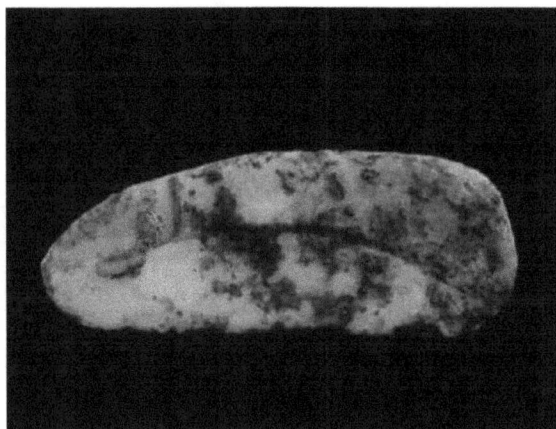

3

Figure 2.9. Examples of Variable 9. Agricultural Tools. 1. Lithic knife *shi dao* 石刀 (*Zhongguo 2014*, colorful plate 292:4); 2. Lithic sickle *shi lian* 石镰 (*Zhongguo 2014*, colorful plate 299:4); 3. Shell sickle *bang lian* 蚌镰 (*Zhongguo 2014*, colorful plate 390:1).

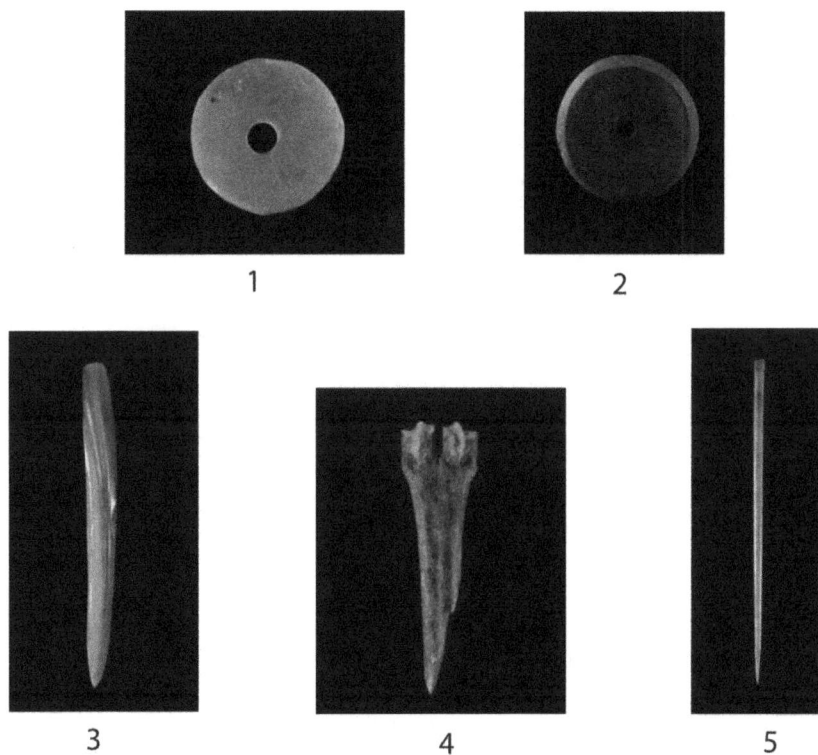

Figure 2.10. Examples of Variable 10. Textile Tools. 1. lithic spindle whorls *shi fanglun* 石纺轮 (*Zhongguo 2014*, colorful plate 315:3); **2. Pottery spindle whorls** *tao fanglun* 陶纺轮 (*Zhongguo 2014*, colorful plate 262:5); **3. Shell awl** *bang zhui* 蚌锥 (*Zhongguo 2014*, colorful plate 391:4); **4. Bone awl** *gu zhui* 骨锥 (*Zhongguo 2014*, colorful plate 348:5); **5. Bone needle** *gu zhen* 骨针 (*Zhongguo 2014*, colorful plate 358:7).

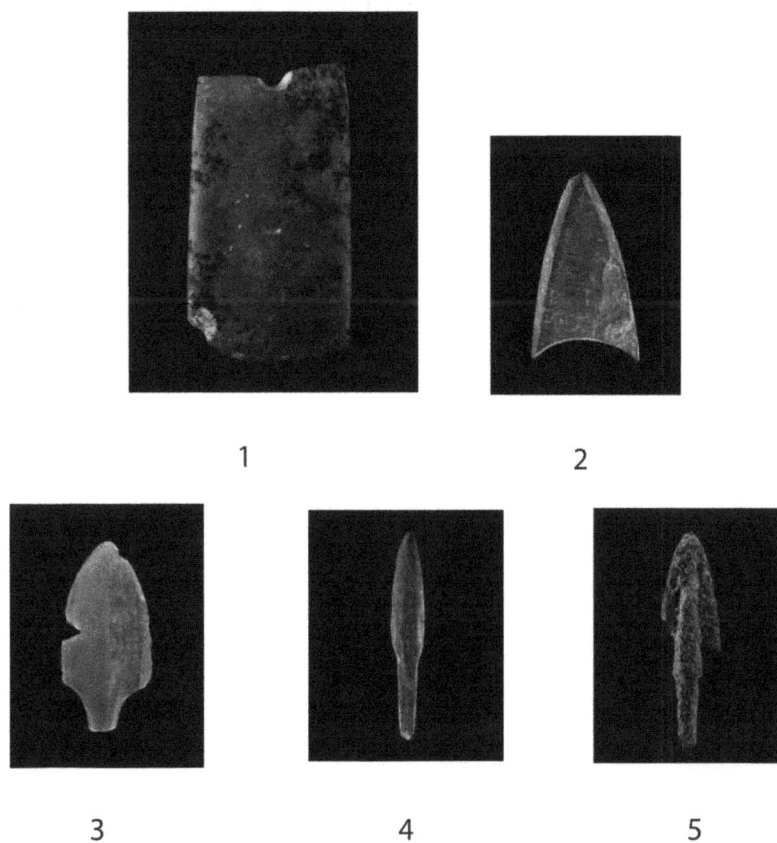

Figure 2.11. Examples of Variable 11. Weapon/Hunting Tools. 1. Lithic axes *yue* 钺 (*Zhongguo 2014*, colorful 325:1); **2. Lithic arrowhead** *shi zu* 石镞 (*Zhongguo 2014*, colorful plate 328:4); **3. Shell arrowhead** *bang zu* 蚌镞 (*Zhongguo 2014*, colorful plate 392:6); **4. Bone arrowhead** *gu zu* 骨镞 (*Zhongguo 2014*, colorful plate 363:8); **5. Bronze arrowhead** *tong zu* 铜镞 (*Zhongguo 2014*, colorful plate 283:4).

procure natural resources, and competitive pressures from the Erligang polity (Liu and Chen 2003; Zhongguo 1999; Liu 2006). Recent archaeological studies have further shed light on subsistence patterns during this era: across both the Erlitou and Erligang periods, the remains of wild animals accounted for no more than 25% of all identifiable mammal bones, while domesticated animal remains constituted over 80% of the total (Zhongguo 2014). This proportional distribution strongly suggests that the inhabitants of the Erlitou site prioritized domesticated animals as their primary source of meat. Although hunting may have still contributed marginally to food supplies, its role in subsistence was secondary. Against this backdrop, the weapons/hunting tools recovered from household contexts are more likely to have functioned as weapons rather than hunting implements, even though arrowheads (a common category within this artifact group) could still be used for hunting to a limited extent. This interpretation also implies that non-elite households at Erlitou may have retained weapons within their residences, a detail that bears significance for understanding the distribution of defensive or military-related resources across different social strata.

Variable 12. Resharpening Tools

In this study, resharpening tools specifically refer to whetstones (*lishi* 砺石) (Figure 2.12). The majority of whetstones included in this research are those collected during excavations and documented under the designation "whetstone (*lishi* 砺石)" in the archaeological report (Zhongguo 2014). Scholarly research has argued that this type of whetstone was used in the processing of lithic, bone, antler, shell, jade, or turquoise items and tools, with a particular focus on sharpening or resharpening other practical tools featuring blades. Notably, this variable also encompasses 4 lithic saws (*shiju* 石锯), which are categorized under "whetstones" in this analysis. These lithic saws could have functioned in item and tool processing alongside other whetstones: they were likely used to slice rocks, turquoises, or jades for further refinement, and in

some cases, may have also been employed directly for the immediate sharpening or resharpening of other items.

In addition, there is one other whetstone collected during excavations and documented under the designation "lithic rotary grinder (*shizhoucheng* 石轴承)" in the archaeological report. A body of scholarly literature has debated the functional purpose of a specific type of whetstone, often referred to as lithic rotary grinders, discovered at archaeological sites across China. Several archaeologists argue that certain whetstones classified as rotary grinders were used in conjunction with wheeled machinery, functioning as gears or motion transmitters to assist drill tools in boring holes into jade or lithic materials (Xu, Tang and Ye 2018). In contrast, other researchers (Li 2019) contend that these so-called rotary grinders should still be categorized as whetstones, positing that they were directly used for drilling or smoothing drilled surfaces, rather than serving as rotary components within a larger instrument. Regardless of the specific function of this type of whetstone, the single example of such a whetstone (or so-called lithic rotary grinder) identified in Erlitou's household contexts likely played a role in item and tool processing. Thus, the resharpening tools examined in this study are understood to be primarily associated with item and tool processing, most commonly for sharpening or resharpening, though a small subset may also have been used for slicing and/or drilling tasks.

Variable 13. Fishing Tools

Fishing tools identified in this study include bone darts (*gu biao* 骨镖) and pottery net sinkers (*tao wangzhui* 陶网坠) (Figure 2.13). These two types of fishing tools are functionally associated with fishing activities, which served as a subsistence strategy for acquiring food resources at the Erlitou site. Both bone darts and pottery net sinkers represent specialized implements tailored to fishing: bone darts would have been used for spearing fish, while pottery net sinkers, designed to weigh down fishing nets, facilitated the capture of aquatic organisms.

1

2

Figure 2.12. Examples of Variable 12. Resharpening Tools. 1. Whetstone *lishi* 砺石 (*Zhongguo 2014*, colorful plate 320:7); 2. Whetstone *lishi* 砺石 (*Zhongguo 2014*; colorful plate 331:3).

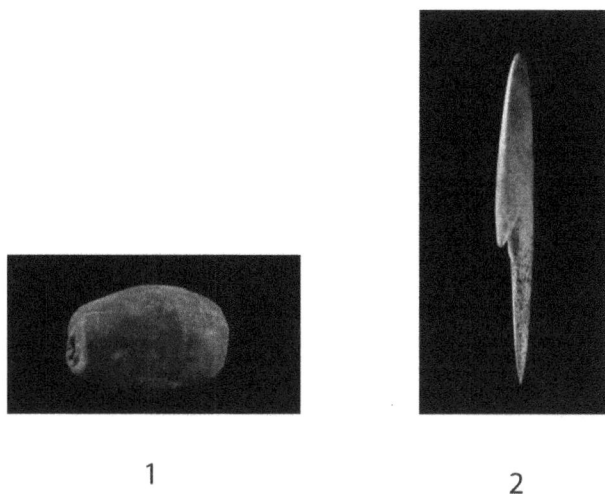

1   2

Figure 2.13. Examples of Variable 13. Fishing Tools.
1. Pottery net sinker *tao wangzhui* 陶网坠 (*Zhongguo 2014*,
colorful plate 263:2); **2. Bone dart** *gu biao* 骨镖 (*Zhongguo*
2014, colorful plate 347:2).

Their presence in household contexts further suggests that
fishing may have been a localized subsistence practice,
contributing to the food procurement of individual Erlitou
households alongside other activities such as agriculture
and animal husbandry.

In contrast to agriculture and animal husbandry, fish
accounted for no more than 1% of the total identifiable
animal remains throughout both the Erlitou period and the
Erligang period (Zhongguo 2014). This low proportion
strongly suggests that fish were not heavily consumed by
the inhabitants of the Erlitou site, and further indicates that
fishing likely did not constitute a primary or emphasized
subsistence strategy for procuring food resources at the
site. Notably, this minimal contribution of fish to the
overall animal remains aligns with the earlier observation
that domesticated animals dominated meat procurement
(accounting for over 80% of identifiable mammal bones)
during the same periods. Together, these data highlight
a clear subsistence priority on agriculture and animal
husbandry at Erlitou, with fishing functioning as a
secondary or supplementary practice rather than a core
component of the site's food economy.

Variable 14. Ritual Paraphernalia

The majority of ritual paraphernalia examined in this
study consists of oracle bones (*bu gu* 卜骨) (Figure 2.14).
Divination represents a key religious practice documented
at the Erlitou site, with scapulimancy (divination using
animal scapulae) identified in various contexts, including
garbage pits, ash ditches, earthen layers, the enclosing
walls of the palatial complex, and the footings or walls of
buildings. Some archaeologists argue that during the early
phase of state formation in China, elites monopolized
communication with ancestors and deities; non-elite
individuals, if seeking to contact these supernatural
entities, would have relied on the intermediary of shamanic
elites (Chang 1989). Based on an analysis of 160 oracle

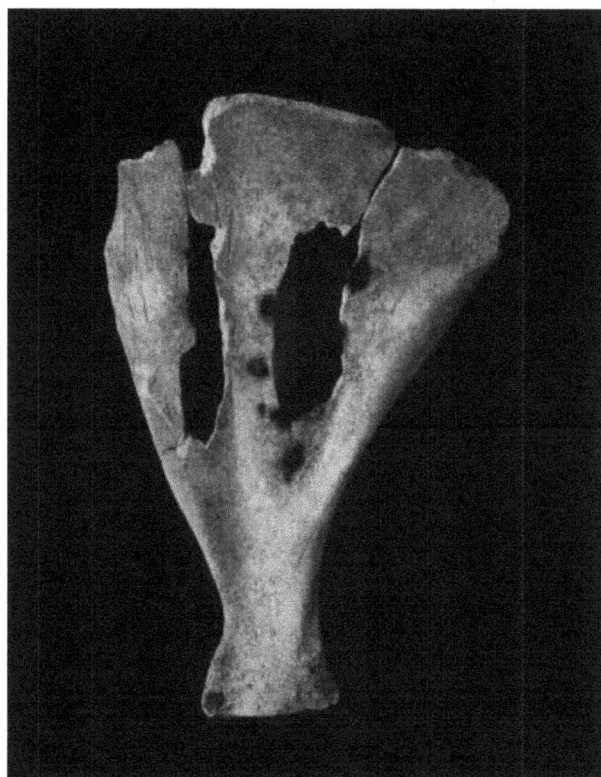

Figure 2.14. Example of Variable 14. Ritual Paraphernalia.
Oracle bone *bu gu* 卜骨 (*Zhongguo 2014*, colorful plate 402:2).

scapulae unearthed during the 1999–2006 excavations,
Chen and Li (2013) note that bovid scapulae are the most
abundant, accounting for approximately 50% of the total.
Pig and sheep/goat scapulae follow in frequency, while
deer scapulae constitute only about 6.25%. Given that
the majority of cattle, pigs, and sheep/goats identified at
the site have been confirmed as domesticated (Zhongguo
2014), it is likely that the pyromancy (fire-based divination)
practiced at Erlitou primarily utilized the remains
of domesticated animals. While most scapulimancy
specimens from Erlitou lack preparatory modifications,
such as drilled hollows on the scapula surface or the
leveling of the rear surface by removing the spine, the
emergence of pre-prepared scapulae for divination starting
in Erlitou Phase 3 may indicate that diviners began to exert
intentional influence over the interpretation of divination
results (Chen and Li 2013). Drawing on these findings,
Chen and Li (2013) further propose that the Erlitou society
may have had professionalized diviners, reflecting a degree
of specialization in religious practice.

In addition to oracle bones, one household unit yielded
another type of pottery ritual paraphernalia: a hollow-
bottomed vessel (*toudiqi* 透底器). This pottery artifact,
consistent with three other examples documented in
collections predating the 1999–2006 excavations and a
small number found at other Early Bronze Age sites across
China, is characterized by the absence of a solid base (Du
2006; Wang 2019). The lack of a bottom clearly indicates
that this type of pottery was not designed for practical
daily functions such as holding, storing, or containing
substances. For this reason, several archaeologists have

argued that such artifacts should be classified as ritual paraphernalia, as their form directly excludes utilitarian use (Du 2006; Wang 2019). Given this functional attribution, the presence of a greater quantity of ritual paraphernalia (including both oracle bones and hollow-bottomed vessels) in a household unit may suggest two key implications: first, that the household was more extensively involved in or specialized in ritual worship activities; and second, that the household likely held a higher or more socially respected status within the Erlitou community. This correlation between ritual artifact abundance and social status aligns with broader archaeological understandings of early state societies, where access to and use of ritual paraphernalia often served as markers of elite identity or religious authority.

Variable 15. Lithic Production

The majority of lithic production data analyzed in this study were collected during excavations and documented under the category of "lithic raw materials (石料)" in the archaeological report, while a smaller portion was recorded under the designation of "broken lithic artifacts (石器残件)" (Figure 2.15). According to Anne Ford (2004), the reduction sequence for stone tools such as spades, axes, chisels, adzes, and knives typically includes three key stages: flaking, hammer dressing and grinding, and the final finished product. For the purposes of this research, two of these stages (i.e., flaking, and hammer dressing and grinding) are combined into a single category termed "blank" (a semi-finished stage of lithic production). Additionally, this study classifies lithic raw materials into five distinct types: unworked stone, cores, flakes, blanks, and indeterminate lithic materials. It is noteworthy that the analysis also identified some broken lithic artifacts as lithic blanks, further refining the classification of semi-finished production remains. For the variable measuring lithic production activity, only lithic cores, flakes, and blanks are counted, these three categories directly reflect active involvement in the lithic reduction process, as opposed to unworked raw materials or unidentifiable fragments. The presence of such lithic production data

within the household unit samples strongly suggests that specific families at the Erlitou site were involved in lithic production, providing evidence of household-level craft activity related to stone tool manufacturing.

At the Erlitou site, several types of rocks were widely utilized for lithic production, with sandstone accounting for 36.5%, andesite 22.75%, limestone 7.3%, and additional rock types making up the remaining proportion (Qian et al. 2014). In terms of raw material procurement, andesite is the only one of these rock types that could be sourced locally, specifically from the riverbed of the Old Luo River (古洛河), located south of the Erlitou site. By contrast, limestone, sandstone, dolomite, and other associated rock types could only be obtained from the northern and eastern piedmonts of Mount Song (嵩山), which lie to the south and east of the Erlitou site respectively (Qian et al. 2014; Zhongguo and Zhongaomei 2019). Two key sites, Huizui (灰咀) and Shaochai (稍柴), are geographically positioned as critical intermediaries in this raw material supply network. Huizui is situated between the Erlitou site and the northern piedmont of Mount Song, while Shaochai lies between Erlitou and the eastern piedmont of the same mountain. Scholarly research suggests that both sites likely functioned as nodes for the Erlitou state, facilitating the procurement and transportation of rock materials to the core site. Notably, Huizui may have also operated as a specialized lithic workshop, with evidence indicating it exported surplus lithic products, particularly lithic spades, to the Erlitou site. This conclusion is supported by the observation that lithic spades from Erlitou and Huizui share identical rock types and exhibit consistent lithic reduction technologies, indicating a direct production and supply relationship between the two sites (Chen et al. 2003; Ford 2004; Chen, X. 2006; Zhongguo 2010; Liu and Chen 2012).

Variable 16. Bone Production

The bone production data analyzed in this study were collected during excavations and documented under the category of "bone raw materials (骨料)" in the archaeological report (Figure 2.16). In accordance with

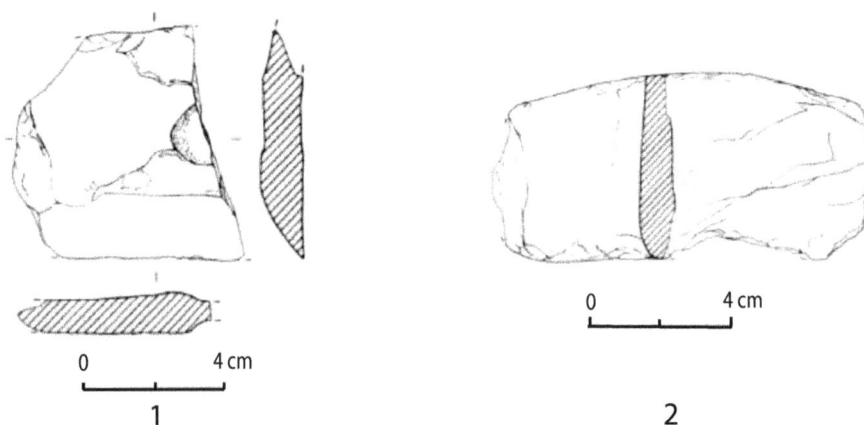

Figure 2.15. Examples of Variable 15. Lithic Production. 1. Blank – lithic knife *shidao pijian* 石刀坯件 (*Zhongguo 2014*, pp 461, figure f5-5-1-38-2: 2); 2. Blank – lithic sickle (handle) *shilianbing pijian* 石镰(柄)坯件 (*Zhongguo 2014*, pp 456, figure f5-5-1-32-2:1).

Figure 2.16. Examples of Variable 16. Bone Production. Bone raw materials *gu liao* 骨料 (*Zhongguo* 2014, colorful plate 380:1).

established archaeological frameworks, bone raw materials and artifacts can be categorized into distinct stages of the production process based on processing marks: cores, blanks, waste, semi-finished products, and finished products (Xu, Zhou and Yi 2021; Wang 2018). For the specific purposes of this research, two of these stages (i.e., blanks and semi-finished products) are consolidated into a single category referred to as "blank," as both represent intermediate phases of bone working prior to the completion of a final artifact. This study focuses exclusively on three production-related categories: cores, blanks (the consolidated category), and waste, as these directly reflect active engagement in bone tool/item manufacturing. To ensure clarity in classification, each category is defined explicitly: Bone cores refer to the diaphyses (shafts) of animal bones that have been separated from the joint ends, serving as the primary raw material base for shaping bone artifacts. Blanks are bone fragments exhibiting clear processing traces, including cutting or sawing marks and evidence of cancellous bone (spongy bone) removal, modifications that indicate the initial shaping of the raw material into a form suitable for further refinement. Bone waste encompasses discarded components generated during production, such as cut-off joint ends and debris (fine fragments) resulting from cutting, sawing, or scraping processes. Notably, bone raw materials (骨料) that lack sufficient processing marks to confirm their association with bone tool/item production are classified as "indeterminate" and excluded from the production-related analysis. For the variable measuring bone production activity, only bone cores, blanks, and waste are counted. These three categories reliably indicate direct involvement in the bone working process, distinguishing them from unmodified raw materials or unidentifiable fragments. The presence of such bone production data within the household unit samples strongly suggests that specific families at the Erlitou site

were involved in bone production, providing concrete evidence of household-level craft specialization related to the manufacturing of bone tools or artifacts. This finding aligns with the broader pattern of household-based craft activities observed at the site, including lithic production, and contributes to our understanding of domestic economic diversity in Erlitou society.

Variable 17. Antler Production

The antler production data analyzed in this study were collected during excavations and documented under the category of "antler raw materials (角料)" in the archaeological report (Figure 2.17). In line with established archaeological classification systems for osseous materials, antler raw materials and artifacts can be categorized into distinct stages of the production process based on processing marks: cores, blanks, waste, semi-finished products, and finished products (Wang 2018; Yu 2016). For the specific objectives of this research, two intermediate stages (i.e., blanks and semi-finished products) are consolidated into a single category termed "blank," as both represent formative phases of antler working that precede the creation of a final artifact. This study focuses exclusively on three production-relevant categories: cores, blanks (the consolidated category), and waste, as these directly reflect active engagement in antler tool/item manufacturing. To eliminate ambiguity in classification, each category is defined explicitly: Antler cores refer to the main beams of antlers from which the coronets (the bulbous base connecting the antler to the skull) have been removed, serving as the primary raw material foundation for shaping antler artifacts. Antler blanks are antler fragments bearing clear processing traces, including cutting or sawing marks and evidence of cancellous bone (spongy bone) removal, modifications that signal the initial shaping of raw antler into a form ready for further refinement. Antler waste encompasses

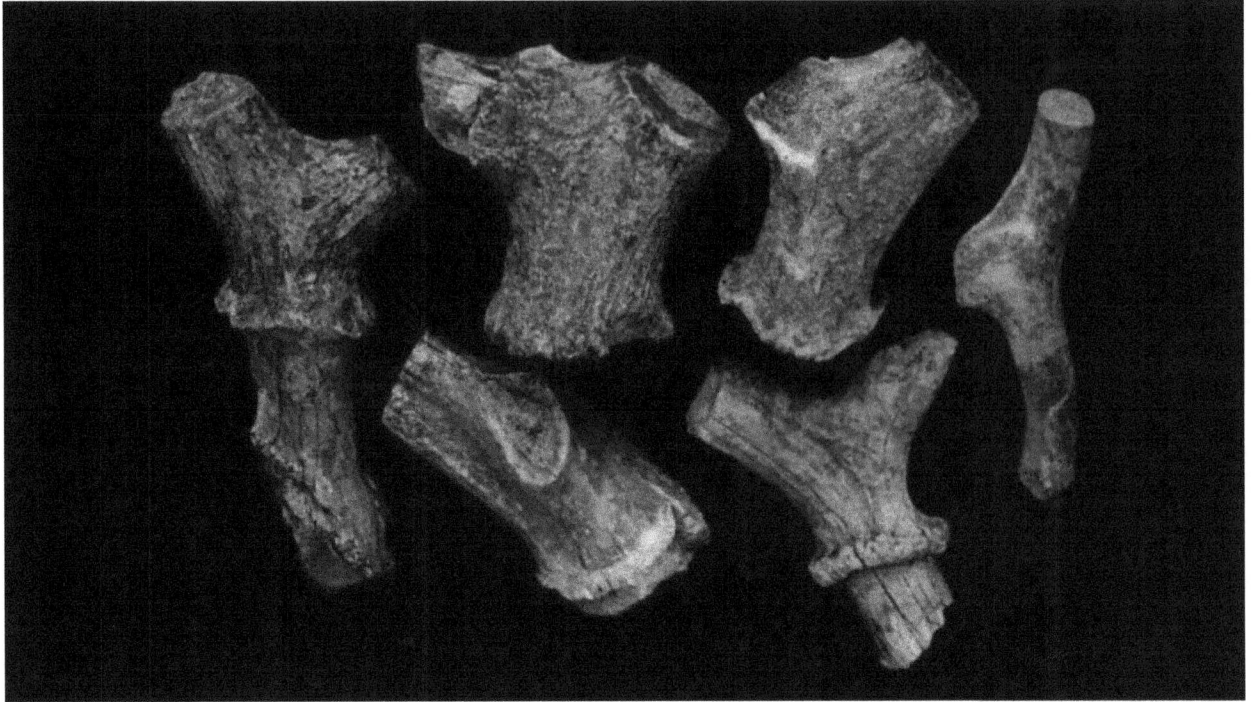

Figure 2.17. Examples of Variable 17. Antler Production. Antler raw materials *jiao liao* 角料 (***Zhongguo 2014***, colorful plate 380:2).

discarded byproducts generated during production, such as cut-off coronets and other debris resulting from cutting, sawing, or scraping processes. Notably, antler raw materials (角料) that lack sufficient processing marks to confirm their association with antler tool/item production are classified as "indeterminate" and excluded from the production-related analysis. For the variable measuring antler production activity, only antler cores, blanks, and waste are counted. These three categories reliably indicate direct involvement in the antler working process, distinguishing them from unmodified raw materials or unidentifiable fragments. The presence of such antler production data within the household unit samples strongly suggests that specific families at the Erlitou site were involved in antler production, providing concrete evidence of household-level craft specialization related to the manufacturing of antler tools or artifacts. This finding aligns with the broader pattern of household-based craft activities observed at the site (including lithic and bone production) and further enriches our understanding of the diverse domestic economic practices that sustained Erlitou society.

Variable 18. Shell Production

The shell production data analyzed in this study were collected during excavations and documented under the category of "shell raw materials (蚌料)" in the archaeological report. Unlike lithic, bone, or antler materials, where production stages can be clearly differentiated based on processing marks, shell raw materials pose unique challenges: their fragmented state and limited diagnostic features make it difficult to determine their exact position within the production sequence. For this reason, all shell raw materials included

in this research are collectively categorized as either "blanks" or "wastes," with the defining criterion being the presence of clear processing traces (such as grinding or cutting marks), which confirm their association with shell tool/item manufacturing.

For the variable measuring shell production activity, these categorized shell blanks and wastes are the primary data points, and their presence directly indicates active engagement in shell working processes, distinguishing them from unmodified shell remains. The occurrence of such shell production data within the household unit samples strongly suggests that specific families at the Erlitou site were involved in shell production, providing evidence of household-level craft specialization related to the manufacturing of shell artifacts or tools. Notably, all these shell raw materials are derived from river mussels, further indicating that they were intended for the production of practical tools, such as shell knives, sickles, arrowheads, or other utilitarian implements common in Early Bronze Age contexts.

To contextualize the raw material supply for shell production, it is important to note that river mussels (*Unionidae*) were not a key food resource for the inhabitants of the Erlitou site. Archaeological evidence shows that the Erlitou people likely did not prioritize river mussels for subsistence: among the total identifiable aquatic invertebrate remains (which include *Viviparidae*, *Unionidae*, and *Veneridae*), *Unionidae* account for less than 4% (Zhongguo 2014). This low consumption rate contrasts with prehistoric China more broadly, where scholarly research has documented that shell tools were frequently crafted from the shells of

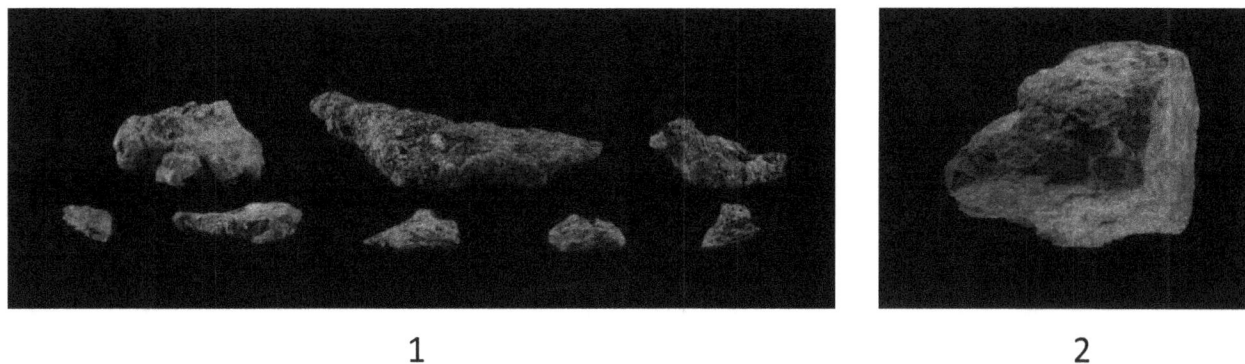

Figure 2.18. Examples of Variable 19. Bronze Working. 1. Slag *tong zha* 铜渣 (*Zhongguo 2014*, colorful plate 287:1); 2. Ore *tong kuangshi* 铜矿石 (*Zhongguo 2014*, colorful plate 287:4).

Lamellibranchia (a class that includes *Unionidae*) (Lv and Fu 2010; Hu 2018).

A critical implication of this low dietary reliance on river mussels is that the supply of raw materials for shell artifact/tool production at Erlitou may have been either unstable or limited in quantity. Unlike contexts where shellfish are consumed extensively (generating abundant byproducts for tool production), the Erlitou site's minimal use of river mussels for food would have required intentional procurement of shells specifically for craft purposes, adding another layer of complexity to the organization of household-based shell production.

Variable 19. Bronze Working

Bronze smelting and casting constituted a pivotal industry within the economic and technological system of the Erlitou site, representing one of the most sophisticated craft activities of the Early Bronze Age in China. Over the course of 55 years of archaeological excavation, researchers have identified one specialized bronze-casting workshop and multiple bronze-melting locations at the site, findings that underscore the scale and institutional organization of bronze production at Erlitou (Zhongguo 1999, 2003; Chen 2016).

Scholarly debates highlight the strategic significance of bronze production for the Erlitou polity: several archaeologists argue that the expansion of Erlitou's political influence was partly driven by the demand for and procurement of copper resources, as access to this critical raw material was essential for sustaining large-scale bronze production (Liu and Chen 2003, 2012). The bronze artifacts unearthed at Erlitou further reflect the social and ritual importance of this industry, with recovered items primarily falling into two categories: ritual paraphernalia and prestige goods, objects closely tied to elite identity, religious practice, and political authority (Zhongguo 2003).

While large-scale bronze casting was concentrated in specialized workshop areas, evidence of household-level engagement in bronze working has also been identified. Specifically, the presence of copper raw materials within

household units strongly suggests that certain families at Erlitou may have been involved in aspects of bronze production. Within the household sample analyzed in this study, the copper raw materials documented include copper ores and smelting slag (Figure 2.18), two key materials that directly indicate participation in bronze production (i.e., ore processing and smelting). This finding aligns with the broader pattern of household-based craft specialization observed for lithic, bone, antler, and shell production at Erlitou, while also highlighting the hierarchical organization of bronze technology: specialized workshops likely handled complex casting of ritual and prestige goods, while households may have contributed to raw material processing or small-scale secondary working.

2.3. General Patterns of the Erlitou Households Revealed by Multidimensional Scaling

To measure the patterning among household samples using multidimensional scaling (MDS), similarity scores between all cases were calculated via a method tailored to the intrinsic nature of the variables. In statistical analysis, the selection of a dissimilarity/similarity measurement method is contingent on the type of variables being analyzed, with distinct approaches corresponding to different variable characteristics: If all variables are true measurements (e.g., continuous or ratio-scale data), Euclidean distance is the most widely used metric for quantifying dissimilarity between cases. For variable sets consisting *only* of presence/absence (binary) variables, the Simple Matching Coefficient and Jaccard's Coefficient are the preferred tools — each accounting for the presence or absence of attributes across cases, though Jaccard's Coefficient excludes cases where both attributes are absent (a key distinction in binary data analysis). For mixed variable sets (incorporating true measurements, presence/absence variables, categorical variables, and/or ordinal variables), Gower's Coefficient and Anderberg's Coefficient are recognized as optimal choices, as they can handle multiple variable types simultaneously by normalizing differences across distinct data formats. In the context of this study, Euclidean distance was selected to calculate similarity scores among the household samples. This choice was justified by the fact that all 19 variables included in the analysis are true measurements of the ratio scale.

A critical consideration in multidimensional scaling (MDS) is the identification of the optimal configuration. Based on the calculated similarity scores, MDS can generate multiple sets of configurations across different dimensionalities (i.e., varying numbers of dimensions). A standard approach to determining the best configuration involves evaluating rank-order correlations, which are quantified as stress values in MDS analysis. While different stress values may not always yield substantially divergent configurations, lower stress values consistently indicate a stronger rank-order correlation between the original similarity scores and the distances represented in the MDS configuration, meaning the configuration more accurately reflects the pairwise similarities/dissimilarities among cases. However, it is important to note that lower stress values or an increase in the number of dimensions do not necessarily result in meaningful improvements to the interpretability of case-to-case relationships in visualizations. Adding more dimensions may reduce stress numerically but can complicate the intuitive understanding of patterns, as human cognition is limited in processing configurations beyond 2–3 dimensions. A widely accepted rule of thumb in MDS practice is that stress values of approximately or the-first-lower-than 0.15 are typically associated with the most interpretable configurations (Drennan 2010). This threshold balances the need for statistical accuracy (lower stress) and practical interpretability, ensuring that the MDS output effectively condenses the multidimensional similarity data into a visualizable format that retains meaningful patterns among household unit samples.

The stress values corresponding to the dissimilarity scores of the 34 household units (based on 19 variables) are presented in Table 2.3. The stress value for the two-dimensional configuration is 0.037, the first value below the 0.15 threshold and exhibiting a distinct, interpretable "elbow" in the stress-dimensionality plot (Figure 2.19). In statistical terms, an "elbow" in such plots denotes the point at which increasing dimensionality no longer yields a substantial reduction in stress, signifying the optimal choice for interpretation. Following the two-dimensional configuration, the stress value does decrease further in the three-dimensional model, but the magnitude of this reduction is negligible. For configurations with four or five dimensions, the stress value begins to rise again; this upward trend is attributed to the impact of random noise on the iterative procedure inherent to MDS. This pattern

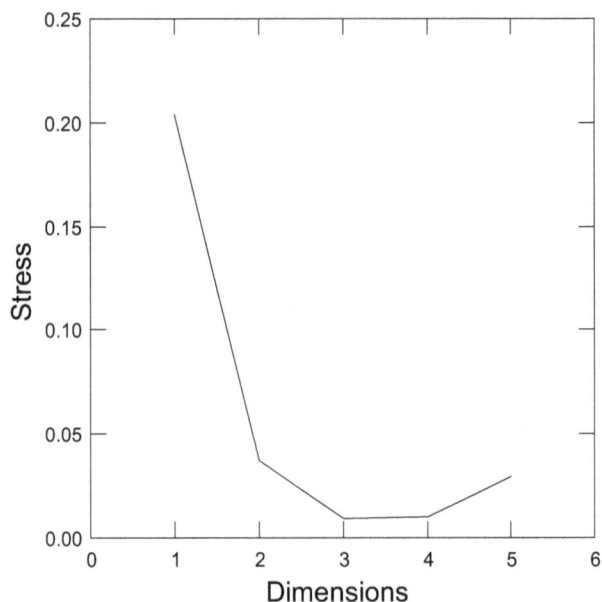

Figure 2.19. Graph of final stress values for analysis of Erlitou household units sample with increasing number of dimensions.

of stress values reveals that configurations with three or more dimensions do not provide a more interpretable visualization or enhance the identification of meaningful household-level patterns compared to the two-dimensional configuration, failing to improve the patterning's explanatory power. Thus, based on the first-less-than-the-threshold stress value (0.037 < 0.15), and the presence of a clear "elbow" at two dimensions, this study selects the two-dimensional scaling solution to analyze the patterning of the Erlitou household sample.

Figure 2.20 illustrates the distribution of the 34 household units in the sample within the two-dimensional scaling plot derived from MDS analysis. Each square in the plot represents the artifact assemblage of a single household unit, with the position of each square determined by the unit's correlation to the 19 variables included in the analysis. As evident from the plot, a distinct cluster is present in the right-center region; this cluster encompasses the majority of the household units, indicating a group of households that exhibit broad similarity across the multiple factors (i.e., the 19 variables) measured in this study. To the contrast, there is a smaller number of household units standing farther away in several directions from this cluster, deviating substantially from the norm represented by the central cluster. Such deviations in artifact assemblages likely reflect differentiations in the social and economic dimensions among the households. The specific nature of this unusualness, including potential differences in craft specialization, ritual involvement, or subsistence strategies, will be addressed and discussed in detail in subsequent chapters of this study.

Figure 2.20 further displays the 34 household units from four chronological phases, with each phase represented by a distinct color. This color-coding was implemented to

Table 2.3. Final stress values for analysis of the Erlitou household sample across increasing dimensions.

Dimension(s)	Stress value
1	0.204
2	0.037
3	0.009
4	0.010
5	0.029

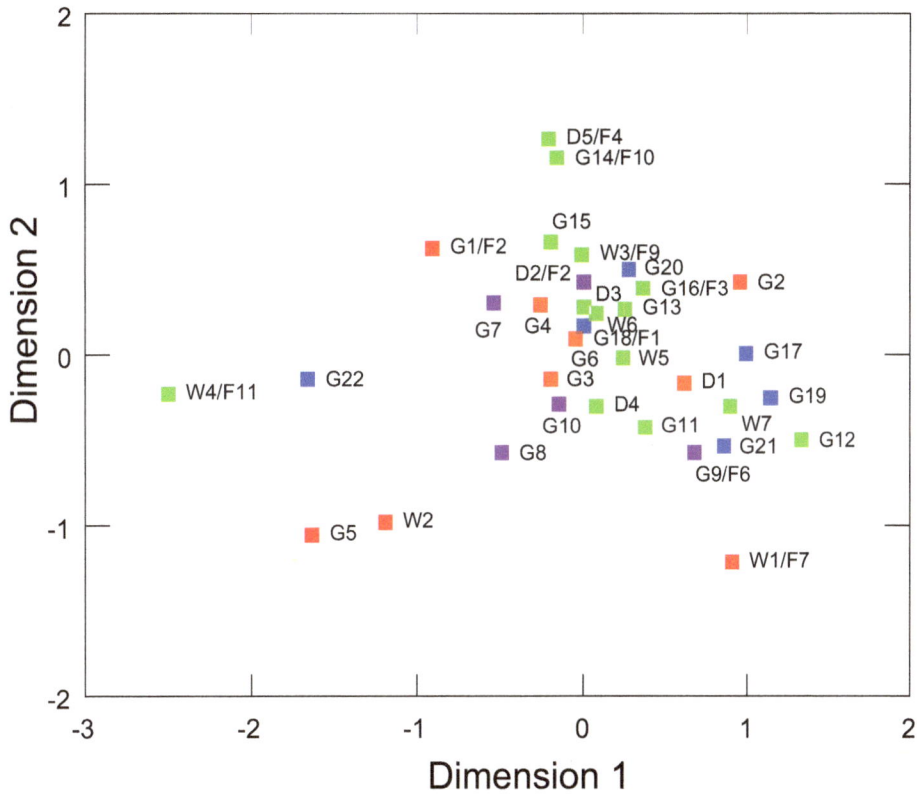

Figure 2.20. Two-dimensional configuration of the 34 household units. (Household units from Erlitou Phase 2 in red, from Erlitou Phase 3 in purple, from Erlitou Phase 4 in green, and from Erligang phase in blue).

investigate whether differences in household assemblages might be attributed to diachronic fashion changes. Specifically, the color assignments are as follows: household units from Erlitou Phase 2 are in red, household units from Erlitou Phase 3 are in purple, household units from Erlitou Phase 4 are in green, and household units from Erligang phase are in blue (Figure 2.2). As observed in the plot, household units from the four different phases are thoroughly intermingled, with no tendency to separate into sections by phases. This distribution pattern indicates that household assemblages of one phase are not more similar to each other than they are to assemblages from another phases. In other words, there is no evidence of substantial phase-specific changes in household assemblages across the Erlitou and early Erligang periods. So, the overall patterning of household assemblages, as reflected in the MDS configuration, remained relatively stable throughout the occupational span of the Erlitou site. Thus, it is methodologically legitimate to interpret the patterns observed in the two-dimensional configuration as indicators of various forms of economic or social differentiation between households rather than as outcomes of temporal change in fashions or preferences. Building on this, a set of characteristics visualized through the two-dimensional scaling configuration may provide insights into the differentiation of Erlitou households along dimensions such as wealth, prestige, ritual involvement, and craft production.

Wealth Differentiation within the Erlitou Household Sample

3.1. Patterns of the Variables Correlated to Wealth in the Two-dimensional Configuration

In this chapter, we explore the patterning of household assemblage variables related to wealth differentiation, as reflected in the two-dimensional multidimensional scaling configuration presented in Chapter 2. Such variables include *Variable 2* (*Incising/Stamping in Complex Patterns*), *Variable 5* (*Storage Vessels*), *Variable 6* (*Food Preparation Artifacts*), and *Variable 7* (*Ornaments*).

3.1.1. Variable 5. Storage Vessels

Figure 3.1 presents the two-dimensional MDS configuration plot of the 34 household units in this sample, with the plot illustrating the values of Variable 5 (Storage Vessels). Each square in the figure represents a ratio of the number of storage vessel sherds divided by the number of sherds from identifiable vessel forms within a household unit. Larger squares correspond to household units with higher

proportions of storage vessel sherds, which indicates a greater quantity of storage vessels.

As shown in the plot, every household unit in the sample contains storage vessels, with the proportion of storage vessel sherds relative to total identifiable vessel sherds ranging from approximately 30% to 60% (Table 3.1). This range is considerable, spanning from a relatively small share of identifiable vessels to a clear majority. Such variation may reflect significant differences in the amount of stored goods, and thus, by extension, in wealth, among the household units.

Actually, the sizes of the samples of sherds from the 34 household units range from around 100 to thousands of sherds in total. In order to consider carefully the potential bias caused by small sample sizes, this study estimated the minimum total sherd count needed to be considered a highly reliable indicator of the proportional composition of the ceramic assemblages of each household unit. With

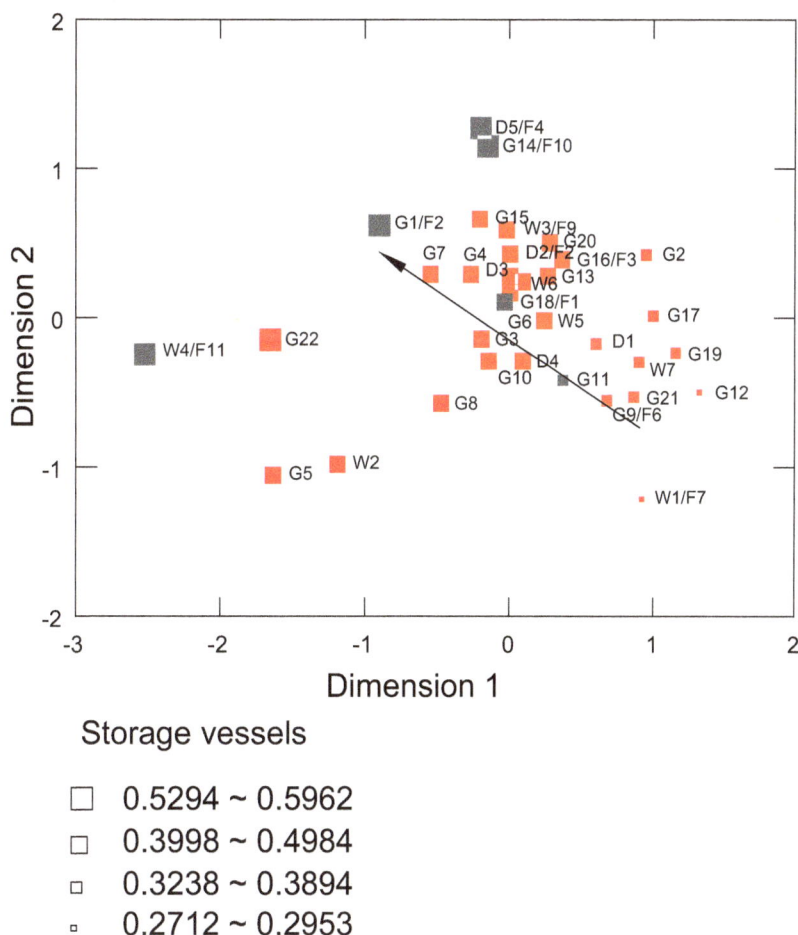

Figure 3.1. Plot of Variable 5. Storage Vessels (larger squares representing higher proportions of storage vessels; grey squares are the household units with fewer than 384 sherds of various vessel forms).

Table 3.1. Proportions of the variables related to wealth differentiation in the 34 household units.

Household unit	Incising/stamping in complex patterns	Storage vessels	Food preparation artifacts	Ornaments
G1/F2	0.0000	0.5427	0.0000	0.0061
G2	0.0000	0.3894	0.0133	0.0000
G3	0.0008	0.4356	0.0066	0.0000
G4	0.0024	0.4732	0.0063	0.0032
G5	0.0021	0.4693	0.0080	0.0013
G6	0.0000	0.4400	0.0267	0.0000
G7	0.0016	0.4984	0.0076	0.0011
G8	0.0007	0.4223	0.0080	0.0004
G9/F6	0.0000	0.3360	0.0102	0.0000
G10	0.0006	0.4192	0.0218	0.0000
W1/F7	0.0006	0.2712	0.0032	0.0016
W2	0.0000	0.4466	0.0032	0.0000
D1	0.0021	0.3776	0.0050	0.0025
D2/F2	0.0023	0.4629	0.0000	0.0089
G11	0.0040	0.3681	0.0055	0.0000
G12	0.0000	0.2953	0.0034	0.0000
G13	0.0003	0.4283	0.0020	0.0020
G14/F10	0.0000	0.5294	0.0000	0.0000
G15	0.0007	0.4907	0.0244	0.0044
G16/F3	0.0000	0.4331	0.0029	0.0000
W3/F9	0.0011	0.4765	0.0098	0.0020
W4/F11	0.0000	0.5962	0.0192	0.0000
W5	0.0010	0.4100	0.0059	0.0007
W6	0.0000	0.4424	0.0050	0.0000
W7	0.0000	0.3393	0.0030	0.0030
D3	0.0005	0.4511	0.0153	0.0012
D4	0.0015	0.3998	0.0062	0.0004
D5/F4	0.0101	0.5385	0.0154	0.0000
G17	0.0027	0.3560	0.0039	0.0006
G18/F1	0.0006	0.4419	0.0080	0.0040
G19	0.0013	0.3238	0.0050	0.0025
G20	0.0014	0.4473	0.0113	0.0000
G21	0.0000	0.3240	0.0078	0.0000
G22	0.0000	0.5306	0.0018	0.0000

a conservative guess of 50% of sherds from various vessel forms (i.e., a maximum variance for proportional estimates) and a 95% confidence level, a random sample of sherds regardless of vessel forms from a household unit must include at least 384 sherds to be deemed highly reliable. This calculation is based on the *t*-value for unknown degrees of freedom at a 95% confidence level ($t = 1.96$), a standard statistical parameter for estimating sample size requirements in proportional analysis. This threshold implies that any household unit with more than 384 sherds in total can be considered a highly reliable representation of actual ceramic assemblage. Conversely, in Figure 3.1, household units with a total sherd sample size of fewer than 384 are displayed in grey. This color coding explicitly indicates that

their ceramic assemblage proportional estimates are less reliable, allowing readers to contextualize the interpretive limitations of these units when analyzing the distribution of Variable 5 (Storage Vessels).

Although 6 household units are considered less reliable due to their total sherd sample sizes, no sharp division is observed in this two-dimensional plot. Instead, there is a gradual variation in the proportion of storage vessel sherds: proportions are fairly low in the lower-right region of the plot, moderate in the middle, and highest along the upper-left edge of the two-dimensional configuration. This distribution pattern suggests that wealth among the household sample corresponds to the proportion of storage vessel sherds. Specifically, households positioned in the lower-right region (with low storage vessel sherd proportions) likely represent lower wealth levels, while those broadly in the left region (with higher proportions) correspond to higher wealth levels. Variations in the quantity of stored goods across these households further imply differences in three key capacities: first, the ability to procure necessary or socially valued goods; second, the capacity to consume such goods; and third, access to exchanged services. These differences collectively reflect the wealth differentiation observed among the household sample.

3.1.2. Variable 7. Ornaments

A two-dimensional plot for Variable 7 (Ornaments) (Figure 3.2) illustrates the distribution of values calculated for each household unit in the sample: specifically, the ratio of the number of ornaments to the number of sherds from identifiable vessel forms. In this plot, larger squares represent household units with higher proportions of ornaments relative to identifiable vessel sherds. Ornaments are notably rare in the sample compared to storage vessels, with their proportions ranging from approximately 0.04% to 0.9% (Table 3.1). To contextualize this rarity: for household units that contain ornaments, the ratio of ornaments to identifiable vessel sherds ranges from

roughly 1 ornament per 2,500 identifiable vessel sherds to 1 ornament per 111 identifiable vessel sherds.

However, it must be noted that the number of sherds from identifiable vessel forms ranges from only approximately 34 to several thousand, and no ornaments were found in some household units. If a rate of 1 ornament per 2,500 sherds of identifiable vessel forms is considered low, we cannot confidently conclude that a household unit with 50 identifiable vessel sherds and no ornaments truly has a lower ornament ratio than a household unit with 1 ornament per 2,500 sherds.

To rigorously account for the effects of zero ornament counts and small sample sizes, this study further analyzes the ornament ratios of only those household units in which ornaments were found. The median of these ratios, calculated as the number of ornaments divided by the number of identifiable vessel sherds, is 0.002. This median ratio implies that one or more ornaments would be expected only when the number of identifiable vessel sherds exceeds 500 (derived from $1/0.002 = 500$).

Thus, when no ornaments are found in household units with fewer than 500 identifiable vessel sherds, there is a significant likelihood that these zero counts are merely random noise inherent in small samples. For this reason,

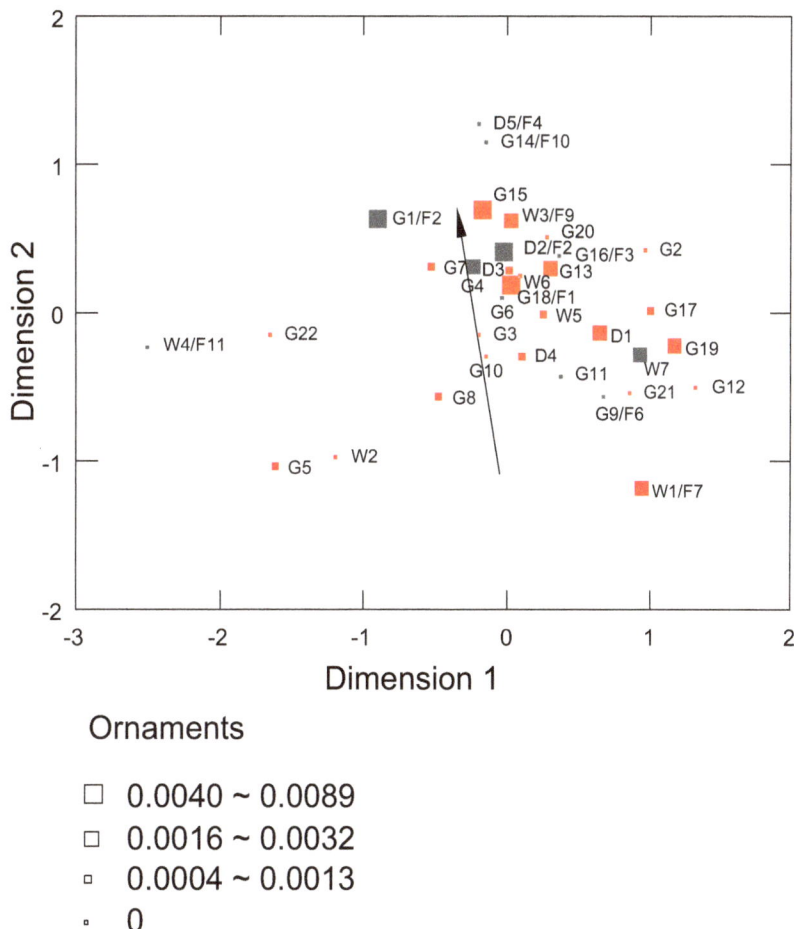

Ornaments

- ☐ 0.0040 ~ 0.0089
- ☐ 0.0016 ~ 0.0032
- ▫ 0.0004 ~ 0.0013
- ▪ 0

Figure 3.2. Plot of Variable 7. Ornaments (larger squares representing higher proportions of Ornaments; grey squares are the household units with fewer than 500 sherds of identifiable vessel forms).

the 11 household units with fewer than 500 identifiable vessel sherds are displayed in grey in Figure 3.2, explicitly indicating the reduced reliability because of their zero ornament counts.

The low ratio range indicates a very small consumption of ornaments among this household sample. Such access to ornaments, even in small amounts, still indicates the capacity for consuming valuable goods and this capacity would represent wealth. Only 19 household units in this sample (including 4 less reliable cases) consumed ornaments, more or less.

Although the proportions of ornaments are low, their distribution across the two-dimensional configuration follows a clear gradient: ratios start low in the lower-right region, rise gradually through the middle, and reach their highest values along the upper-left edge. Such gradual variation behaves just like Variable 5 (Storage Vessels), suggesting that the number of ornaments also indicates wealth among the household sample in conjunction with storage vessels.

3.1.3. Variable 6. Food Preparation Artifacts

A similar trend is observable in the two-dimensional scaling plot illustrating the proportions of Variable 6 (Food Preparation Artifacts; Figure 3.3). Each square in the plot represents a ratio of the number of food preparation artifacts to the number of identifiable vessel sherds for an individual household unit in the sample, with larger squares indicating household units that have higher proportions of food preparation artifacts.

As shown in Table 3.1, the proportions of food preparation artifacts range from approximately 0.2% to 2.7% for nearly every household unit, with the exception of three units that yielded no food preparation artifacts. Notably, two of these three units are represented by very small total sherd samples, which may account for the absence of such artifacts.

However, the ratios of food preparation artifacts (relative to identifiable vessel sherds) range from approximately 1 food preparation artifact per 500 identifiable vessel sherds to 1 food preparation artifact per 37 identifiable vessel sherds. If a ratio of 1 food preparation artifact per 500 identifiable vessel sherds is defined as low, then household units with 34 to 300 identifiable vessel sherds and no recorded food preparation artifacts may potentially be the product of substantial random noise in small samples. Thus, the zero counts and the small sample size of the sherds of identifiable vessel forms must be carefully dealt with. Among household units in which food preparation

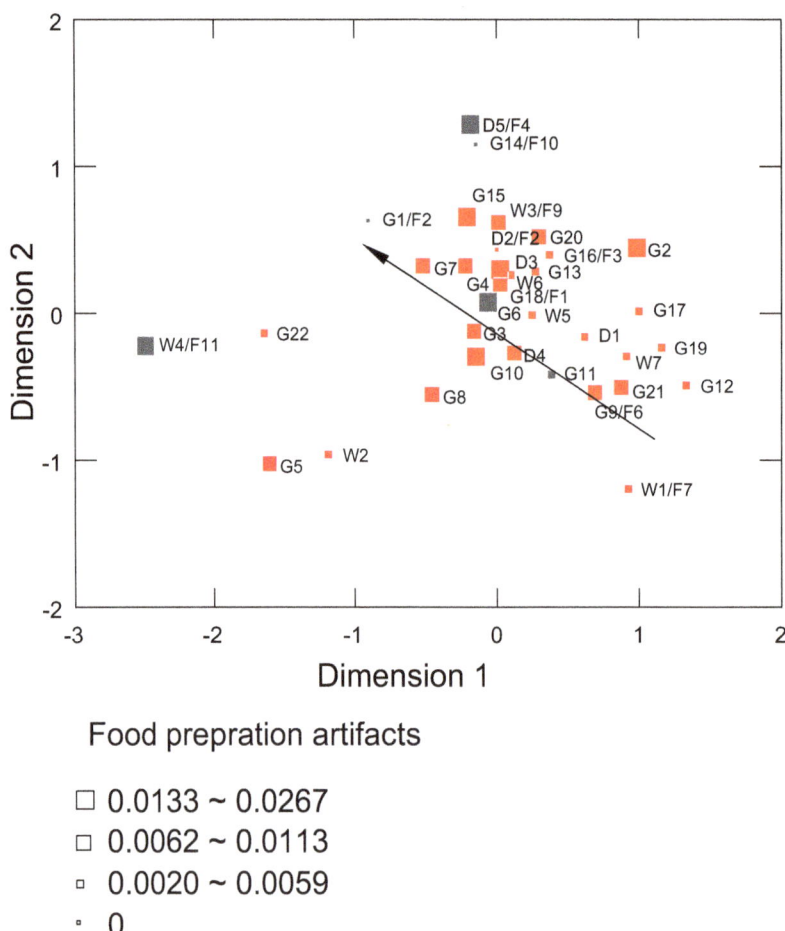

Food prepration artifacts

☐ 0.0133 ~ 0.0267
☐ 0.0062 ~ 0.0113
▫ 0.0020 ~ 0.0059
▫ 0

Figure 3.3. Plot of Variable 6. Food Preparation Artifacts (larger squares indicate higher proportion of food preparation artifacts; grey squares are the household units with fewer than 348 sherds of various vessel forms).

artifacts were found, the median ratio (calculated as the number of food preparation artifacts divided by the number of identifiable vessel sherds) is 0.007. This median value implies that one or more food preparation artifacts would typically be expected for every 143 identifiable vessel sherds (derived from 1/0.007 ≈ 143). Thus, the 3 household units with fewer than 143 identifiable vessel sherds are considered less reliable compared to units with larger sample sizes. Notably, there are 6 household units with a total sherd sample size (regardless of vessel form) below the threshold for reasonable confidence (384 sherds), and these 6 units include the 3 units with fewer than 143 identifiable vessel sherds. To ensure consistency in reliability assessment, it is methodologically safer to classify all 6 units collectively as less reliable cases. In Figure 3.3, these less reliable cases are displayed in grey to explicitly indicate their reduced interpretive confidence.

Variations in the quantity of food preparation artifacts across household units suggest two key differences: first, variation in the demand for food preparation activities, and second, potential variation in the capacity to diversify food recipes. In the two-dimensional configuration, there is no sharp division in the distribution of food preparation artifact proportions; instead, a gradual gradient is observed. Proportions start fairly low in the lower-right region of the

plot and increase steadily, reaching their highest values in the upper-left region. This gradual distribution pattern mirrors that of Variable 5 (Storage Vessels), indicating that the quantity of food preparation artifacts also serves as an indicator of greater wealth among the household sample.

3.1.4. Variable 2. Incising/Stamping in Complex Patterns

Variable 2 (Incising/Stamping in Complex Patterns) exhibits a distribution pattern similar to that of Variable 5 (Storage Vessels; Figure 3.4). Each square in the plot represents a household unit, and larger squares indicate higher proportions of sherds with incising/stamping in complex patterns. As shown in Table 3.1, the proportions of such decorated sherds are relatively low, ranging from approximately 0.03% to 1% across the household sample.

In addition, it must be noted that the denominator for Variable 2 (Incising/Stamping in Complex Patterns) is the total number of sherds. The rate of 0.03% means about one sherd with incising/stamping in complex patterns per 3,000 sherds. If this is true low rate for Variable 2, the household units with only hundreds of sherds may still have some sherds or vessels decorated with incising/ stamping in complex patterns decoration. For this reason, the effects of zero counts (i.e. no decorated sherds) and

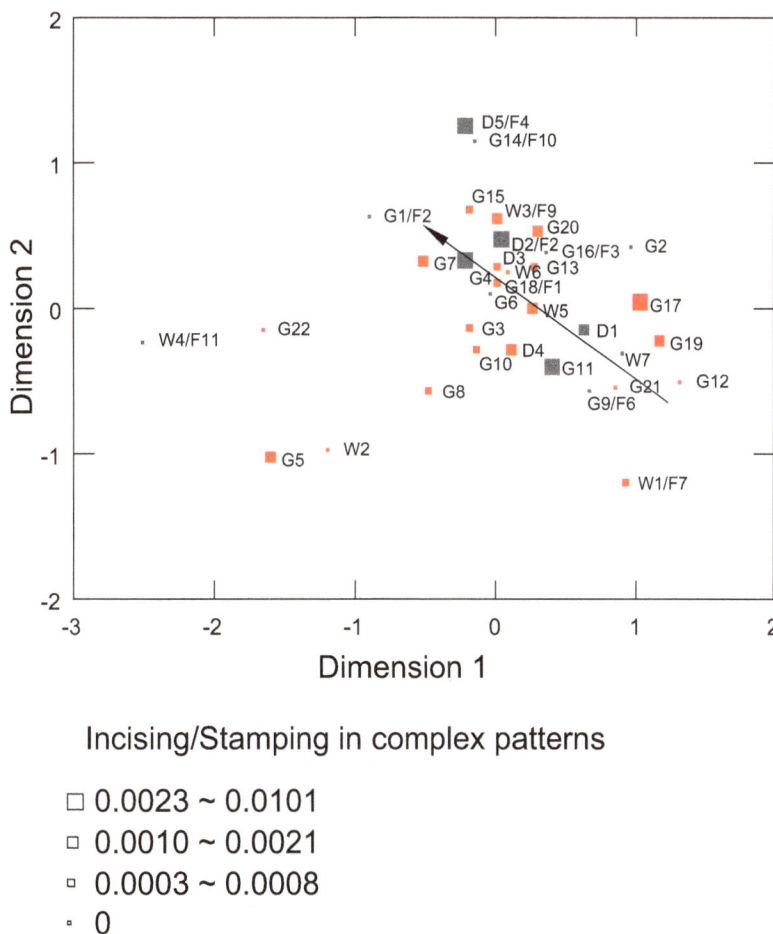

Figure 3.4. Plot of Variable 2. Incising/Stamping in Complex Patterns (larger squares indicate higher proportions of sherds with incising/stamping in complex patterns; grey squares are the household units with fewer than 1,000 sherds of various vessel forms).

small sample sizes must be considered carefully. Among the household units in which vessels or sherds decorated with incising/stamping in complex patterns were found, the median ratio (the number of sherds with incising/stamping in complex patterns divided by the total number of sherds of each household unit) is 0.001. This means that probably every 1,000 sherds will have at least one sherd with incising/stamping in complex patterns (derived from $1/0.001 = 1,000$). Thus, household units (13) with sample sizes lower than 1,000 sherds regardless of vessel forms would be less reliable than others represented by larger samples. These less reliable cases are displayed in grey in Figure 3.4. Compared to Variable 6 (Food Preparation Artifacts) and Variable 7 (Ornaments), the rate of sherds decorated with incising/stamping in complex patterns seems less rare.

There are 21 household units (including 5 less reliable cases) in this sample found with ceramic vessels decorated with incising/stamping in complex patterns. The proportions of sherds bearing such decoration also show a relatively gradual variation across the two-dimensional plot, starting from fairly low proportions at the lower right and rising gradually toward the upper part of the configuration. This distribution pattern, to some extent, echoes the gradual variation observed in the proportions of storage vessels (Variable 5), and suggests that higher proportions of ceramic vessels decorated with incising/stamping in complex patterns are also an indicator of greater wealth among the household units.

These four variables, then, pattern in a similar way in the space defined by the two-dimensional configuration. The four variables all form a gradual variation, to some extent, running from lower values in the lower right to higher values in the upper left across the plot of Dimensions 1 and 2. Household units with high proportions of storage vessels (Variable 5) are likely to have high proportions of the ornaments (Variable 7), food preparation artifacts (Variable 6), and sherds with incising/stamping in complex patterns (Variable 2). This correlation suggests the household units with high proportions of storage vessels tend strongly to be those that consumed greater quantities of ornaments, food preparation artifacts, and ceramic vessels with incising/stamping in complex patterns. All four variables can reasonably be connected to economic well-being or standard of living. This shared distribution pattern probably reflects the wealth differentiation among the 34 household units in the sample.

A question might be raised: could the co-occurrence of high proportions of storage vessels alongside high proportions of food preparation artifacts and ornaments represent larger household sizes rather than greater wealth? The underlying argument here is that more people would require a larger food supply, greater storage capacity, and more food-sharing activities, and, thus, generate more refuse. However, this interpretation is undermined by three key lines of evidence: First, the consistently small housing structures at Erlitou were likely to be occupied by nuclear families with very limited variation in the number of household members. This minimizes the possibilities that differences in household size could explain the observed variation in artifact proportions. Second, the variables of this study are proportions, indicating the relative abundance of one type of artifact against artifacts for other purposes. They are not absolute frequencies or numbers of objects. For example, the storage vessel variable does not measure a household's total storage capacity, but the share of storage vessels relative to other vessel types. In this way, even if a larger family needed a larger storage capacity, it would also require more serving vessels and other kinds of vessels, so the proportion of storage vessels would not be necessarily higher in larger households than in smaller ones. Third, the proportions of storage vessels and food preparation artifacts correlate with the proportions of ornaments and sherds with incising/stamping in complex patterns, lending further support to the idea that these variables represent a consistent package of artifacts related most convincingly to wealth differentiation.

3.2. Discussion

The Erlitou settlement has been interpreted as a capital with complex functional divisions (Xu 2009, 2022). The palatial enclosure, standing at the center of the site, was occupied by the ruling elites and their families. Ruling elites' families and intermediate elites are expected to be tremendously wealthy household units characterized by high consumption of storage vessels, food preparation artifacts, vessels with incising/stamping in complex patterns, and luxury ornaments. If the non-elites were completely excluded from the palatial enclosure, thus, we would expect to see some clear gap between household units in or near the palatial enclosure and those from other locations. The household units in or near the workshop enclosure and in the eastern end of the site also may be expected to distinctly separated from the cluster of household units in or near the palatial enclosure. However, the household units studied in this research do not show a clear separation by locations in the level of wealth. And they must fall quite low on the wealth scale, certainly below the realm of the truly impressive wealth of Eritou elites.

The household units in or near the palatial enclosure, in or near the workshop enclosure, and at the eastern end of the site are respectively displayed in different colors in Figure 3.5. The household units from the three locations are all thoroughly mixed together, with no tendency to form location-based clusters.

As we can see in the Figure 3.5, The household units in or near the palatial enclosure (blue squares) are scattered in several directions; although most are located in the middle of the plot, some are standing out to the upper left corner, possibly the wealthy ones, and some are standing in the right with some even reaching out to the lower right, possibly the less wealthy ones. There is no clear cluster consisting only of palatial-enclosure-adjacent

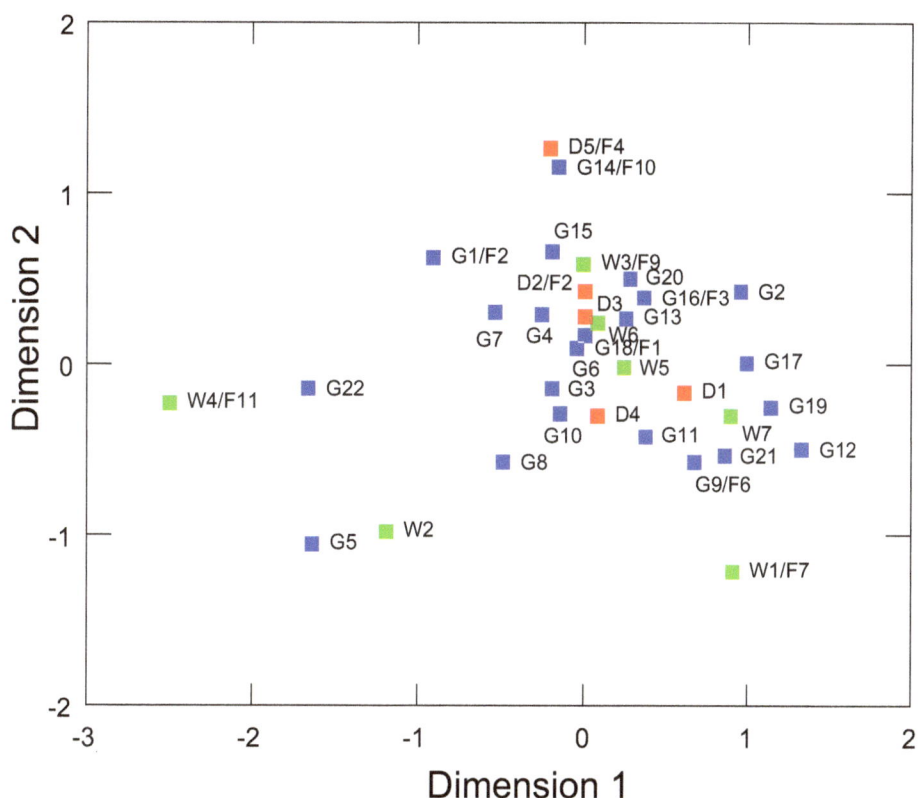

Figure 3.5. Household units from different regions in different colors. (Household units in or near the palatial enclosure in blue, household units in or near the workshop enclosure in green, and household units at the eastern end of the site in red).

household units near the left, or upper-left corner of the configuration.

The household units in or near the workshop enclosure and at the eastern end (green squares and red squares), although only a small number in this sample, also scatter in several directions in this two-dimensional plot; some are reaching out to the upper left, while some are standing in the lower right. There is also no cluster of only household units in or near the workshop enclosure, or at the eastern end of the site, forming in the lower right. In a word, the household units from the three locations are mixed together in terms of the wealth distribution pattern in the configuration space. There is no clear cluster consisting solely of workshop-enclosure-adjacent or eastern-end household units in the lower right corner. Such patterning suggests all the 34 household units in this sample regardless of their locations, probably shared a general range of wealth. They must fall quite low on the wealth scale, certainly below what would be expected of "intermediate elites" and entirely outside of the realm of the truly impressive wealth of Eritou elites.

At the same time, the 34 household units are spread quite widely across the wealth distribution pattern in the configuration space. The scattering also suggests that the 34 household units in this sample varied in opportunity to accumulate wealth and did not share the exact same wealth levels in terms of standard of living.

There has been an assumption that people living in on-the-ground housing structures, especially the medium- or small-sized rammed earth buildings, should be higher in rank than those sheltered in semi-subterranean house structures at Erlitou. However, such a "higher rank" assumption does not make any distinction between wealth and prestige: whether such rank stems from greater wealth or from higher prestige; it conflates the two, suggesting higher rank involves with both wealth and prestige without differentiating which of the two dimensions constitutes the basis of that elevated status (Zhongguo 2014, 2019; Xu 2009, 2022). It is true that an on-the-ground housing structure requires more labor to construct. According to Xu (2009, 2022), Palatial Platform No. 1, with an area of about 10,000 m², including a 900 m² main palace building and a courtyard of about 5,000 m², took 200,000 working days to complete this construction. This calculation assumes 1,000 laborers, each producing 0.1 m³ of rammed earth volume per day. It also seems superficially obvious that those occupying small on-the-ground housing structures, despite being much smaller than the palatial structures, must have been wealthier than those living in semi-subterranean structures. In Figure 3.6, the household units living in small on-the-ground housing structures are displayed in red and those occupying semi-subterranean housing structures are in green. It is quite clear that the household units living in small on-the-ground housing structures are concentrated more toward upper left (the wealthier part) than those living in semi-subterranean housing structures in the configuration space. Such patterning indicates that the artifact assemblages consumed by the household units in small on-the-ground housing structures indeed differed from those consumed by the

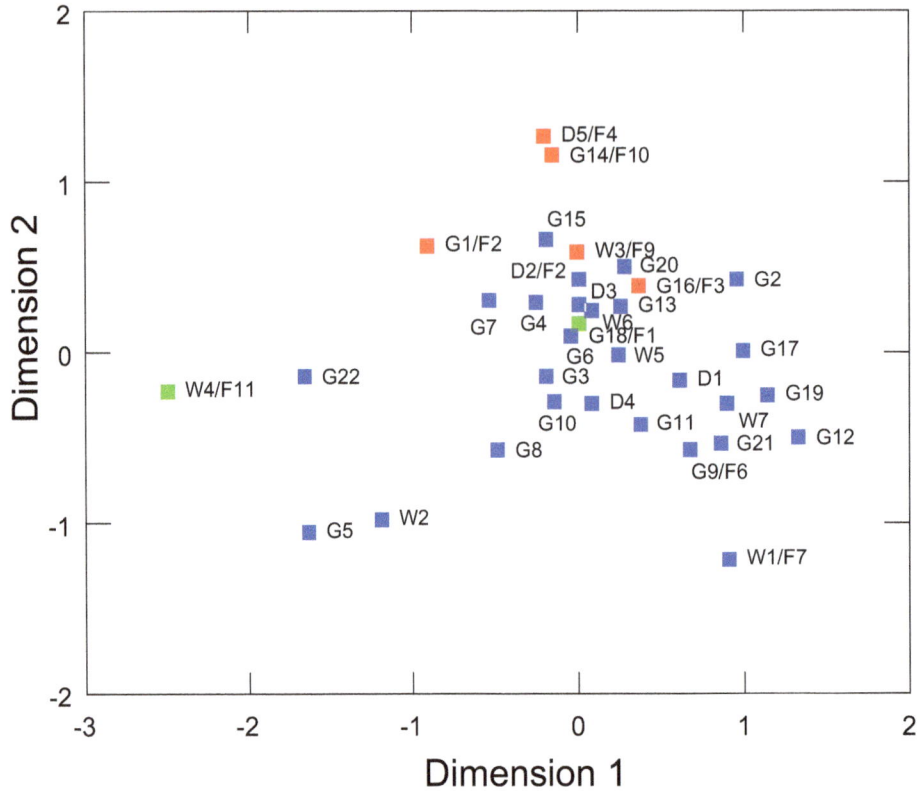

Figure 3.6. Household units colored by different housing structures. (Household units living in small on-the-ground housing structures in red, household units occupying semi-subterranean housing structures in green, household units with unknown housing structures in blue.).

household units in semi-subterranean housing structures, to some extent; in other words, the household units in small on-the-ground housing structures were wealthier than the household units in semi-subterranean housing structures. Thus, there is a correspondence between the wealth indicators derived from household artifact assemblages and residential architecture. However, this conclusion remains suggestive and tentative, in that it is based on a very small sample, especially of the household units with clear identifiable housing structures; only 2

household units were sheltered in semi-subterranean housing structures, only 5 household units were living in small on-the-ground structures, 3 household units had indeterminate structures because of poor preservation, and the other 24 household units are only represented by artifact samples from locations where no housing structures were recovered. And although the 5 household units in small on-the-ground structures fall in the high-wealth part of the scaling space, 3 of them are represented by the less reliable small artifact samples.

Prestige Differentiation within the Erlitou Household Sample

4.1. Patterns of the Variables Correlated to Prestige in the Two-dimensional Configuration

This chapter will explore the patterning of household assemblage variables related to prestige differentiation in the two-dimensional multidimensional scaling configuration presented in Chapter 2. These variables include *Variable 1 (Fingernail Incising)*, *Variable 3 (Polishing)*, and *Variable 4 (Feasting Utensils and Vessels)*.

4.1.1. Variable 3. Polishing

Figure 4.1 is the two-dimensional configuration illustrating values of Variable 3 (Polishing) showing how the proportions (calculated as the number of polished vessels or sherds divided by the number of sherds regardless of vessel forms for each household unit) behave in this sample. Each square in the plot represents a household unit with polished vessels or sherds, and larger squares indicate higher proportions of such polished vessels or sherds. As shown in Table 4.1, the proportions of sherds with polishing are relatively low, ranging

from about 3.3% to about 34%. Such variation reflects differences among the household units in this sample in their capacity to serve and store food and fermented beverages using polished vessels. Although every household unit in this sample has at least some polished vessels or sherds, the effects of small sample size must still be considered carefully. The median ratio is 12.4%. This means that, on average, for every 8 sherds there is at least one polished sherd. Thus, those household units with a sample size fewer than 8 sherds regardless of vessel forms would be considered less reliable. In fact, there is no household unit in the sample with only 8 or fewer sherds. But, according to the conservative estimation outlined in the Chapter 3, this study takes a random sample of sherds, regardless of vessel forms, to be more reliable if it has at least 384 (based on a *t*-value of 1.96 for unknown degrees of freedom at 95% confidence). In total, 6 household units have a sherd sample size of fewer than 384 sherds. For consistency, these 6 household units are classified as less reliable cases, compared to those with larger sample sizes. In Figure 4.1, these less reliable cases are displayed in grey.

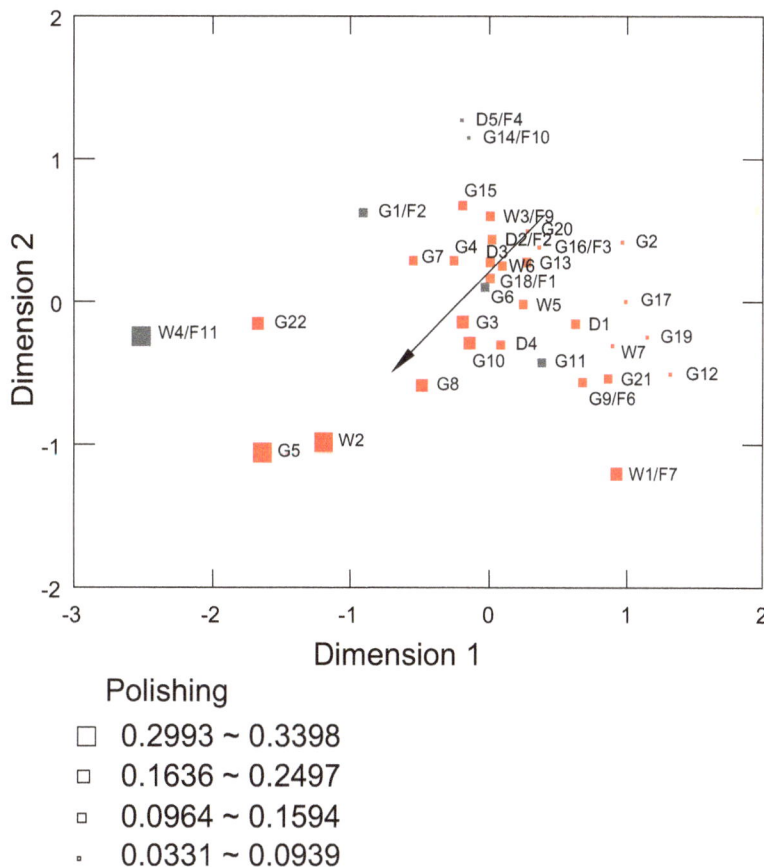

Figure 4.1. Plot of Variable 3. Polishing (larger squares indicate higher proportions of polished sherds; grey squares are the household units with fewer than 384 sherds of various vessel forms).

Table 4.1. Proportions of the variables related to prestige differentiation in the 34 household units.

Household unit	Fingernail incising	Polishing	Feasting utensils & vessels
G1/F2	0.0000	0.1564	0.0732
G2	0.0000	0.0331	0.0499
G3	0.0045	0.1669	0.0508
G4	0.0024	0.1357	0.0568
G5	0.0152	0.3393	0.0828
G6	0.0138	0.1330	0.0467
G7	0.0049	0.1594	0.0529
G8	0.0034	0.2138	0.0844
G9/F6	0.0000	0.1297	0.0570
G10	0.0034	0.1733	0.0503
W1/F7	0.0074	0.1636	0.0363
W2	0.0000	0.2993	0.0730
D1	0.0085	0.0983	0.1019
D2/F2	0.0069	0.1098	0.0237
G11	0.0000	0.1389	0.0549
G12	0.0009	0.0823	0.0148
G13	0.0081	0.0994	0.0319
G14/F10	0.0000	0.0658	0.0294
G15	0.0034	0.0998	0.0664
G16/F3	0.0092	0.0809	0.0552
W3/F9	0.0028	0.0964	0.0342
W4/F11	0.0097	0.3398	0.0577
W5	0.0057	0.1267	0.0223
W6	0.0070	0.1169	0.0322
W7	0.0076	0.0939	0.0417
D3	0.0047	0.1217	0.0247
D4	0.0059	0.1542	0.0576
D5/F4	0.0000	0.0553	0.0615
G17	0.0032	0.0653	0.0272
G18/F1	0.0074	0.1262	0.0471
G19	0.0024	0.0704	0.0408
G20	0.0042	0.0807	0.0320
G21	0.0020	0.1126	0.0566
G22	0.0187	0.2497	0.1532

Although 6 household units may be less reliable due to small sample sizes, there is no sharp division in this two-dimensional plot. Instead, a gradual variation is revealed in the two-dimensional MDS plot: proportions of polished vessels or sherds start from fairly low in the upper right, rises moderately across the middle and then reaches their highest values at the lower left edge of the two-dimensional configuration. Thus, the consumption of polished vessels in the household sample is relatively lower in the upper right but higher on the left. This pattern suggests, among the households in this sample, those standing more to the lower left tend to be more capable of serving and storing food and fermented beverages using polished vessels.

4.1.2. Variable 4. Feasting Utensils and Vessels

Figure 4.2 is a two-dimensional configuration plot showing the 34 household units in this sample, with each unit's position representing the values of Variable 4 (Feasting Utensils and Vessels). Each square in this figure corresponds to a ratio of the number of feasting utensils and feasting vessels sherds divided by the number of sherds of identifiable vessel forms for each household unit. Larger squares indicate household units with higher proportions of feasting utensils and feasting vessel sherds. All household units in this sample have some feasting utensils and vessels, with proportions ranging from about 1.5% to about 15% (Table 4.1). This substantial range could indicate real differences in the capabilities of organizing feasting activities for the purpose of gaining prestige.

The median ratio of feasting utensils and feasting vessels sherds (relative to identifiable vessel form sherds) is 0.051. This means that there is probably at least one feasting utensil or feasting vessel sherd per 20 identifiable vessel form sherds. No household unit in the sample has 20 or fewer identifiable vessel form sherds. However, the potential effects of small sample sizes still require careful consideration.

There are 6 household units with a sherd sample size (regardless of vessel forms) below the confidently representative threshold of 384. Thus, these 6 household units are considered less reliable than those represented by larger sample sizes, and they are displayed in grey in the plot.

Although 6 household units are considered less reliable in terms of their small sample sizes, no sharp division is shown in this two-dimensional plot, but rather a gradual variation. The gradual variation starts with fairly low proportions of feasting utensils and vessels in the upper right, rises moderately through the middle, and then moves to the highest values at the lower left edge of the two-dimensional configuration.

This suggests that household units with lower prestige are in the upper right and those with higher prestige are broadly distributed on the left side of the configuration. Variations in the quantity of feasting utensils and vessels suggests different capacities in arranging and hosting feasting activities, sharing food and fermented beverages, and participating in ancestral venerations and other festive ceremonies among the households in this sample.

4.1.3. Variable 1. Fingernail Incising

Variable 1 (Fingernail Incising) behaves in a similar manner to Variable 3 (Polishing) and Variable 4 (Feasting Utensils and Vessels) (Figure 4.3). Each square in the plot represents a household unit containing the sherds decorated with fingernail incising, and larger squares indicate higher proportions of sherds decorated by fingernail incising. The proportions of sherds with fingernail incising decoration are relatively low, ranging from about 0.1% to about 1.9% (Table 4.1).

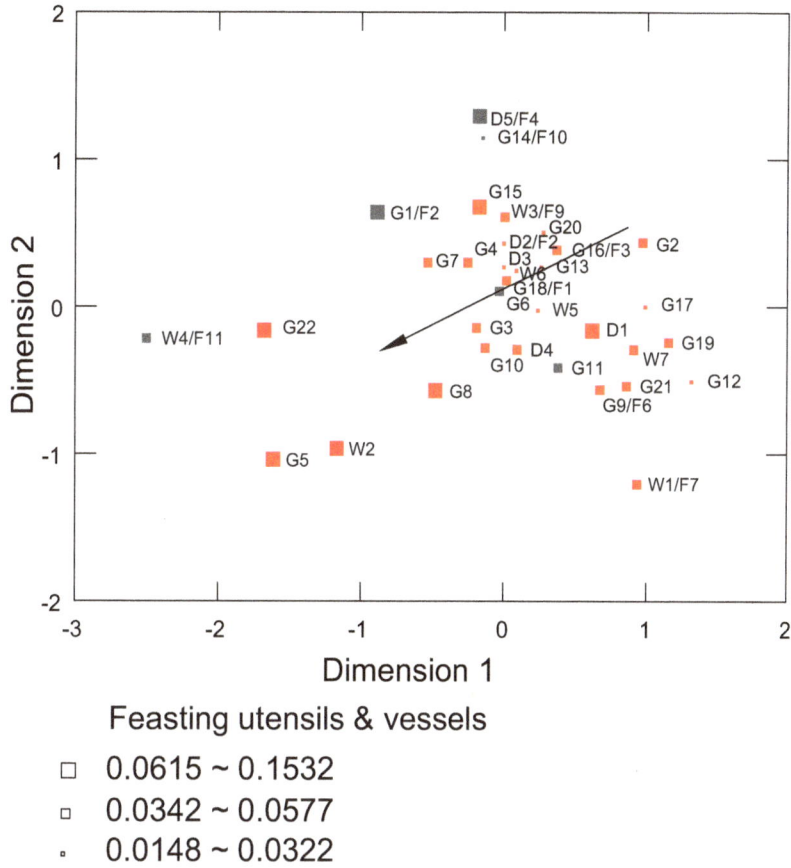

Feasting utensils & vessels

- □ 0.0615 ~ 0.1532
- ▫ 0.0342 ~ 0.0577
- ▫ 0.0148 ~ 0.0322

Figure 4.2. Plot of Variable 4. Feasting Utensils and Vessels (larger squares representing higher proportions of feasting utensils and vessels; grey squares are the household units with fewer than 384 sherds of various vessel forms).

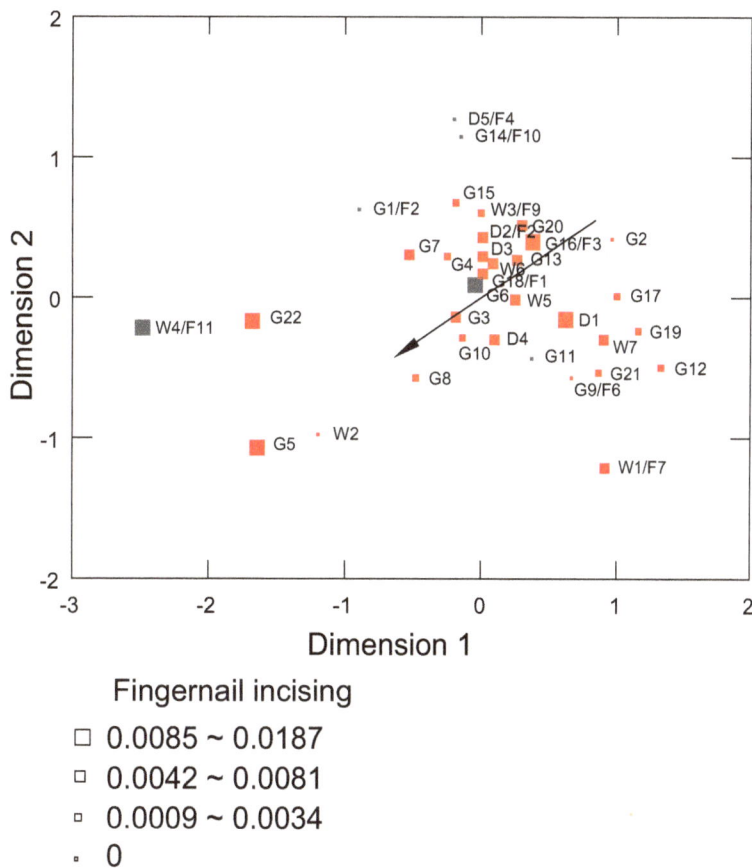

Fingernail incising

- □ 0.0085 ~ 0.0187
- ▫ 0.0042 ~ 0.0081
- ▫ 0.0009 ~ 0.0034
- ▪ 0

Figure 4.3. Plot of Variable 1. Fingernail Incising (larger squares indicate higher proportion of sherds decorated with fingernail incising; grey squares are the household units with fewer than 384 sherds regardless of vessel forms).

In contrast to Variable 4 (Feasting Utensils and Vessels), the denominator for Variable 1 (Fingernail Incising) is the total number of sherds. The rate of 0.1% means about one sherd with fingernail incising per 1,000 sherds. If this is a true low rate for Variable 1, household units with only several hundred sherds and no sherds or vessels decorated with fingernail incising are simply the result of the significant random noise in small samples. Thus, the effects of zero counts (i.e., no decorated sherds) and small sample sizes must be taken into consideration carefully.

The median of the ratios (number of sherds with fingernail incising decoration divided by the total number of sherds of each household unit), among the household units in which vessels or sherds decorated by fingernail incising were found, is 0.6%. This means that there is likely at least one sherd with fingernail incising for every 167 sherds. Thus, household units with a total sherd sample size (regardless of vessel forms) less than 167 sherds are considered less reliable.

There are 6 household units with a sample of fewer than 384 sherds, and these are considered as less reliable cases, compared to those with larger samples. In Figure 4.3, these less reliable cases are displayed in grey.

In this sample, 27 household units (including 2 less reliable cases) are found with ceramic vessels or sherds decorated with fingernail incising. The proportions of such vessels or sherds with fingernail incising exhibit a relatively gradual variation, starting from fairly low proportions at the upper right and rising to higher proportions in the lower left part of the two-dimensional plot. This pattern, to some extent, echoes the gradual variation shown by the proportions of polished vessels (Variable 3) and feasting utensils and vessels (Variable 4). This similarity suggests that more prestigious household units also consumed more ceramic vessels decorated with fingernail incising, perhaps serving and storing food and fermented beverages in these vessels.

These three variables, then, pattern in a relatively similar way in the space defined by the two-dimensional configuration. The three variables all display a gradual variation, running from lower values in the upper right to higher values in the lower left across the plot of Dimensions 1 and 2. The households with high proportions of feasting utensils and vessels (Variable 4) are likely to have high proportions of polished vessels or sherds (Variable 3) and fingernail incised vessels or sherds (Variable 1). One may question why polishing and fingernail incising are treated as prestige indicators here instead of as wealth indicators in Chapter 3. Generally, extra labor in ceramic production by decoration application would increase the value or cost of the pottery (Smith 1987; Costin and Earle 1989). However, in the scaling space of this Erlitou household sample, polishing and fingernail incising correlate with feasting utensils and vessels rather than with storage vessels (Variable 5), food preparation artifacts (Variable 6), ornaments (Variable 7), or incised/stamped complex patterns (Variable 2), suggesting that polishing and fingernail incising at

Erlitou did not simply correlate with the labor value or represent a household's economic capacity in consuming fine ceramics; instead, they were more closely connected to feasting and prestige. Thus, all three variables serve together as indicators of prestigious social status.

One may also question whether a greater number of feasting utensils and vessels may be because of larger household sizes rather than because of their prestige. It is possible that the proportion of utensils and vessels simply for eating and drinking may be correlated to the number of residents in a household. But if the family sizes were generally similar, the wealthier or more prestigious families would consume more such objects and produce more refuse. As Chapter 1 shows, the consistently small housing structures at Erlitou were likely occupied by nuclear families. In addition, feasting utensils and vessels do not run in the same direction as wealth differentiation goes (see further discussion comes below), making them more indicative of prestige differentiation. Moreover, feasting utensils and vessels are measured as a proportion, not as absolute abundance or frequency. Even if a larger family consumed more feasting utensils and vessels, it would also need more storage vessels and other forms of vessels, so the proportion of feasting utensils and vessels would not necessarily be greater in larger households than in smaller ones. Feasting utensils and vessels correlate strongly with polishing (Variable 3) and fingernail incising (Variable 1), further suggesting that these two variables are also indicators of prestige differentiation.

4.2. Discussion

The ruling elites' families of the Erlitou state, who are presumed to occupy the palatial enclosure, and the intermediate elites would be expected to form highly prestigious household units. They would likely consume more exquisite feasting utensils and vessels and have greater capacity in serving and storing food and fermented beverages in polished vessels or ceramic vessels decorated with fingernail incising (or perhaps other complex, elaborate decorative patterns). If the palatial enclosure were completely forbidden to the non-elites, we would expect to see a clear gap in terms of prestige between household units inside or near the palatial enclosure and those from other locations. Household units inside or near the workshop enclosure and at the eastern end of the site might also stand apart from the cluster of household units in or near the palatial enclosure. However, the household units in this sample do not show a clear separation by location in terms of prestige. And they must fall relatively low on the prestige scale, certainly below the realm of the truly impressive prestige associated with Erlitou's elites.

Displayed in different colors in Figure 4.4, the household units in or near the palatial enclosure, in or near the workshop enclosure, and at the eastern end of the site are all thoroughly mixed together in the plot of Dimensions 1 and 2. The household units in or near the palatial enclosure (blue squares) are scattered in several directions; although most are located in the middle of the

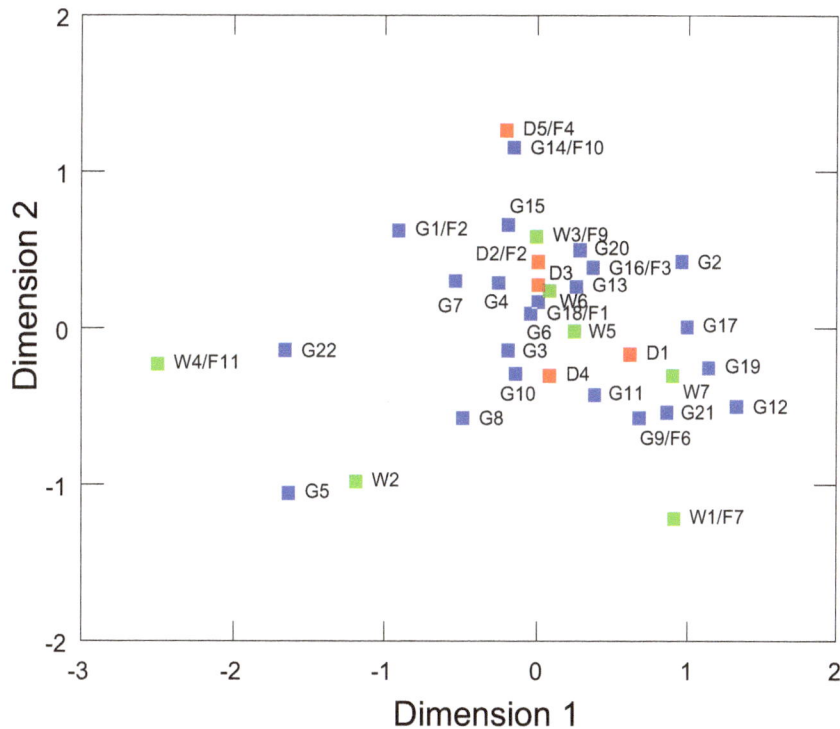

Figure 4.4. Household units from different regions in different colors. (Household units in or near the palatial enclosure in blue, household units in or near the workshop enclosure in green, and household units at the eastern end of the site in red).

plot, some stand out in the lower left corner, possibly the most prestigious ones, while some are in the right section, even reaching out to the upper right, possibly the less prestigious ones. There is no clear cluster consisting of only household units in or near the palatial enclosure near the left or even farther to lower left corners. The household units in or near the workshop enclosure (green squares), although small in number in this sample, also scatter in several directions across this two-dimensional plot; some reach out to the lower left, while some are in the right section. However, the household units at the eastern end of the site (red squares) tend to only appear in the middle and upper right of the plot, possibly representing low to moderate level of prestige. In a word, most of the household units from the three locations in this sample are intermingled in the prestige scale in the configuration space. There are still four of the most prestigious household units in this sample in the lower left corner of the scaling space: 2 from the palatial enclosure and 2 from the workshop enclosure, although one of the highly prestigious household units has issues with a small sample size. Such patterning suggests all the 34 household units in this sample from the three locations occupied a quite low social rank on the prestige scale, almost certainly below the expected level of "intermediate elites" and entirely outside of the realm of the truly significant prestige associated with Eritou elites.

In the meantime, the 34 household units are widely distributed across the prestige pattern in the configuration space. The scattering pattern also suggests that the household units in this sample varied in their opportunities to negotiate and gain prestige, and did not share the same level of prestige in terms of feasting activities. But, such

negotiation of prestige among the non-elites represented by this household sample was not based on economic power, or wealth; indeed, prestige did not correspond to wealth at all but crosscut it. As shown in the study of wealth differentiation in Chapter 3, relatively wealthy household units are located in the upper left of this plot, not in the lower left where more prestigious households are situated. Wealthier households were not more prestigious, and more prestigious households were not wealthier. Wealth and prestige were differentiated under different and unrelated mechanisms. Some prestigious household units are in the palatial enclosure, and others are in the workshop enclosure. In contrast, household units at the eastern end of the site, although they tended to have relatively higher (at least moderate to high) wealth, seem to be only low to moderate in prestige. This indicates that there must be other principles or mechanisms through which non-elites in this household sample negotiated and gained prestige. It is possible that some relatively prestigious non-elite families served ruling elites and their families on a daily basis alongside other non-elite families in the palatial enclosure, and formed a hierarchical attendant group. It is also possible that some prestigious non-elite families, possibly specialized elite-oriented workers in the workshop enclosure, formed an administrative system in the elite-oriented worker communities, and the less prestigious families at the eastern end of the site, despite their relative wealth, possibly had only a distant relationship with the royal court, and ruling elites and their families. Prestigious household units in this sample were more likely to be in or near the palatial enclosure and the workshop enclosure rather than at the eastern end of the site. Residing in or near the palatial enclosure and the workshop enclosure may have signaled prestige among non-elites, to some extent. Such a tendency in residences may have contributed to maintaining and protecting ruling elites and their governance, as well as enhancing royal control over elite-oriented craft production and the monopolized consumption of high-quality artifacts such as turquoise and bronze, both of which have been identified in the workshop enclosure. Thus, prestige among non-elites was probably tied to their relationship with the royal court. It aligns with recent studies that elites (that is, families far more prestigious than non-elites in the Erlitou community) were distributed in a centripetal pattern, more concentrated around the palatial enclosure than in areas farther from the site's center (Xu, Chen and Zhao 2004; Zhao 2020). In contrast, being in or near the palatial enclosure and workshop enclosure was not a prerequisite for household units in this sample to be wealthy. Wealthier families could be found not only in or near the palatial enclosure and workshop enclosure, but also at the eastern end of the site.

On the other hand, people living in on-the-ground housing structures, especially the medium- or small-size rammed earth buildings, have been assumed to be higher in rank than those in semi-subterranean housing structures at Erlitou (Zhongguo 2014, 2019; Xu 2009, 2022). It is common to conjecture that those occupying small on-the-ground housing structures, despite being much smaller than the palatial structures, must have been more prestigious than those living in semi-subterranean structures. This assumption is derived from the idea that prestige could enable the families to procure wealth, which is then represented by their standard of living in some cases, and, in other cases, wealthy families could also gain their prestige through their economic power.

However, this study suggests that probably prestige was not gained through high wealth among the non-elite households in this sample, nor could wealth systematically generate prestige. In fact, prestige did not correspond to wealth at all. In Figure 4.5, the household units living in small on-the-ground housing structures are displayed in red and those occupying semi-subterranean housing structures are in green. The household units in semi-subterranean housing structures stand more towards lower left (the more prestigious part of the configuration) than those living in small on-the-ground housing structures; in other words, the household units living in semi-subterranean housing structures in this sample tend to be relatively more prestigious than those living in small on-the-ground housing structures. The analysis presented in Chapter 3 suggests that the household units living in small on-the-ground housing structures are wealthier, and the household unis living in semi-subterranean housing structures are less wealthy. But this chapter finds that non-elite households who lived in semi-subterranean structures could be more prestigious than those living in small on-the-ground structures. This suggests that the standard of living of a non-elite household unit at Erlitou cannot be confidently taken as a proxy for its prestige. It is noteworthy that household units living in semi-subterranean housing structures could be more prestigious than those living in small on-the-ground housing structures. But it must be remembered that this conclusion is based on a very small sample of clearly defined housing structures, with only two semi-subterranean housing structures identified. In addition, some of the household units with identifiable housing structures are represented by less reliable small sherd samples.

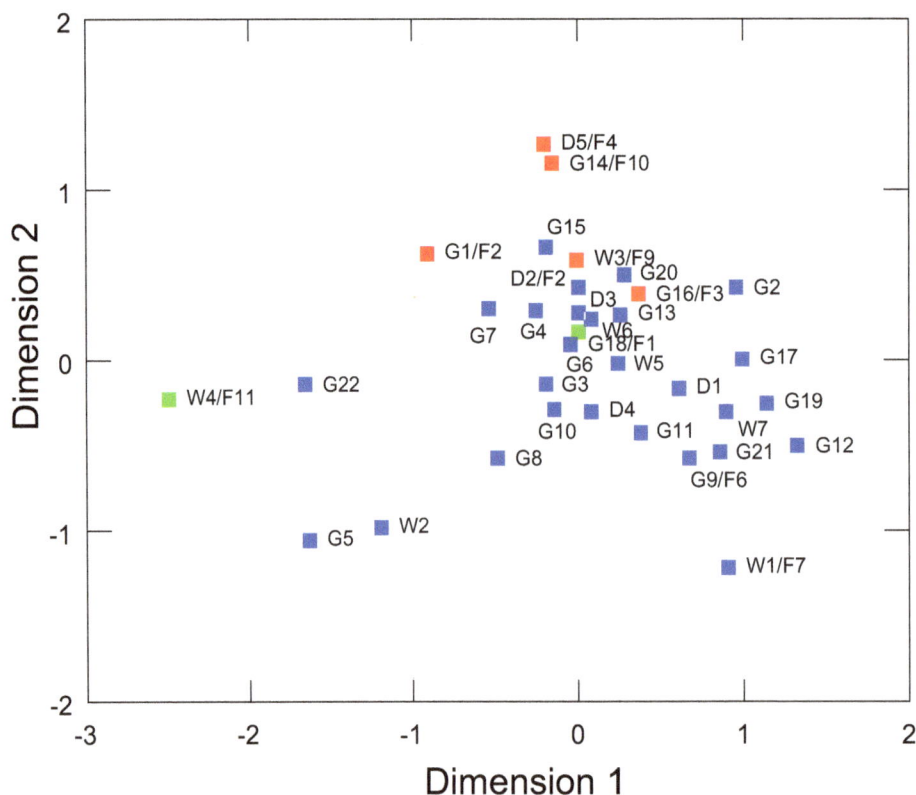

Figure 4.5. Household units colored by different housing structures. (Household units living in small on-the-ground housing structures in red, household units occupying semi-subterranean housing structures in green, household units with unknown housing structures in blue.)

Ritual Differentiation within the Erlitou Household Sample

5.1. Pattern of the Variable Correlated to Ritual in the Two-dimensional Configuration

This chapter will explore the patterning of the single household assemblage variable related to ritual differentiation in the two-dimensional multidimensional scaling configuration presented in Chapter 2. This is *Variable 14* (*Ritual Paraphernalia*).

Figure 5.1 is a two-dimensional configuration plot showing the relative values of Variable 14 (Ritual Paraphernalia) (Table 5.1). Each square in this figure represents a ratio of the number of ritual paraphernalia divided by the number of identifiable vessel form sherds in a household unit. Larger squares represent household units with higher proportions of ritual paraphernalia. In this plot, about 18 households were found with ritual paraphernalia, whose proportions ranging from around 0.04% to around 0.67%. These proportions are quite small, and vary in quite a narrow range. A ratio of 0.04% means about one item of ritual paraphernalia per 2,500 sherds of identifiable vessel forms. If this is a true low rate for Variable 14, household units with only several hundred sherds of identifiable vessel forms and no ritual paraphernalia may possibly be the result of the large amount of random noise in small samples. Thus, the effects of zero counts (that is, ritual paraphernalia) and small sample sizes must be considered carefully. Among the household units in which ritual paraphernalia were found, the median of the ratios (the number of ritual paraphernalia items divided by the number of identifiable vessel form sherds per household unit) is 0.1%. This means that there is probably at least one item of ritual paraphernalia per 1,000 sherds of identifiable vessel forms. Thus, those household units with sample sizes of fewer than 1,000 identifiable vessel form sherds are considered less reliable than those cases represented by larger sample sizes. In Figure 5.1, these less reliable cases are displayed in grey.

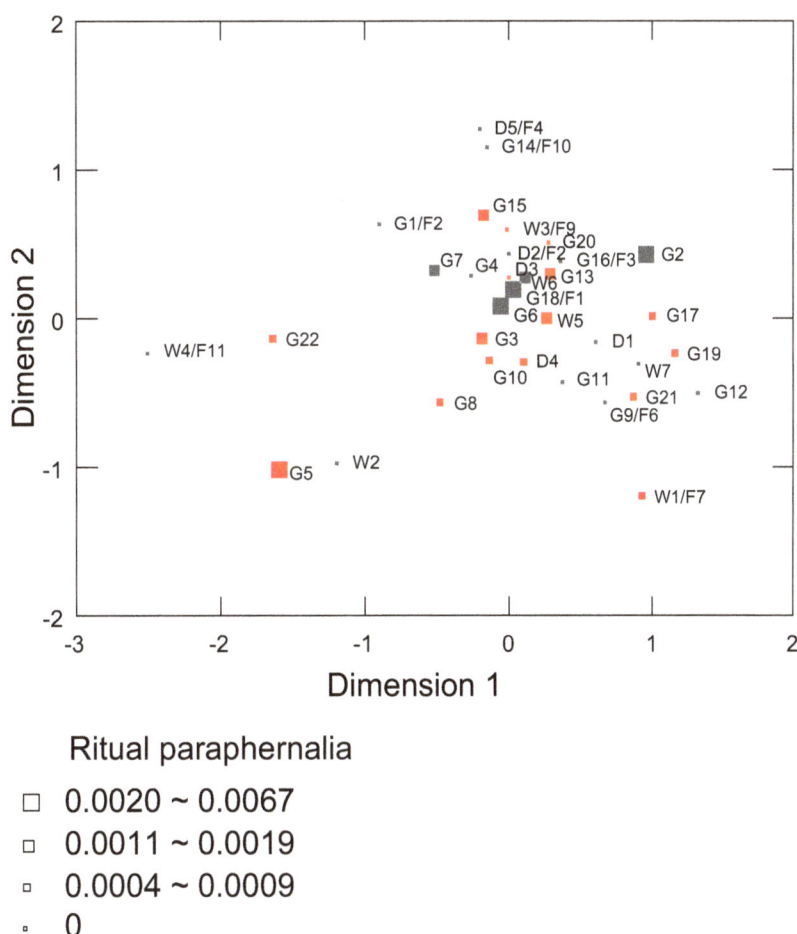

Figure 5.1. Plot of Variable 14. Ritual Paraphernalia (larger squares represent higher proportions; grey squares are the household units with fewer than 1,000 sherds of various vessel forms).

Table 5.1. Proportions of ritual paraphernalia in the 34 household units.

Household unit	Ritual paraphernalia
G1/F2	0.0000
G2	0.0050
G3	0.0019
G4	0.0000
G5	0.0020
G6	0.0067
G7	0.0011
G8	0.0004
G9/F6	0.0000
G10	0.0008
W1/F7	0.0008
W2	0.0000
D1	0.0000
D2/F2	0.0000
G11	0.0000
G12	0.0000
G13	0.0012
G14/F10	0.0000
G15	0.0015
G16/F3	0.0000
W3/F9	0.0000
W4/F11	0.0000
W5	0.0013
W6	0.0012
W7	0.0000
D3	0.0000
D4	0.0004
D5/F4	0.0000
G17	0.0006
G18/F1	0.0030
G19	0.0004
G20	0.0000
G21	0.0009
G22	0.0009

5.2. Discussion

In the early phase of state formation in China，religious activities are believed to have been monopolized by the elites (Wang, Z. 2006; Chang 1989). Elites specialized in communicating with ancestors and gods, and engaged in heavenly worship, through both of which they maintained their sovereignty and stabilized their political hierarchy. According to burial data, Erlitou elites consumed high-quality ritual paraphernalia in jade, turquoise, bronze, and lacquerwares (Cai 2006; Deng 2017; Yan 2020; Gao 2022; Ye and Li 2001; Xu 2016b). Bronze plaques inlaid with turquoise sheets, including the dragon-shaped

turquoise artifact, are believed to be exclusive elite ritual items (Cai 2006; Ye and Li 2001; Xu 2016b; Gao 2022). The animal patterns formed by the bronzes and turquoises probably enabled ruling elites to communicate with gods and supernatural spirits. In conjunction with musical instruments, like bronze bells and lacquer drums, Erlitou elites or specialized elite shamans might dance with these bronze-turquoise ritual paraphernalia in their hands to appease ancestors and supernatural spirits in exchange for prosperity and good fortune (Cai 2006; Du 2006; He 2018; Gao 2022). Jades in animal shapes and other non-utilitarian forms have been identified as ritual jades (玉祭器), which served as intermediaries in worshiping and communicating with gods and other supernatural spirits during religious and sacrificial activities since Neolithic China, and those in practical forms have been regarded as ceremonial jades (玉瑞器), which served as symbols of social status while also complementing rituals (Deng 2017, 2021). For example, lacquer cups (*gu* 觚) and handle-shaped jades (柄形器) may have been used together to perform *Guan ritual* (祼礼), toasting to gods and supernatural spirits in religious and sacrificial activities (Yan 2020). Jade serrated blades (*yazhang* 牙璋), which are in a practical-tool form with sharp blades, may have complemented worshiping practices and prayers for good harvests through ritual killing and blood offering (Wang 2002; Deng 2021). Such ritual paraphernalia crafted from luxury raw materials and in diverse forms demonstrate that Erlitou elites engaged in multiple types of ritual activities beyond oracle divination by scapulimancy. It was possibly true that some ritual activities were monopolized by elites, and non-elites were excluded from such ritual activities. The ruling elites' families of the Erlitou state, who are presumed to occupy the palaces inside of the palatial enclosure, and the intermediate elites would have been tremendously, highly ritualized groups with greater capacity in engaging in ritual activities evidenced by large quantities of ritual paraphernalia.

In this sample, 18 household units (including 5 less reliable cases) were found with ritual paraphernalia. The ritual paraphernalia seen in this household sample consists entirely of oracle bones, with the exception of one ceramic hollow-bottomed vessel (透底器). Although the function of the hollow-bottomed vessel is still unknown, the ritual activities among the household units in this sample are almost entirely limited to oracle divination by scapulimancy. Thus, compared to elites' access to a wide range of ritual activities and luxury, high-quality ritual paraphernalia, the household units in this sample must share a quite low rank on the ritual scale, almost certainly below the expected level of "intermediate elites" and entirely outside the realm of the truly prominent ritual status of Erlitou elites.

As Figure 5.1 shows, there is also no clear tendency of the ritual paraphernalia increasing from low to high values, but a relatively random scattering pattern. Household units with more ritual paraphernalia and those with less or even no ritual paraphernalia are thoroughly mixed with each other, showing no tendency to increased engagement in ritual activities (represented by the proportion of ritual paraphernalia) in any particular direction, unlike patterns of wealth differentiation and prestige differentiation.

If ritual activities among the household units vary significantly but gradually, the ratio of the ritual paraphernalia would form a tendency, starting from low values in one part of the two-dimensional configuration and rising up to higher values in another part. Even if no such tendency or other spatial pattern formed in the scaling configuration, the ratios should vary substantially more than the most reliable samples indicate that they do.

However, Figure 5.1 shows that some household units with more ritual paraphernalia stand in both the lower left part and the upper right part of this two-dimensional configuration, while the cases with relatively moderate level of ritual paraphernalia stand in the upper left and the lower right. Units with zero ritual paraphernalia are scattered in the middle, among those with the relatively largest and moderate proportions.

The household units with ritual paraphernalia are not limited to areas in or near the palatial enclosure; they also appear in or near the workshop enclosure and at the eastern end of the site although the number of cases from the latter two locations is quite small. In the meantime, only two household units with no ritual paraphernalia are represented by large enough samples to be considered reliable, while most household units with high values and those without any ritual paraphernalia are represented by small less reliable samples.

Such patterning indicates that the access to ritual paraphernalia and ritual activities varied little across the household units in this sample. These household units had evenly distributed but quite modest access to certain ritual paraphernalia, meaning that non-elite households participated only in scapulimancy to a similarly small extent. Ritual activities or duties do not appear to be a significant factor in differentiating these non-elite households.

Almost all these household units had a modest opportunity to engage in the divination by scapulimancy and were very little differentiated in ritual activities and status. The consumption of oracle divination by non-elite families indicates that scapulimancy was not the exclusive prerogative of top elites, although ritual paraphernalia (the consumed oracle bones) were not abundant in the non-elite household units in this sample during the Erlitou period.

This echoes recent findings from the Shang period that scapulimancy was shared by the royal elites and non-royal families during the Bronze Age, allowing both groups to communicate with spirits and ancestors through pyromancy (Poo 1998; Pu 2007). Thus, ritual activities, at least oracle divination by scapulimancy, were also probably shared,

to some extent, by the royal elites and non-elites in the Erlitou state. Erlitou non-elites had limited access to ritual activities, possibly restricted solely to oracle divination by scapulimancy, based on the multidimensional scaling of the 34 household units and the quite low quantity of ritual paraphernalia involving almost entirely of materials for scapulimancy.

Taking it from another point of view (Figure 5.2), if non-elites were completely excluded from the palatial enclosure, we expect to see a clear gap in terms of ritual paraphernalia between the household units in or near the palatial enclosure and those from other locations, forming a cluster of oracle divination artifacts and activities composed of only household units within the palatial enclosure where the proportions of ritual paraphernalia representing access to ritual activities should be dramatically high. It is also expected that if non-elites were excluded from the oracle divination, a cluster of no divination activities should be composed of all the non-elite families from the workshop enclosure and the eastern end of the site in this sample. However, there is no clear clustering by different locations; household units with ritual paraphernalia from the three locations are mixed together thoroughly. On the other hand, the household units with the ritual paraphernalia in or near the palatial enclosure are far more than the other two locations; among the 18 household units with ritual paraphernalia, 14 are in or near the palatial enclosure, 3 are from the workshop enclosure, and 1 is at the eastern end of the site. Meanwhile, even though the modest proportions of ritual paraphernalia are shared across the household units from the three locations, the four household units with the highest proportions of ritual paraphernalia in this sample are all from the palatial enclosure. Additionally, more household units with medium (4) and low (6) proportions were in the palatial enclosure than in the workshop enclosure (2 medium and 1 low) and the eastern end of the site (1 low). In this sample, about 64% of the household units in or near the palatial enclosure have modest proportions of ritual items and about 18% have high proportions; Only about a third of the household units elsewhere (about 43% in or near the workshop enclosure and 20% at the eastern end of the site) have modest proportions with none having high proportions. So, being near the palaces is not the only way that non-elite households were able to participate in scapulimancy, but household units near the palaces were definitely more involved in this activity than others (at least in this sample). Household units with greater access to oracle divination by scapulimancy tended to be closer to the ruling elites. Some household units in the palatial enclosure thus slightly more focused on divination in the hope of more auspicious futures than those from the other two locations. But the absence of evidence of storage of unused oracle bones (only used ones were found) suggests that all the household units in this sample regardless of their locations might still have relied on professional diviners

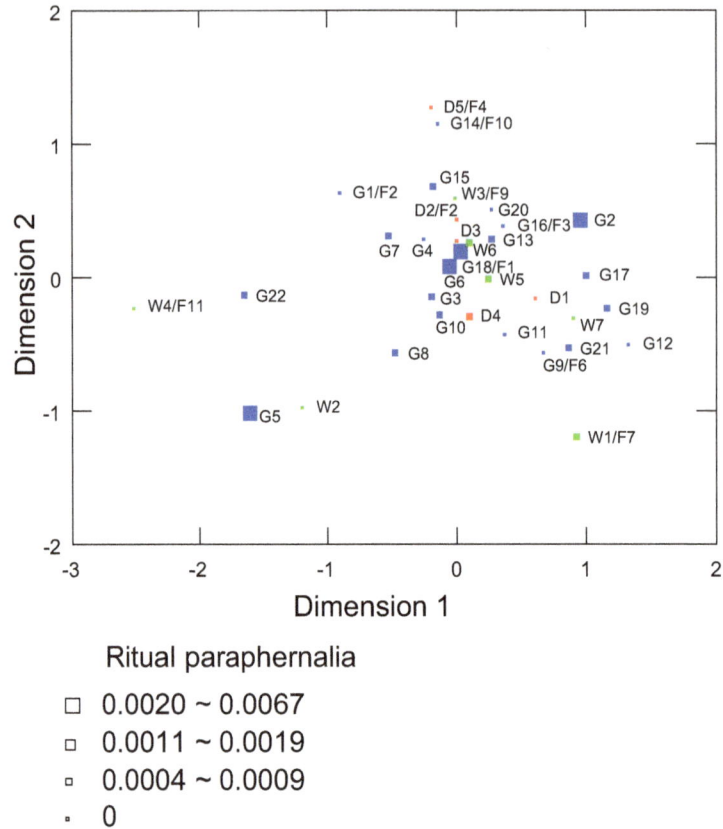

Figure 5.2. Household units indicating the proportions of ritual paraphernalia from different regions in different colors. (Larger squares represent higher ratios of ritual paraphernalia; Household units in or near the palatial enclosure in blue, household units in or near the workshop enclosure in green, and household units at the eastern end of the site in red).

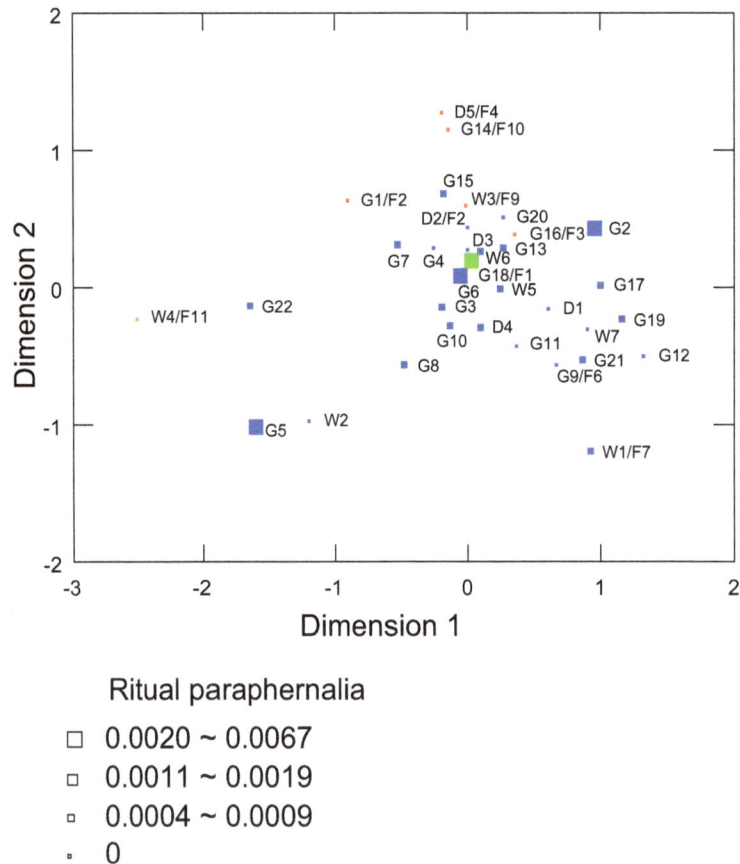

Figure 5.3. Household units indicating proportions of ritual paraphernalia colored by different housing structures. (Larger squares represent higher ratios of ritual paraphernalia; household units living in small on-the-ground structures in red, household units occupying semi-subterranean structures in green, household units with unknown structures in blue.).

to practice and interpret divinations. Of the household units in or near the palatial enclosure who had modest access to oracle divination by scapulimancy, most (13) are near the No.2 and No. 4 palaces (Figure 1.4 and 1.5), which are thought to be royal ancestral temples (Du 2007a and 2007b). The non-elite families from the palatial enclosure in this sample who had access to oracle divination by scapulimancy, although modest, tended to be close to these ancestral temples. This also suggests that non-elites' access to divination in this household sample was probably part of a relationship to the veneration of royal ancestors.

On the other hand, Figure 5.3 displays how the proportions of ritual paraphernalia behave across the household units with different housing structures. Only two household units with recorded housing structures were found with ritual paraphernalia; one (G18/F1) resided in a semi-subterranean structure, and one (W1/F7) was in an unknown type of housing structure.

Meanwhile, most household units living in small on-the-ground housing structures and semi-subterranean housing structures, those with no ritual paraphernalia, and the one living in a semi-subterranean housing structure (G18/F1) with modest access to ritual activities are represented by small less reliable samples.

Thus, the only form-identified housing structure with ritual paraphernalia was semi-subterranean. But this single observation is not sufficient to sustain conclusions about how the ritual differentiation occurred among the non-elite families living in clearly identifiable housing types in this sample.

Productive Differentiation within the Erlitou Household Sample

6.1. Patterns of the Variables Correlated to Production in the Two-dimensional Configuration

This chapter will explore the patterning of household assemblage variables related to productive differentiation in the two-dimensional multidimensional scaling configuration presented in Chapter 2. These variables are *Variable 8 (Carpentry/Construction Tools), Variable 9 (Agricultural Tools), Variable 10 (Textile Tools), Variable 11 (Weapons/Hunting Tools), Variable 12 (Resharpening Tools), Variable 13 (Fishing Tools), Variable 15 (Lithic Production), Variable 16 (Bone Production), Variable 17 (Antler Production), Variable 18 (Shell Production)* and *Variable 19 (Bronze Working)*.

6.1.1. Variable 9. Agricultural Tools

Figure 6.1 is a two-dimensional configuration plot showing the 34 household units in this sample with values of Variable 9 (Agricultural Tools). Each square in this plot represents a ratio of the number of agricultural tools to the number of sherds of identifiable vessel forms for each household

unit (Table 6.1). Larger squares represent household units with higher proportions of agricultural tools, indicating larger involvement in agricultural activities. In this plot, 23 household units were found to have agricultural tools, with proportions ranging from about 0.04% to about 0.70%.

A ratio of 0.04% means about one agricultural tool per 2,500 sherds of identifiable vessel forms in one household unit. If this is a true low rate for Variable 9, household units with only several hundred sherds of identifiable vessel forms and no agricultural tools may simply be the result of significant random noise in small samples. For this reason, the effects of zero counts and small samples must be carefully considered. The median ratio of agricultural tools among the household units found with agricultural tools is about 0.2%, meaning that there could be at least one agricultural tool per 500 sherds of identifiable vessel forms. Thus, household units with sample sizes of fewer than 500 sherds of identifiable vessel forms are less reliable than those represented by larger samples. In Figure 6.1, these less reliable cases are displayed in grey.

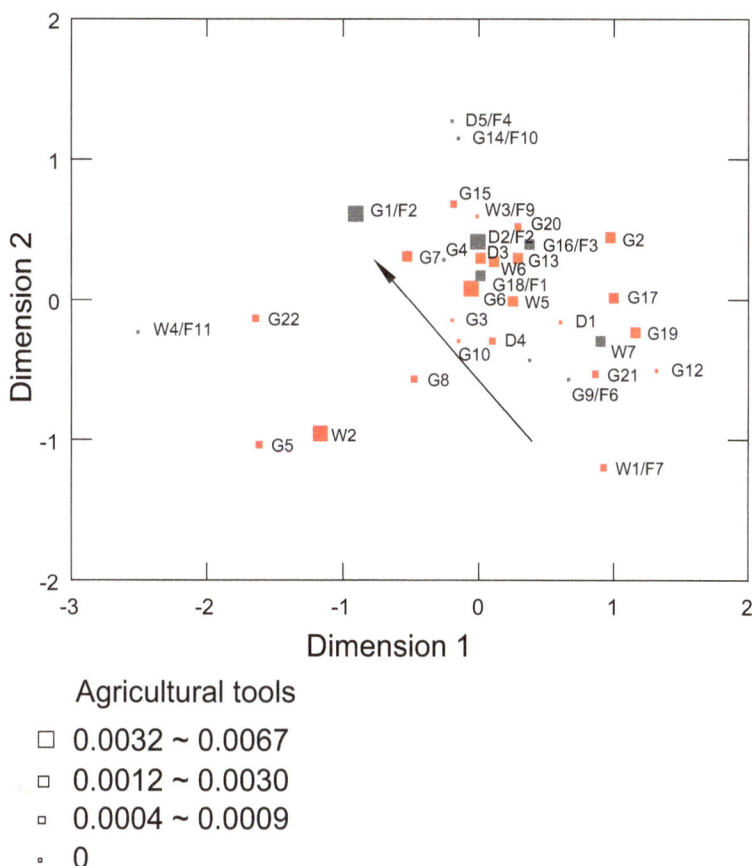

Figure 6.1. Plot of Variable 9. Agricultural Tools (larger squares represent higher proportions; grey squares are the household units with fewer than 500 sherds of various vessel forms).

Table 6.1. Proportions of the variables related to productive activities engaged in by the 34 household units (the largest proportions of each household unit are in red).

Household unit	Carpentry/ construction tools	Agricultural tools	Textile tools	Weapons/ hunting tools	Resharpening tools	Fishing tools	Lithic production	Bone Production	Antler production	Shell production	Bronze working
G1/F2	0.0122	0.0061	0.0061	0.0061	0.0000	0.0000	0.0122	0.0061	0.0122	0.0000	0.0000
G2	0.0000	0.0017	0.0000	0.0000	0.0017	0.0017	0.0000	0.0017	0.0000	0.0000	0.0000
G3	0.0000	0.0000	0.0000	0.0000	0.0000	0.0000	0.0000	0.0000	0.0009	0.0000	0.0000
G4	0.0000	0.0000	0.0000	0.0000	0.0000	0.0000	0.0000	0.0000	0.0000	0.0000	0.0000
G5	0.0007	0.0007	0.0000	0.0007	0.0007	0.0000	0.0000	0.0000	0.0007	0.0020	0.0000
G6	0.0067	0.0067	0.0067	0.0000	0.0000	0.0000	0.0000	0.0000	0.0000	0.0000	0.0000
G7	0.0000	0.0022	0.0011	0.0011	0.0000	0.0000	0.0011	0.0011	0.0022	0.0000	0.0011
G8	0.0000	0.0004	0.0000	0.0000	0.0004	0.0000	0.0000	0.0009	0.0000	0.0004	0.0000
G9/F6	0.0000	0.0000	0.0000	0.0000	0.0000	0.0000	0.0020	0.0000	0.0000	0.0020	0.0000
G10	0.0008	0.0000	0.0000	0.0000	0.0008	0.0000	0.0000	0.0000	0.0000	0.0000	0.0000
W1/F7	0.0000	0.0008	0.0016	0.0000	0.0032	0.0000	0.0008	0.0024	0.0000	0.0008	0.0000
W2	0.0000	0.0032	0.0000	0.0000	0.0011	0.0000	0.0000	0.0000	0.0011	0.0011	0.0000
D1	0.0012	0.0000	0.0037	0.0000	0.0025	0.0012	0.0025	0.0000	0.0000	0.0000	0.0000
D2/F2	0.0000	0.0059	0.0030	0.0030	0.0030	0.0000	0.0000	0.0000	0.0000	0.0000	0.0000
G11	0.0000	0.0000	0.0000	0.0110	0.0055	0.0000	0.0000	0.0000	0.0000	0.0000	0.0000
G12	0.0011	0.0000	0.0011	0.0011	0.0000	0.0011	0.0000	0.0046	0.0000	0.0000	0.0000
G13	0.0016	0.0012	0.0008	0.0032	0.0004	0.0000	0.0004	0.0059	0.0008	0.0004	0.0024
G14/F10	0.0000	0.0000	0.0000	0.0000	0.0000	0.0000	0.0000	0.0000	0.0000	0.0000	0.0000
G15	0.0005	0.0005	0.0000	0.0005	0.0000	0.0000	0.0015	0.0024	0.0000	0.0005	0.0000
G16/F3	0.0000	0.0029	0.0000	0.0087	0.0029	0.0000	0.0000	0.0000	0.0000	0.0000	0.0000
W3/F9	0.0029	0.0000	0.0000	0.0020	0.0010	0.0000	0.0010	0.0000	0.0000	0.0000	0.0000
W4/F11	0.0000	0.0000	0.0000	0.0000	0.0000	0.0192	0.0000	0.0000	0.0000	0.0000	0.0000
W5	0.0009	0.0016	0.0012	0.0010	0.0039	0.0001	0.0006	0.0025	0.0000	0.0003	0.0003
W6	0.0025	0.0012	0.0000	0.0000	0.0000	0.0000	0.0000	0.0025	0.0000	0.0000	0.0000
W7	0.0000	0.0030	0.0000	0.0000	0.0000	0.0000	0.0000	0.0060	0.0000	0.0000	0.0000
D3	0.0012	0.0024	0.0035	0.0012	0.0024	0.0006	0.0047	0.0000	0.0000	0.0000	0.0000
D4	0.0018	0.0009	0.0000	0.0000	0.0026	0.0000	0.0022	0.0018	0.0000	0.0000	0.0000
D5/F4	0.0000	0.0000	0.0000	0.0000	0.0000	0.0000	0.0000	0.0000	0.0000	0.0000	0.0000
G17	0.0013	0.0026	0.0026	0.0006	0.0006	0.0019	0.0006	0.0006	0.0000	0.0000	0.0000
G18/F1	0.0010	0.0030	0.0000	0.0040	0.0000	0.0000	0.0000	0.0010	0.0000	0.0000	0.0000
G19	0.0014	0.0025	0.0018	0.0014	0.0007	0.0000	0.0007	0.0007	0.0000	0.0000	0.0000
G20	0.0009	0.0009	0.0000	0.0000	0.0000	0.0000	0.0000	0.0000	0.0009	0.0000	0.0000
G21	0.0017	0.0009	0.0017	0.0000	0.0009	0.0009	0.0000	0.0000	0.0017	0.0009	0.0000
G22	0.0009	0.0009	0.0000	0.0009	0.0000	0.0000	0.0000	0.0000	0.0000	0.0000	0.0000

In this sample, 23 household units (including 5 less reliable cases) were found to have agricultural tools. The variation in the proportions of agricultural tools shows a relatively gradual tendency, starting from fairly low proportions at the lower right and rising toward the upper left part of the two-dimensional plot. Such variation suggests that among the household units who participated in agricultural activities, those in the upper left part of the configuration space were more intensively focused on these activities. Chapter 3 established that wealth among the non-elite

families in this sample also increases gradually towards the upper left of the configuration space. Thus, Figure 6.1 shows that household units more intensively involved in agricultural production tended strongly to be wealthier than other households in this sample. On the other hand, not all the households in the wealthier corner of the configuration plot were highly involved in agricultural production. Such patterning suggests that some household units might have increased their wealth by focusing on agricultural production, but this was not the only way by which household units accumulated their wealth in this sample.

6.1.2. Variable 8. Carpentry/Construction Tools

Figure 6.2 is a two-dimensional configuration plot showing the 34 household units in this sample with values of Variable 8 (Carpentry/Construction Tools). Each square in this figure represents a ratio of the number of carpentry/construction tools divided by the number of identifiable vessel form sherds in each household unit (Table 6.1). Larger squares represent household units with higher proportions of carpentry/construction tools, indicating larger involvement in carpentry or construction activities. In this plot, 19 household units were found with carpentry/construction tools, with proportions ranging from around 0.05% to around 1.22%.

A ratio of 0.05% means about one carpentry/construction tool can be expected for every 2,000 identifiable vessel form sherds in a household unit. If this is a true low rate for Variable 8, the household units with only several hundred identifiable vessel form sherds and no carpentry/construction tools are simply the result of the large amount of random noise in small samples. The effects of zero counts and small samples must be taken into consideration carefully. The median ratio of carpentry/construction tools among the household units found with such tools is about 0.1%. This means that probably there is at least one

carpentry/construction tool per 1,000 sherds of identifiable vessel forms. Thus, those household units with fewer than 1,000 sherds of identifiable vessel forms should be considered less reliable than those cases represented by larger sample sizes. In Figure 6.2, these less reliable cases are displayed in grey.

There are 19 household units (including 6 less reliable cases) found with carpentry/construction tools. There is no sharp division shown in this two-dimensional plot, but a gradual variation starting from fairly low proportions of carpentry/construction tools in the lower right, rising moderately in the middle and then reaching the highest values at the upper left of the two-dimensional configuration. Among the household units involved in carpentry or construction activities, those who focused more intensely on these activities tend to appear in the upper left, a region that Chapter 3 established as the area where the wealthier households in this sample are clustered. Similar to agricultural production, some households seem to have increased their wealth through carpentry or construction activities, but this was not the only means of accumulating wealth because some of the wealthier households were not highly involved in carpentry or construction activities.

6.1.3. Variable 11. Weapons/Hunting Tools

The two-dimensional plot indicating the values of Variable 11 (Weapons/Hunting Tools) (Figure 6.3) displays how

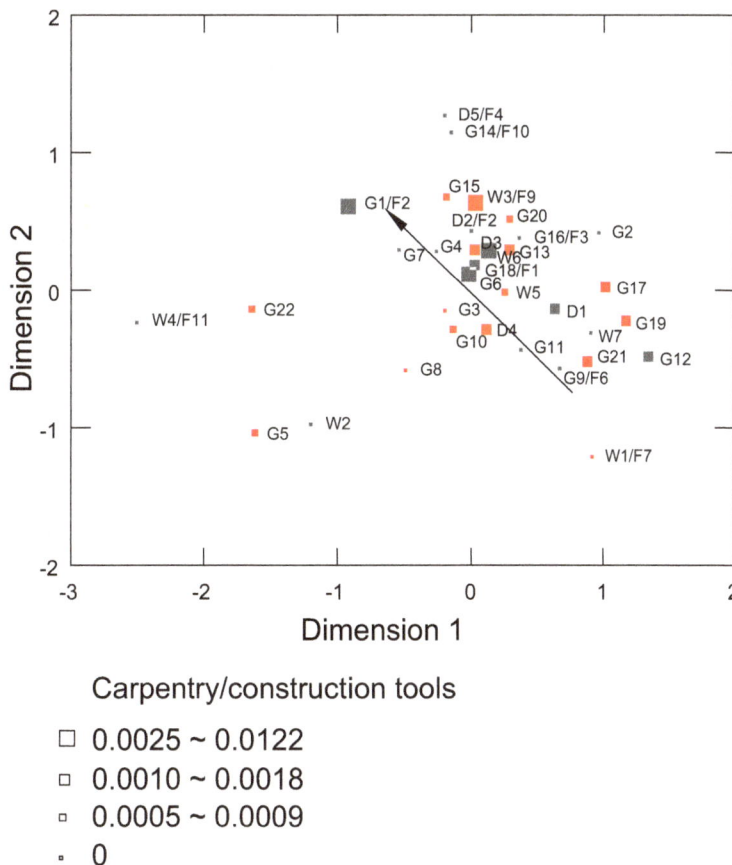

Figure 6.2. Plot of Variable 8. Carpentry/Construction Tools (larger squares represent higher proportions; grey squares are the household units with fewer than 1000 sherds of various vessel forms).

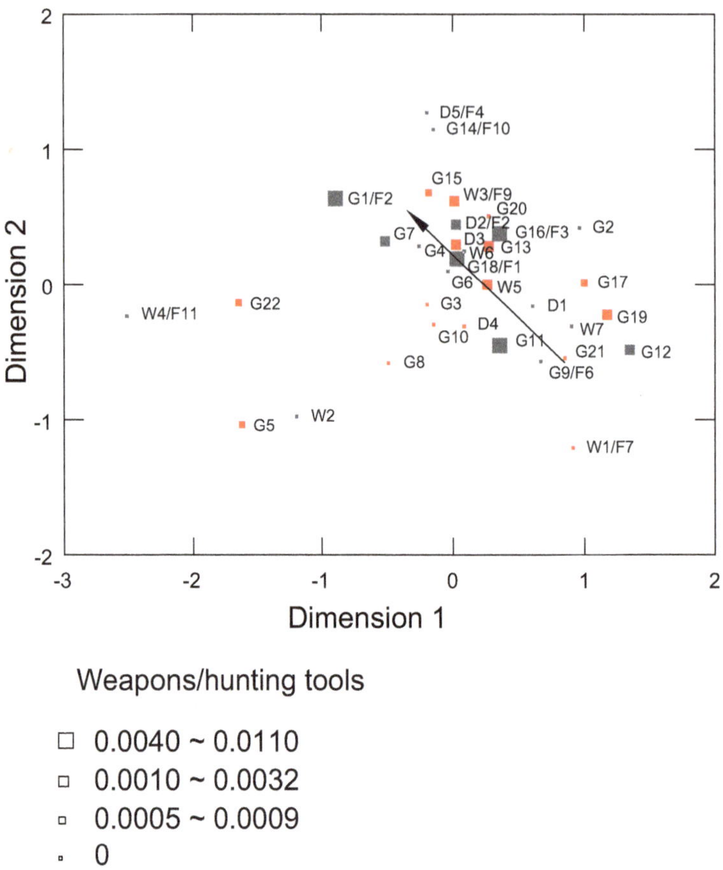

Weapons/hunting tools

☐ 0.0040 ~ 0.0110
▫ 0.0010 ~ 0.0032
▫ 0.0005 ~ 0.0009
▪ 0

Figure 6.3. Plot of Variable 11. Weapons/Hunting Tools (larger squares represent higher proportions; grey squares are the household units with fewer than 1000 sherds of various vessel forms).

the proportions of weapons/hunting tools (the number of weapons/hunting tools divided by the number of sherds of identifiable vessel forms for each household unit in this sample) are distributed. Each square represents one household unit. Larger squares represent household units with higher proportions of weapons/hunting tools. In this sample, 16 household units were found with weapons or hunting tools, all with quite low proportions ranging from around 0.05% to around 1.10%; in other words, the ratios range from about one weapon or hunting tool per 2,000 sherds of identifiable vessel forms to about one weapon or hunting tool per 91 sherds (Table 6.1).

If the ratio, about one weapon or hunting tool per 2,000 sherds of identifiable vessel forms, is truly low, then, we cannot say that the household units with only several hundred sherds of identifiable vessel forms and no weapon or hunting tools really have a lower weapon/hunting tool ratio than those with one weapon or hunting tool per 2,000 sherds. The median ratio of weapons or hunting tools among the household units found with such tools is about 0.1%. Then household units with a sample of fewer than 1,000 sherds of identifiable vessel forms should be considered as less reliable than those represented by larger sample sizes. These less reliable cases are colored grey in Figure 6.3.

Sixteen household units (including 7 less reliable cases) were found with weapons or hunting tools. The proportions of these tools among these household units form a gradual

tendency, increasing from low values in the lower right to higher values in the upper left (the wealthier) part of the two-dimensional configuration. Once again, this pattern suggests that some household units might have increased their wealth through military activities or hunting, but the non-elite families in this sample also had other ways to accumulate wealth as well, implying involvement in military activities or hunting was not the only path to greater wealth.

6.1.4. Variable 15. Lithic Production

Figure 6.4 is a two-dimensional configuration showing the 34 household units in this sample with the values indicating Variable 15 (Lithic Production). Each square in this plot represents a ratio calculated as the number of lithic tool production remains divided by the number of sherds of identifiable vessel forms in a household unit. Larger squares correspond to household units with higher proportions of lithic tool production remains, indicating greater engagement in lithic production. In this plot, 13 household units are found with lithic tool production remains, with proportions ranging from about 0.04% to about 1.22% (Table 6.1).

A ratio of 0.04% means that there is possibly one lithic tool production remain per 2,500 sherds of identifiable vessel forms. If this is a true low rate, then the household units with only several hundred sherds of identifiable vessel

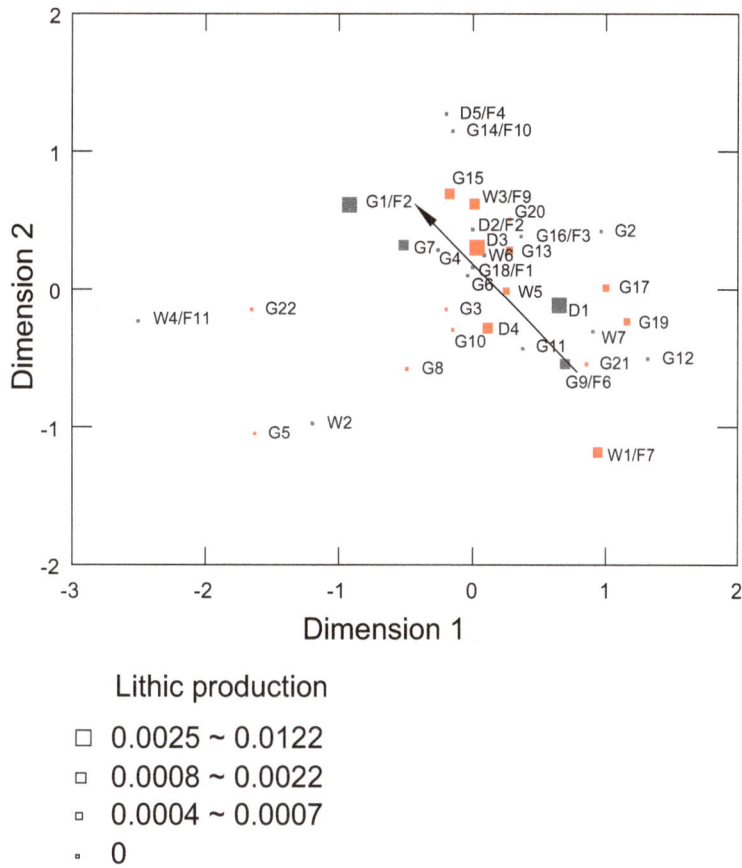

Lithic production

☐ 0.0025 ~ 0.0122
▫ 0.0008 ~ 0.0022
▫ 0.0004 ~ 0.0007
▫ 0

Figure 6.4. Plot of Variable 15. Lithic Production (larger squares represent higher proportions; grey squares are the household units with fewer than 1,000 sherds of various vessel forms).

forms and no lithic tool production remains are possibly the result of significant random noise in small samples. The median ratio of lithic tool production remains among the household units found with such remains is about 0.1%, meaning that there could be at least one lithic tool production remain per 1,000 sherds of identifiable vessel forms. Thus, household units with sample sizes of fewer than 1,000 sherds of identifiable vessel forms should be less reliable than those represented by larger sample sizes. The less reliable cases are displayed in grey in Figure 6.4.

The proportions of lithic tool production remains show a gradual tendency, rising from low proportions in the lower right to higher proportions in the upper left part of the two-dimensional plot. This suggests that household units more involved in lithic tool production tend to stand in the upper left (wealthier) part of this plot. However, there are still some household units in the wealthy area of the scaling space that do not have higher proportions of lithic tool production. Such patterning once again suggests that some non-elite families in this sample might have accumulated wealth by focusing on lithic tool production while other non-elite families accumulated wealth by focusing on other productive activities.

6.1.5. Variable 16. Bone Production

The two-dimensional configuration indicating the values of Variable 16 (Bone Production) (Figure 6.5) shows

how the proportions of bone artifact production remains divided by the number of sherds of identifiable vessel forms are distributed across the household units in this sample. A larger square represents a household unit with a higher proportion of bone artifact production remains. In this sample, 15 household units were found with bone artifact production remains, all with quite low proportions ranging from about 0.06% to about 0.61%; in other words, the ratios range from about one bone artifact production remain per 1,667 sherds of identifiable vessel forms (for the lowest proportion) to about one bone artifact production remain per 164 sherds of identifiable vessel forms (for the highest proportion) (Table 6.1).

If the rate of one bone artifact production remain per 1,667 sherds of identifiable vessel forms is truly low, then the household units with only several hundreds of sherds of identifiable vessel forms and no bone artifact production remains cannot be deemed confidently to have a lower rate than those with one bone artifact production remain per 1,667. The median ratio of bone artifact production remains among the household units found with such remains is about 0.2%. Then, household units with fewer than 500 sherds of identifiable vessel forms are less reliable than those represented by larger sample sizes. These less reliable cases are displayed in grey in Figure 6.5.

Fifteen household units (including 2 less reliable cases) were found with bone artifact production remains. The

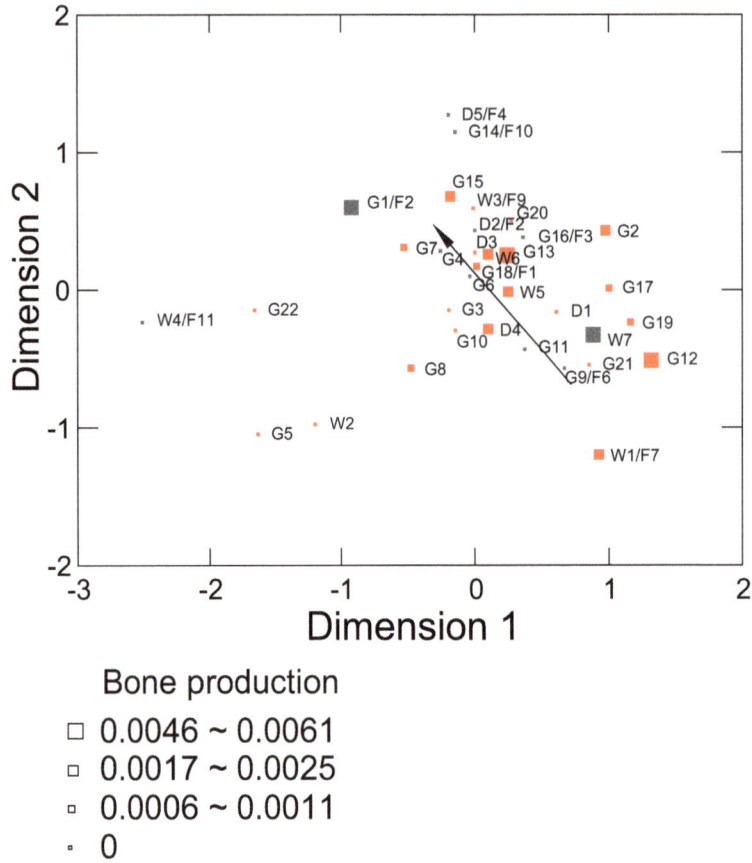

Figure 6.5. Plot of Variable 16. Bone Production (larger squares represent higher proportions; grey squares are the household units with fewer than 500 sherds of various vessel forms).

proportions of these remains among these household units vary in a gradual way, starting from low proportions in the lower right and climbing up to higher proportions in the upper left part of the two-dimensional plot. Household units more involved in bone artifact production tend to be located in the upper left (wealthier) part of this plot. This suggests that some household units in this sample might have accumulated wealth through bone artifact production, but other household units could also accumulate wealth through a focus on other productive activities.

6.1.6. Variable 17. Antler Production

Figure 6.6 is a two-dimensional configuration plot indicating the values of the antler production variable, showing how the proportions (calculated as the number of antler artifact production remains divided by the number of sherds of identifiable vessel forms for each household unit) behave in this sample. Each square in the plot represents a household unit with antler artifact production remains, and larger squares indicate higher proportions of such production remains. Only 8 household units in this sample were found with antler artifact production remains. The proportions of antler artifact production remains are quite low, ranging from about 0.07% to about 1.22% (Table 6.1).

A ratio of 0.07% means that there possibly is one antler artifact production remain per 1,429 sherds of identifiable

vessel forms. If this is a true low rate for Variable 17, household units with only several hundred identifiable vessel form sherds and no antler artifact production remains are possibly the results of the large amount of random noise in small samples. The median ratio of antler artifact production remains among the household units found with such remains is about 0.1%. Household units with fewer than 1,000 sherds of identifiable vessel forms are less reliable than those represented by larger sample sizes. These less reliable cases are displayed in grey in Figure 6.6.

Only 8 household units (including 3 less reliable cases) were uncovered with antler artifact production remains. Such a small sample size suggests that the antler artifact production was not a widely engaged important economic activity among the household sample, and only a few families specialized in it. The proportions of antler artifact production remains also do not form a clear cluster, but show a relatively gradual tendency starting with low proportions in the lower right and rising toward the upper left of the two-dimensional plot. Some household units more involved in antler artifact production tend to appear in the upper left (wealthier) part of the configuration space. Such variation suggests that some household units in this sample could accumulate wealth through emphasizing antler artifact production, but non-elite families still had other ways to increase their wealth.

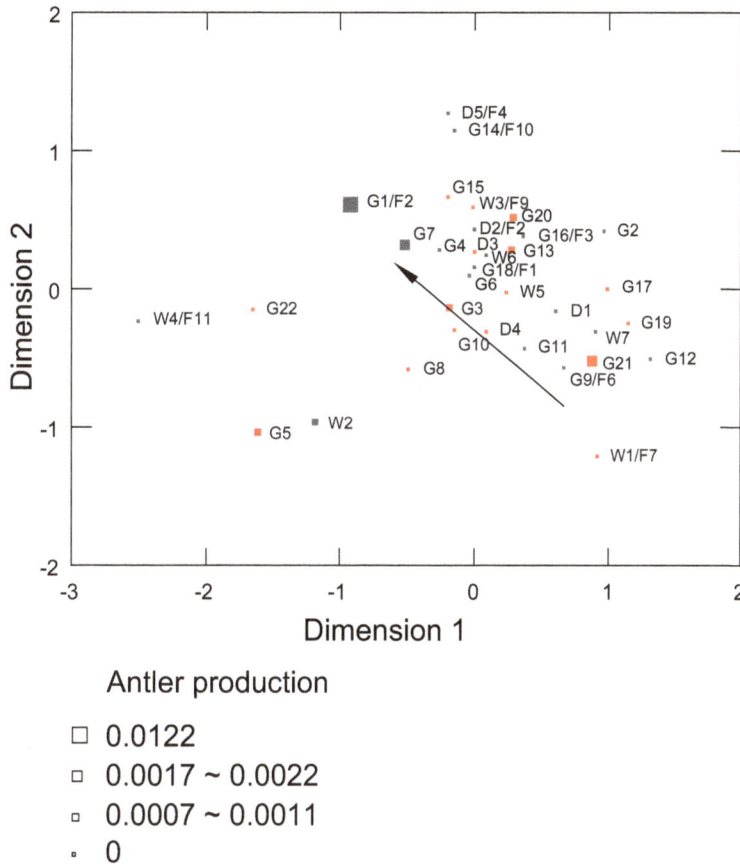

Figure 6.6. Plot of Variable 17. Antler Production (larger squares represent higher proportions; grey squares are the household units with fewer than 1,000 sherds of various vessel forms).

6.1.7. *Variable 19. Bronze Working*

Figure 6.7 is a two-dimensional configuration plot showing the 34 household units in this sample with values indicating Variable 19 (Bronze Working). Each square in this figure represents a ratio of the number of copper ores and slags divided by the number of sherds of identifiable vessel forms in a household unit. Larger squares correspond to household units with higher proportions of bronze working remains, indicating greater involvement in bronze working. In this plot, only 3 household units were found with copper ores and/or slags, with proportions of around 0.03%, 0.11% and 0.24% (Table 6.1).

A ratio of 0.03% means that there is possibly one bronze working remain per 3,333 sherds of identifiable vessel forms in a household unit. If this is a true low rate, household units with only hundreds of sherds of identifiable vessel forms and no bronze working remains are possible results of the large amount of random noise in small samples. Given the effects of small sample sizes and zero counts, this study also examines the median ratio of bronze working remains among household units found with such remains. This median is about 0.1%. Thus, household units with fewer than 1,000 sherds of identifiable vessel forms are counted as less reliable and displayed in grey in Figure 6.7.

Bronze working also raises more complicated issues to consider than the productive activities discussed above. Only

3 household units (including 1 less reliable case) were found with bronze working remains. Bronze smelting and casting is believed to be far more complex productive activities than other household-based production and are usually thought to require high-level specialization and workshop-based production. They require a large and stable supply of ores, furnaces, and other equipment. A bronze-casting workshop has been identified in the southern part of the workshop enclosure. The bronze-casting workshop has been argued as a royal-controlled, elite-oriented production site that supplied bronze items exclusively for elite consumption (Zhongguo 1999, 2003, 2014; Chen 2016; Liu and Chen 2003; Xu 2009, 2022). An array of bronze casting remains including crucibles, ores, slags, lithic and pottery molds, and furnaces have been found in the area of the bronze-casting workshop suggesting that the bronze casting was specialized in that area (Zhongguo 1999; Chen 2016). However, some copper ores and slags have been found associated with household garbage. Such small amounts of materials related to bronze working and no other equipment make us wonder whether such remains might have been from somewhere else and simply been incorporated into the household garbage rather than representing an activity actually carried out at these households. If these copper ores and slags were from somewhere else where bronze-smelting (or, even -casting) was conducted, their incorporation into household garbage would suggest bronze-working activities near the household units where the garbage was found. But, of the three household units with bronze-working remains, two (G7 and

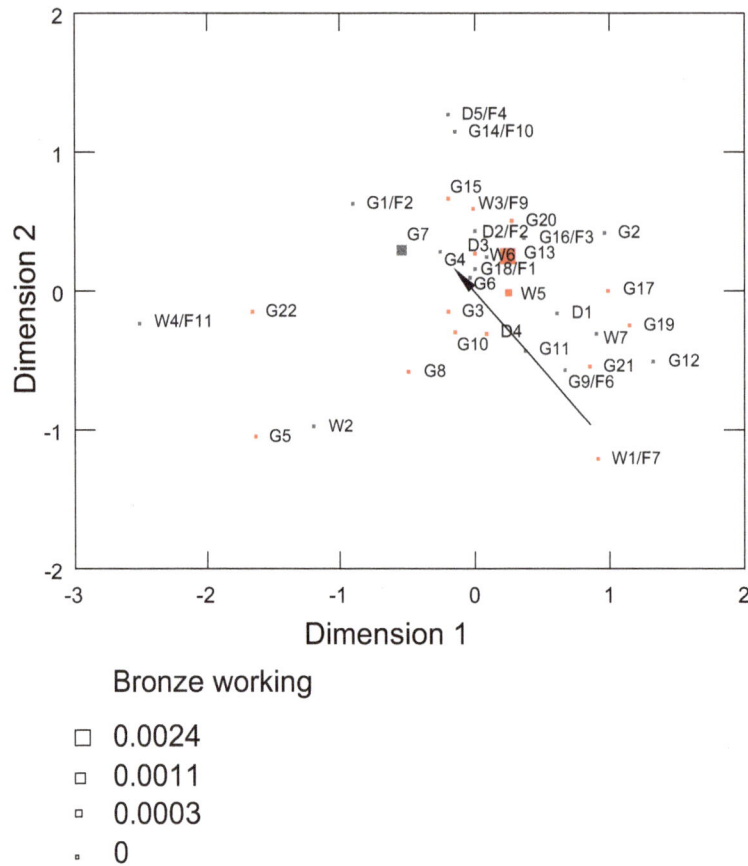

Figure 6.7. Plot of Variable 19. Bronze Working (larger squares represent higher proportions; grey squares are the household units with fewer than 1,000 sherds of various vessel forms).

G13) are in the palatial enclosure, and one (W5) is in the northern part of the workshop enclosure (which is currently known as the turquoise workshop). None of the three is in the vicinity of the bronze-casting workshop which is in the southern part of the workshop enclosure. Before 1999 - 2006, some bronze-working remains including crucibles, slags, and ceramic molds dating to Erlitou Phase 2 had been found both at the northeast of the palatial enclosure and in the area of the later bronze-casting workshop, suggesting that bronze-smelting (or -casting) may have been conducted in more than one spot but closer to the ruling elites before Erlitou Phase 3 by which bronze casting became concentrated in the bronze-casting workshop within the workshop enclosure (Zhongguo 1999; Chen 2016). In Erlitou Phase 4, copper ores and slags began to be seen outside the bronze-casting workshop again suggesting that there might have been other smelting or casting spots at the Erlitou site simultaneous with the specialized bronze-casting workshop (Zhongguo 2014; Chen 2016). Based on the small amount of bronze-working remains, Chen (2016) argues there might have been small-scale smelting or casting spots serving for producing some less complex bronze items or for mending broken ones. Although it seems unusual to conduct bronze working in a household context, for now the possibility of household-level bronze working serving the ruling elites cannot be definitely ruled out.

If the copper ores and slags found in household garbage truly represent household-level bronze working activities,

it suggests that bronze working was not a widely engaged important economic activity among the household sample, being even less widespread than antler artifact production. In this case, only a few families specialized in bronze working, and the non-elite families who engaged or specialized in such activities were likely to be in the moderate level of wealth accumulation.

6.1.8. Discussion of Productive Activities Related to Greater Wealth

Variable 8 (Carpentry/Construction Tools), Variable 9 (Agricultural Tools), Variable 11 (Weapons/Hunting Tools), Variable 15 (Lithic Production), Variable 16 (Bone Production), and Variable 17 (Antler Production) all pattern in a relatively similar way in the space defined by the two-dimensional configuration. The six variables all vary gradually, running from lower proportions in the lower right to higher proportions in the upper left of the plot for Dimensions 1 and 2. The household units with high proportions of carpentry or construction tools, agricultural tools, weapons or hunting tools, lithic tool production remains, bone artifact production remains, and antler artifact production remains tend to stand in the upper left (wealthier) part of the plot. Most household units in the wealthier zone of the scaling space focus on one or another, or even more than just one, of these six productive activities. This pattern suggests that household units could accumulate wealth by intensifying their participation in carpentry or construction activities, agricultural activities, military or hunting activities, lithic tool production, bone artifact production, or antler artifact production, and that such economic activities were likely to offer good economic returns.

6.1.9. Variable 12. Resharpening Tools

The two-dimensional plot indicating the values of Variable 12 (Resharpening Tools) (Figure 6.8) reveals how the proportions calculated as the number of resharpening tools divided by the number of sherds of identifiable vessel forms for each household unit in this sample are distributed. Larger squares represent household units with higher proportions of the resharpening tools, or whetstones. In this sample, resharpening tools are extremely rare, with proportions ranging from only about 0.04% to about 0.55% (Table 6.1). Such ratios can be translated as about one whetstone per 2,500 sherds of identifiable vessel forms (for the lowest proportion) to about one whetstone per 182 sherds of identifiable vessel forms (for the highest proportion).

If the ratio of one whetstone per 2,500 sherds of identifiable vessel forms in a household unit is a true low rate, we cannot say confidently a household unit with only hundreds of sherds of identifiable vessel forms and no whetstone truly has a lower resharpening tool ratio than

the household unit with one whetstone per 2,500 sherds of identifiable vessel forms. Considering the effects caused by zero values for resharpening tools and small sample sizes, this study further examines the resharpening tool ratios among household units found with whetstones and finds the median ratio is about 0.2%. Such a ratio means that one or more whetstones could be expected if the number of sherds of identifiable vessel forms is greater than 500. So, when no whetstones are found in household units with a sample of fewer than 500 sherds of identifiable vessel forms, it is likely that the zero results may merely be the result of significant random noise in small samples. Therefore, household units with a sample size of fewer than 500 sherds of identifiable vessel forms are possibly less reliable cases and are displayed in grey in Figure 6.8.

Eighteen household units (including 3 less reliable cases) were found with whetstones or resharpening tools. The variation in the proportions of resharpening tools is relatively gradual, starting from fairly low proportions in the upper left and increasing toward the lower right part of the two-dimensional plot. So, household units that consumed more resharpening tools and were more engaged in resharpening or smoothing services tend to be in the middle to the lower right part of the plot. In terms of wealth distribution, household units more involved in resharpening or smoothing activities fall in the middle to lower ranges. Such patterning suggests that resharpening or smoothing,

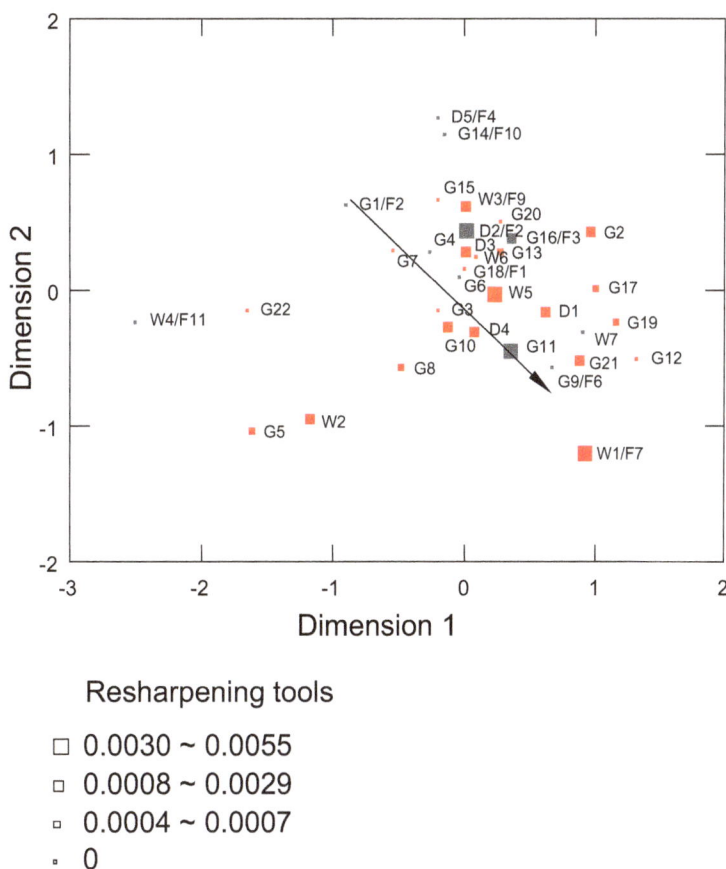

Figure 6.8. Plot of Variable 12. Resharpening Tools (larger squares represent higher proportions; grey squares are the household units with fewer than 500 sherds of various vessel forms).

in contrast to the productive activities considered above, was not an effective activity toward greater wealth for non-elite families in this household sample.

6.1.10. Variable 10. Textile Tools

Figure 6.9 is a two-dimensional configuration plot showing the 34 household units in this sample with the values indicating Variable 10 (Textile Tools). Each square in this figure represents a ratio of the number of textile tools to the number of sherds of identifiable vessel forms in a household unit. Larger squares represent household units with higher proportions of textile tools, indicating greater involvement in textile activities. In this plot, 13 household units were found with textile tools, with quite low proportions ranging from about 0.08% to about 0.67% (Table 6.1).

A rate of 0.08% means that there could be about one textile tool per 1,250 sherds of identifiable vessel forms in a household unit. If this is a true low rate, then household units with only hundreds of sherds and no textile tools are possibly the result of significant random noise in small samples. The median ratio of textile tools among household units found with textile tools is about 0.2%, indicating that there could be at least one textile tool per 500 sherds. Thus, household units with fewer than 500 sherds of identifiable vessel forms are considered less reliable and are colored grey in Figure 6.9.

Thirteen household units (including 3 less reliable cases) were found with textile tools. The proportions of textile

tools behave in a gradual way, starting with low values in the upper left and moving toward higher values in the lower right part of the two-dimensional configuration. This shows that household units more involved in textile production and weaving activities tend to stand in the lower right part of this plot. Although some squares in the plot do not follow this pattern, appearing toward the upper left, these represent less reliable ratios calculated from smaller samples. With reference to the wealth tendency, household units involved more in the textile production or weaving activities are located in the moderate to low ranges of the wealth distribution. This pattern suggests that textile production, like resharpening, was not an activity which led non-elite families to greater wealth.

6.1.11. Variable 18. Shell Production

The two-dimensional configuration indicating the values of Variable 18 (Shell Production) (Figure 6.10) shows how the proportions, calculated as the number of shell artifact production remains divided by the number of sherds of identifiable vessel forms in each household unit, behave in this sample. Larger squares represent household units with higher proportions of shell artifact production remains. In this sample, only 9 household units were involved in shell artifact production, with fairly low proportions ranging from about 0.03% to about 0.20%; in other words, the ratios of shell artifact production remains among the household units engaging in this production are from about one shell artifact production remain per 3,333 sherds of identifiable

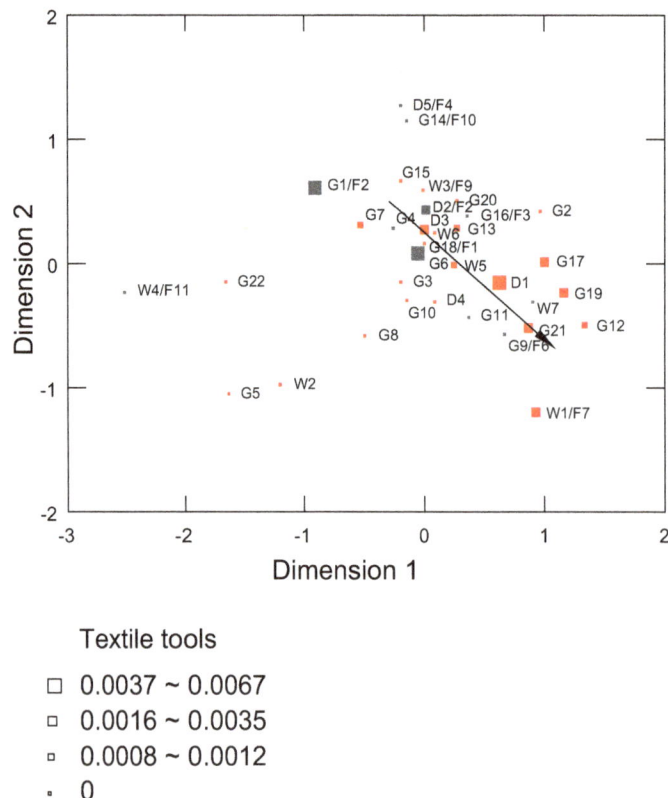

Figure 6.9. Plot of Variable 10. Textile Tools (larger squares represent higher proportions; grey squares are the household units with fewer than 500 sherds of various vessel forms).

vessel forms to about one shell artifact production remain per 500 sherds (Table 6.1).

If the ratio of about one shell artifact production remain per 3,333 sherds of identifiable vessel forms is truly low, then the household units with only hundreds of sherds of identifiable vessel forms and no shell artifact production remains cannot be considered to have a lower rate. The median ratio of shell artifact production remains among household units found with such remains is about 0.1%, which means that there is possibly one or more shell artifact production remains per 1,000 sherds of identifiable vessel forms. Thus, household units with fewer than 1,000 sherds of identifiable vessel forms are less reliable than those represented by larger sample sizes. These less reliable cases are colored grey in Figure 6.10.

Only 9 household units (including 2 less reliable cases) in this household sample were found with shell artifact production remains. The proportions of shell artifact production remains also behave in a gradual way, starting from low values in the upper left and moving to higher values in the lower right part of the two-dimensional plot. This patterning suggests that shell artifact production was also not an important or widespread economic activity among the household sample, and only a few families engaged in this production. Household units more involved in shell artifact production tend to appear in the lower right part of this plot, which corresponds to the moderate to low

ranges of the wealth distribution. Such patterning suggests that shell artifact production was also not a pathway for the non-elite families to greater wealth.

6.1.12. Variable 13. Fishing Tools

The two-dimensional plot indicating the values of Variable 13 (Fishing Tools) (Figure 6.11) reveals how the proportions, calculated as the number of fishing tools divided by the number of sherds of identifiable vessel forms in each household unit, behave in this sample. Larger squares represent household units with larger proportions of fishing tools. In this sample, only 8 household units were found with fishing tools, with proportions ranging from about 0.01% to about 1.92% (Table 6.1). In other words, the ratios range from about one fishing tool per 10,000 sherds of identifiable vessel forms to about one fishing tool per 52 sherds.

If the ratio of about one fishing tool per 10,000 sherds of identifiable vessel forms is truly low, then a household unit with only hundreds of sherds of identifiable vessel forms and no fishing tools cannot be confidently considered with a lower ratio. The median ratio of fishing tools among household units found with fishing tools is about 0.1%. Such a ratio means that there is possibly one or more fishing tools per 1,000 sherds of identifiable vessel forms in a household unit. Thus, household units with fewer than 1,000 sherds of identifiable vessel forms are considered less reliable than

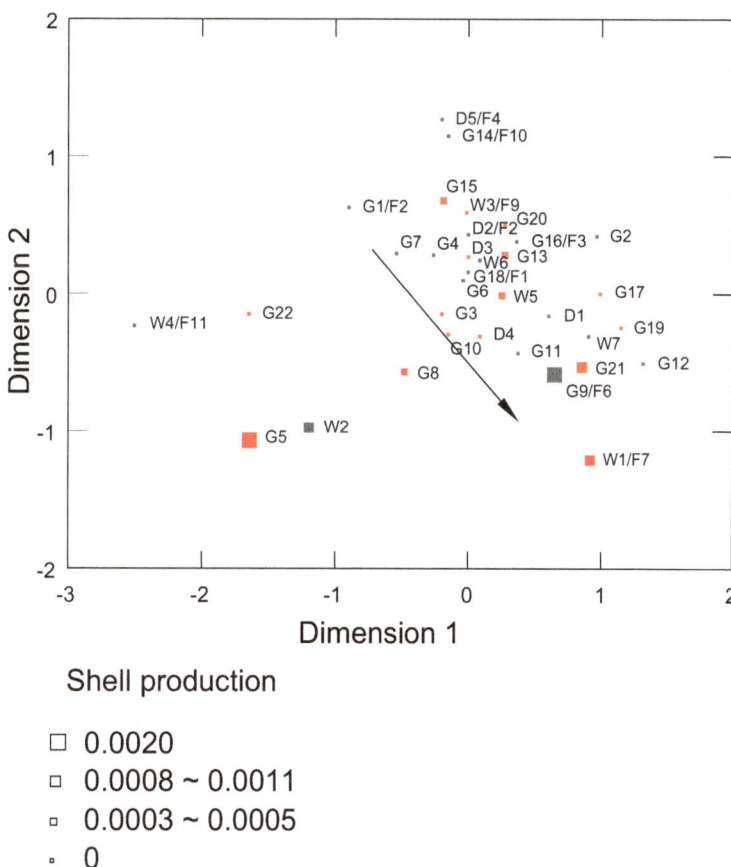

Shell production

□ 0.0020
▫ 0.0008 ~ 0.0011
▫ 0.0003 ~ 0.0005
▫ 0

Figure 6.10. Plot of Variable 18. Shell Production (larger squares represent higher proportions; grey squares are the household units with fewer than 1,000 sherds of various vessel forms).

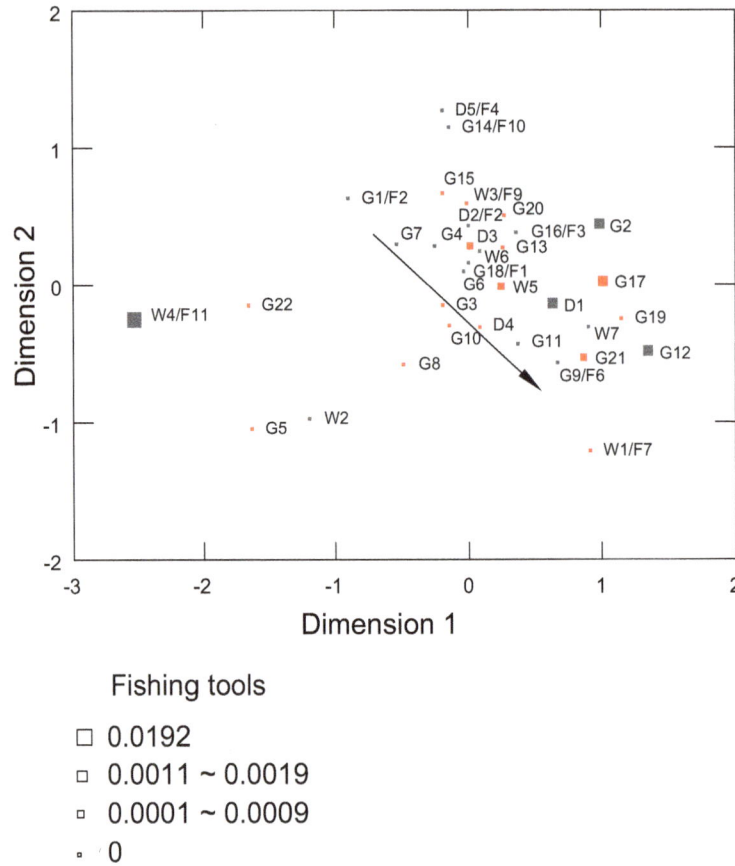

Fishing tools

☐ 0.0192
▫ 0.0011 ~ 0.0019
▫ 0.0001 ~ 0.0009
▫ 0

Figure 6.11. Plot of Variable 13. Fishing Tools (larger squares represent higher proportions; grey squares are the household units with fewer than 1,000 sherds of various vessel forms).

those represented by larger sample sizes. These less reliable household units are displayed in grey in Figure 6.11.

Only 8 household units (including 4 less reliable cases) were found with fishing tools. The proportions of fishing tools in the household sample start with low values in the upper left and rise gradually toward the lower right part of the two-dimensional configuration, although one square representing a less reliable ratio from a small sample stands out in the lower left as a possible exception to this pattern. Such patterning suggests that fishing was not an important economic activity widely engaged in by the household sample, and only a few families in this sample specialized in fishing activities. Household units more engaged in fishing tend to appear in the lower right part of the plot, which corresponds to the moderate to low range of the wealth distribution. This suggests that fishing could not lead the non-elite families to greater wealth as well.

6.1.13. Discussion of Productive Activities Related to Lower Wealth

Variable 10 (Textile Tools), Variable 12 (Resharpening Tools), Variable 13 (Fishing Tools), and Variable 18 (Shell Production) all pattern in a relatively similar way in the space defined by the two-dimensional configuration. The four variables all show gradual variation, to some extent, ranging from low values in the upper left corner to higher values in the lower right corner of the plot for Dimensions 1

and 2. This gradual variation parallels the wealth tendency but in the opposite direction from the productive variables discussed in the first half of this chapter. Household units with high proportions of textile tools, resharpening tools, fishing tools, and shell artifact production remains tend to stand in the lower right (less wealthy) part of the plot. Thus, resharpening or smoothing, textile making or weaving, fishing, and shell artifact production possibly could not offer good economic returns, and non-elite families in the Erlitou state could not accumulate wealth through focusing on these four productive activities.

6.2. Discussion

A set of 11 variables, representing an array of productive activities engaged in by the household units in this sample, are explored in this two-dimensional scaling. Such a study of the productive activities conducted in household contexts and by the household sample can contribute to our understanding of the economic interactions among household units and how the productive activities influenced the non-elite families represented by the household units in this sample in the Erlitou state.

In the plot of Dimensions 1 and 2, there is no clear tendency for any productive activities to cluster together; instead, there is a thoroughly mixed pattern (Figure 6.1 ~ 6.11). The proportions of different kinds of practical tools are also all quite low among the household sample. If there had been a highly specialized productive pattern among the household units, clustering by variables representing correlated productive activities would be expected in the two-dimensional configuration. However, the household units in this two-dimensional configuration do not form any clear clusters by productive activities but mix together thoroughly across a complex array of productive activities. There is also no clear clustering by different locations within the Erlitou site, although bronze working was observed only in the palatial enclosure (G7 and G13) and the workshop enclosure (W5) (Figure 6.12). The intermingled pattern and the quite low proportions of practical tools and remains suggest that productive differentiation was relatively modest in scope across the three locations of the Erlitou site. Such production was widely engaged in by the non-elites in the household sample, although not all household units focused especially intensely on subsistence production. At the same time, some household units were involved in several different productive activities, which combine and recombine in constantly varying ways.

Such economic involvement in both production for themselves and extra commodities for exchange with other households did not promote the prestige of the household units in this sample. As chapter 4 has shown, prestige differentiation within the household sample starts at low values in the upper right corner of the two-dimensional configuration and rises to higher values toward the lower left corner. If productive differentiation had some relevance to prestige negotiation, household units more involved in productive activities for exchange should have appeared

more in the lower left part of this two-dimensional configuration. Instead, most household units involved in different kinds of productive activities for exchange are more likely to stand in the middle and upper part of the configuration space, especially the upper left or the lower right, rather than in the lower left. Household units that participated more intensely in productive activities for exchange, regardless of what the productive activities were, tended to have moderate to low prestige. Some relatively prestigious household units were also engaged in agricultural activities, carpentry or construction activities, military or hunting activities, and the production of antler or shell artifacts. But more prestigious non-elites generally did not emphasize productive activities, compared to less prestigious families in this household sample, although there were some possible exceptions. Thus, prestige was not negotiated or gained by involvement in the productive activities represented by the 11 variables.

On the other hand, engagement in productive activities specially for exchange with other households seems to have made it possible to augment household standards of living within the household sample, that is, to accumulate some degree of wealth (Figure 6.12). The proportions related to some productive activities parallel the pattern of wealth differentiation in the configuration space. Most household units involved in these productive activities stand in the upper-left-to-lower-right scope of the two-dimensional configuration. Variable 8 (Carpentry/Construction Tools), Variable 9 (Agricultural Tools), Variable 11 (Weapons/ Hunting Tools), Variable 15 (Lithic Production), Variable

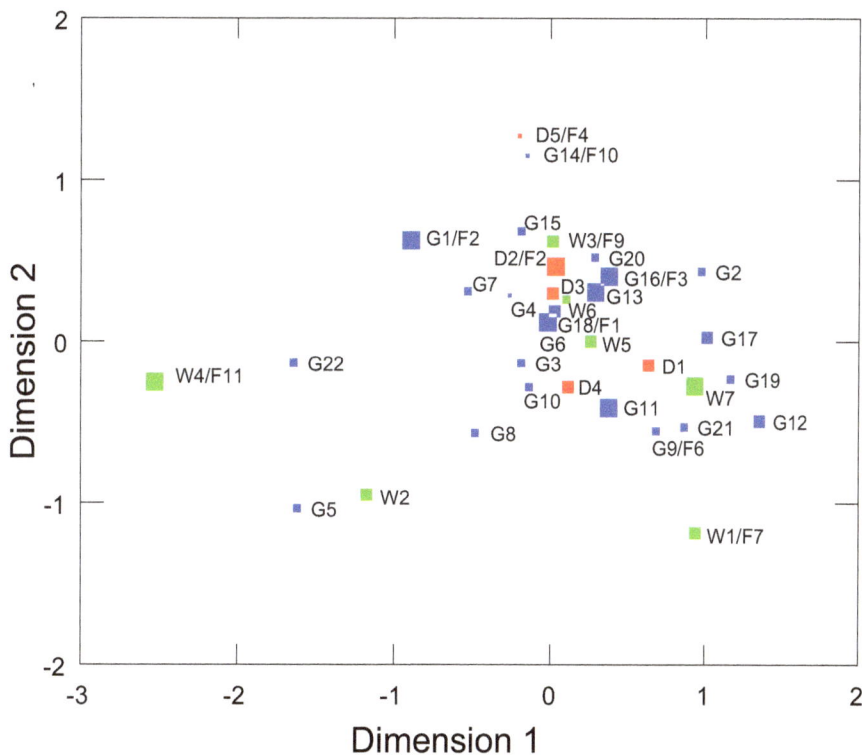

Figure 6.12. Household units with the highest proportion of artifactual evidence of special productive activities from different regions in different colors. (The size of each square indicates the highest proportion of artifactual evidence for any productive activity engaged in by the corresponding household; household units in or near the palatial enclosure in blue, household units in or near the workshop enclosure in green, and household units at the eastern end of the site in red).

16 (Bone Production), Variable 17 (Antler Production), and Variable 19 (Bronze Working) (Figure 6.1 ~ 6.7) occur in higher proportions in the wealthier portion of the configuration plot; in contrast, household units with high proportions of Variable 10 (Textile Tools), Variable 12 (Resharpening Tools), Variable 13 (Fishing Tools), and Variable 18 (Shell Production) (Figure 6.8 ~ 6.11) tend to be in the lower right part of the two-dimensional configuration, suggesting moderate to low wealth (Figure 6.12). This patterning suggests that the productive activities represented by the former seven-variable set offered more economic returns than those represented by the latter four-variable set in the Erlitou economy. Household units emphasizing the first set of productive activities seem to have improved their standards of living while those focusing on the second set did not, although the patterns are complicated. Such different emphases among non-elite families suggest not only that wealth redistribution happened, but also some exchange among household units took place in Erlitou society.

Agriculture was the main source of subsistence for Erlitou people. In this sample, over half of the household units were certainly involved in agriculture, suggesting that agricultural production by residents of the Erlitou settlement was important along with food tribute from the Erlitou rural hinterland in the Yiluo Basin (Liu 2006; Qiao 2010). Construction/carpentry activities were the second most widespread productive activity evidenced by the artifact assemblages of Erlitou household units. Certainly, massive construction from Erlitou Phase 2 to Phase 4 was required to create the enclosed walls of the palatial enclosure and the workshop enclosure, and to build the array of palaces in the palatial enclosure. At the same time, population increase enlarged the demand for shelter. Construction/carpentry activities may have provided good economic returns because of this expanded demand. Weapons/hunting tools are also widely seen among the household units in this sample. Although arrowheads could serve in hunting to some extent, such artifacts, as discussed in Chapter 2, are more likely to be weapons. The presence of weapons in household contexts suggests that many non-elites in the Erlitou state may have served in the armed forces in addition to their economic duties represented by the weapons/hunting tools in household contexts. With elite demands for procurement of natural resources through military expansion and increased demands for defense against the rising political challenge from the Erligang polity (Liu and Chen 2003, 2012; Liu 2006), non-elites might have been paid off well for serving in the armed forces. Patterns of household units engaging in production of lithic tools, bone artifacts, and antler artifacts suggest that some non-elites could also engage in tool manufacturing during the Erlitou period. Such production may have met local demand for productive or practical tools used in agricultural production, carpentry or construction activities, military or hunting activities, and textile making or weaving activities in conjunction with some supply of lithic raw materials and, even, some tools from other settlements in the Erlitou hinterland, like

Shaochai 稍柴 and Huizui 灰咀 (Chen et al. 2003; Ford 2004; Chen, X. 2006; Liu, Chen, and Li 2007; Zhongguo 2014; Qian et al. 2014; Zhongguo and Zhongaomei 2019). Emphases on such production also probably contributed to wealth accumulation. Bronze-casting is believed to be a high-level, complex economic activity and has been identified as an important elite-oriented productive activity in the workshop enclosure. If there was indeed household-based bronze working as well, involvement in bronze-working probably could have enabled non-elite families in the palatial enclosure and the workshop enclosure to be at least in the medium range of the wealth distribution in the scaling space. Similarly, turquoise artifacts were another luxury goods monopolized by the Erlitou elites. A turquoise workshop was identified in the northern part of the workshop enclosure between 1999 and 2006. Including some household units from the possible turquoise workshop area, some household units (G13, G18/F1, W2, W5 and D4) are associated with the turquoise debris in this household sample. Because the huge quantity of turquoise debris (4084 pieces) in W5 would create a large imbalance in the patterns in the scaling space and vastly outnumbers the turquoise debris associated with the other 4 household units (10 in G13, 1 in G18/F1, 1 in W2, and 1 in D4), turquoise production was not included in the multi-dimensional scaling. Given the small size of the turquoise debris in the G18/F1, W2 and D4, it is inconclusive to say they were involved in the turquoise item production, and the turquoise debris might have been casually and occasionally incorporated into household garbage, although W2 is in the area of the turquoise workshop and no other turquoise manufacturing spots have been identified in the palatial enclosure or at the eastern end of the site. In contrast, G13 and W5 were possibly specialized in turquoise item production. W5 was highly specialized in turquoise manufacturing, so W5 might have been an important specialized worker family in the turquoise workshop emphasizing turquoise manufacturing. The much smaller number of turquoise debris in G13 suggests G13 possibly did not focus as much as W5 on turquoise item production and possibly served for mending turquoise items for the royal elites. Just like the possibly specialized bronze-working families, the household units specialized in and involved in turquoise artifact production also were at least in the moderate range of wealth distribution in this household sample. Thus, it is possible that, because of their important contributions to provide subsistence goods, shelter, practical tools, and community safety, some households gained good economic returns from specialized productive activities. Specialization in and involvement with bronze smelting/ casting (if possible) and turquoise production satisfied the royal elites' demands for luxury goods and ritual consumption. In this case, the service to and a relationship with the royal court could also possibly have enabled non-elite families to accumulate some degree of wealth and improve their standards of living.

Other productive activities seem not to produce extra household wealth or are only engaged in by less wealthy household units; these are activities that do not seem to enable households to accumulate wealth. Compared to cultivated plants and herded animals, fish were not heavily consumed by the people at the Erlitou site. This may have limited economic returns from fishing. The less wealthy household units with more fishing tools might have been driven to pursue this less desirable but readily available resource. Similarly, people at the Erlitou site probably did not focus on the consumption of river mussels as food. Such small consumption of river mussels could have led to an unstable or small supply of raw materials for shell artifact/tool production because shell tools were particularly made from the shells of Lamellibranchia in prehistoric China (Lv and Fu 2010; Hu 2018). Lack of stable supply of raw materials might not only have made the Erlitou people less reliant on shell tools compared to lithic tools but also meant that shell artifact/tool production did not offer good economic returns. Some less wealthy non-elite families, as a consequence, may have engaged in shell artifact/tool production merely to get by. Whetstones are believed to have been widely used to resharpen the blades of agricultural tools, carpentry or construction tools, and weapons, and sharpen or smoothen goods made of stone, bone, antler, tooth, shell, turquoise, bronze, and jade. In some non-elite families, whetstones could have been auxiliary to other economic activities. However, some household units were involved in agricultural or other activities but not associated with whetstones, especially those in the higher range of the wealth distribution. Such patterning suggests that relatively wealthy non-elite families might have focused on their own economic

production and turned to less wealthy non-elite families to resharpen their tools, and non-elite families who were in the moderate to low ranges of wealth might have conducted some resharpening or smoothing in addition to the production they were engaged in for survival. Textile or clothing making was also participated in by only a few non-elite families, including some relatively wealthy household units and some household units who are in the moderate to low ranges of the wealth distribution in the scaling space. Non-elite families in the moderate to low ranges of the wealth distribution could have focused more on this activity than relative wealthy non-elite families, possibly suggesting that some less wealthy non-elite families could not accumulate wealth but could manage to survive through focusing on textile or clothing making.

Although some household units living in small on-the-ground housing structures (G14/F10 and D5/F4) were found with no any practical tools at all, and some household units living in small on-the-ground housing structures or semi-subterranean housing structures are represented by small, less reliable samples, household units living in small on-the-ground housing structures were still likely to invest more effort or time in economic activities, especially in those that offered greater returns (Figure 6.13). Furthermore, these household units were more likely to appear in the upper left (the wealthier part) of this two-dimensional plot. Such patterning indicates that involvement in the well paid-off productive activities probably enabled non-elite families to procure wealth and better their standards of living.

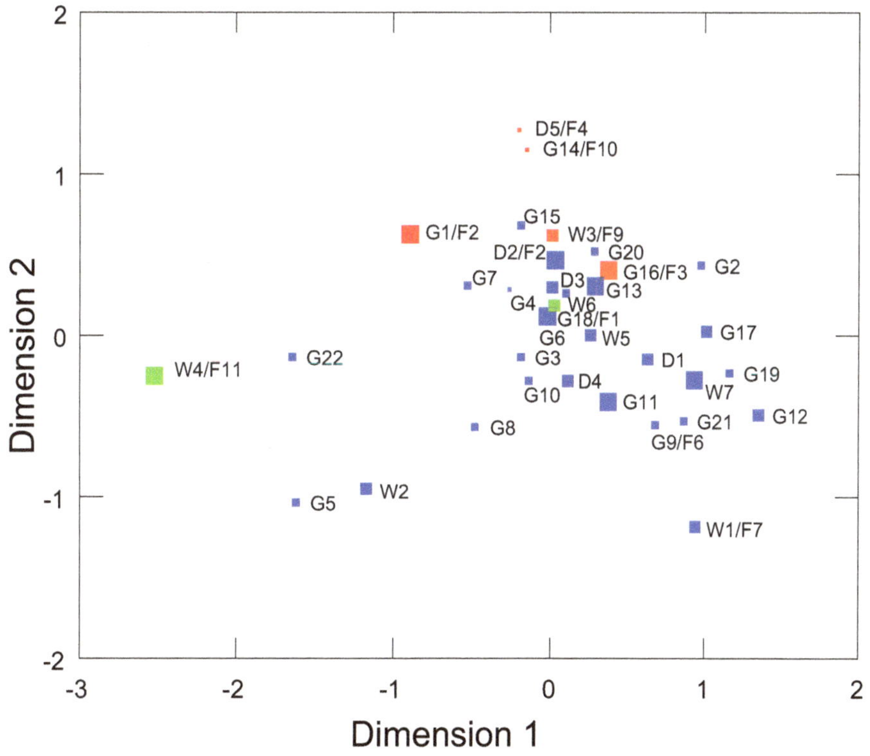

Figure 6.13. Household units indicating the highest proportion of tools for productive activities colored by different housing structures. (The size of each square indicates the highest proportion of artifactual evidence for any productive activity engaged in by the corresponding household; household units living in small on-the-ground housing structures in red, household units occupying semi-subterranean housing structures in green, household units with unknown housing structures in blue.).

Conclusions

7.1. Response to Research Question 1

How much wealth differentiation is detectable among the households in this sample?

Wealth differentiation is detectable from the distribution of artifacts across the 34 households in this sample, although the degree of wealth differentiation is only moderate. Compared to the luxurious standard of living of the elites, the household units studied in this research must fall quite low on the Erlitou wealth scale and entirely outside of the elite group. One might suppose that non-elites in an early city would form a great mass of the population with very little differentiation in wealth (Marcus 2004). However, this sample of households displays that there was enough wealth differentiation among non-elite families to be detectable, and even the limited analytical capacity offered by archaeological household artifact assemblages can identify variations in wealth or standards of living. One may also suppose that less wealthy families, or non-elite families, were totally excluded from the palatial enclosure in that the palaces were occupied only by ruling elites. However, this household sample displays that some non-elite families did live next to the palaces, and non-elite families in or near the palatial enclosure are not all wealthier than non-elite families in the other two locations. As the value of goods is related to multiple factors like beauty, rarity, distance, and labor intensity (Brysbaert 2017), and elite-oriented production only satisfies elites' exclusive demand for high-value, specialized goods, one may suppose that involvement in or specialization in elite-oriented production could enable non-elite workers to accumulate wealth. The known elite-oriented productions at Erlitou are turquoise item production and bronze casting. In this household sample, there is only one non-elite household strongly focusing on turquoise production in the turquoise workshop, one non-elite household involved in turquoise production, and 3 non-elite households possibly involved in bronze working, all of which are in the medium to high range of the wealth distribution. So, elite-oriented production could enable non-elites to accumulate some wealth in the Erlitou state, to some extent. There are still some relatively wealthy non-elites from the eastern end of the site which is farther from the palaces and not specialized in elite-monopolized production. This study finds that some of these households did accumulate more wealth than others, but that the non-elite households in this sample who were somewhat wealthier than others could be located in the palatial enclosure, the workshop enclosure, or the eastern end of the site, and the households that did not get any wealthier than others occurred in all these locations as well. The moderate but gradual differentiation in the

wealth distribution suggests that non-elite families at the Erlitou site possibly had their own pathways to accumulate wealth and improve their standards of living.

7.2. Response to Research Question 2

How much prestige differentiation is detectable among the households in this sample?

Prestige differentiation is detectable across the 34 household units in this sample from the distribution of artifacts, although the detectable differentiation in prestige is only moderate. Compared to the tremendous prestige enjoyed by the elites, the household units studied in this research fall quite low on the scale of the Erlitou prestige spectrum and entirely outside of the elite group. One may suppose that only extremely prestigious families resided in the palatial enclosure, or, in other words, that non-elites in terms of prestige were excluded from the palatial enclosure (Zhongguo 2003; Xu 2009, 2022). However, this household sample displays that some non-elite families still lived adjacent to royal elites in the palatial enclosure. On the other hand, the 34 non-elite households were likely not at the very bottom of the Erlitou "social pyramid" given that some were close to the palaces. Some non-elite families still had some access to the court of the divine rulers and the royal ancestral temple suggested by the spatial organization so that they might still have appreciated some level of prestige.

One might also suppose that non-elites in an early city would be homogeneous with little differentiation in prestige (Marcus 2004). However, the non-elite families in the Erlitou site still might have some pathways to improve their prestige suggested by the small number of the nuanced prestigious non-elite families in this sample, but wealth and prestige were separate and unrelated dimensions. In this sample, wealthy families were not particularly prestigious and prestigious families were not particularly wealthy. This suggests that the ability to gain the respect of others or prestige was not enhanced by accumulation of wealth in this household sample. The Erlitou state might have formed a system through which non-elite families could raise their prestige. On the other hand, this study only investigates a small sample of non-elite households (34) so it still cannot fully rule out the possibility that feasting or other kinds of generosity had the effect of inflicting debt on others and earning respect and reciprocal obligations because such may have been practiced among Erlitou non-elites although such was not clearly observed in this household sample. Thus, it is still inconclusive to say what the system was and how it worked. Although their positions might be related to service to the ruling elites, more work is required to figure out what principles lay behind the negotiation of prestige among Erlitou non-elites.

7.3. Response to Research Question 3

How much ritual differentiation is detectable among the households in this sample?

Ritual differentiation is detectable from the household artifacts across the 34 household units, although the detectable ritual differentiation is limited. One might suppose that Erlitou non-elites were completely excluded from all kinds of ritual activities. Compared to the multiple forms of ritual activities and high-quality ritual paraphernalia of the (ruling) elites, the 34 household units in this sample were involved in very few ritual activities. They did not, for example, participate in the shaman dances with bronze-turquoise ritual paraphernalia, bells, and drums in the hope of prosperity and bliss (Cai 2006; Du 2006; He 2018; Gao 2022). So, non-elites indeed were quite low on the Erlitou ritual spectrum. However, household assemblages suggest that Erlitou non-elites could still participate in oracle divination by scapulimancy. The non-elite households in this sample, as a group, did not engage in scapulimancy very much, but about half of them (18 out of the 34 household units) still participated in scapulimancy. On the other hand, household units more involved in divination tend to be closer to the palatial enclosure, especially to the suggested ancestral temples. Being near the palaces is not the only way that non-elite households could participate in scapulimancy, but household units near the palaces were definitely more involved in this activity than others (at least in this sample), suggesting that some household units in the palatial enclosure might have been slightly more focused on divination in the hope of an auspicious future, and divination might also have been related to (royal) ancestral veneration. It is possibly true that ritual status and involvement in most ritual activities were prestige related in the Erlitou state because elites monopolized most ritual activities and ritual duties, but it is inconclusive what constrained non-elites from divining their own welfare; there is no real detectable difference in ritual participation between wealthy and prestigious non-elite households in the scaling space.

7.4. Response to Research Question 4

How much productive differentiation is detectable among the households in this sample?

Productive differentiation is detectable among the household units in this sample although the detectable productive differentiation is modest. Based on the workshop enclosure, which is composed of the known turquoise workshop and the bronze-casting workshop, and other workshops outside the workshop enclosure, the Erlitou site seems to emphasize a workshop economy through which the population obtained handicrafts and

goods by the workshops and the workshop enclosure provided the monopolized consumption of turquoise items and bronze artifacts for Erlitou elites (Zhongguo 2003; Zhao and Zhang 2021). Meanwhile, the Erlitou site has also been argued to rely on crop tribute from the Erlitou rural hinterland (Liu 2006; Qiao 2010). However, the household assemblages across the 34-household sample suggest that almost all the household units studied in this research participated in the production of daily necessities. Agricultural production was participated in by more than half of the household units in this sample. Some other household units might have focused on the production of daily necessities other than subsistence goods. So, the non-elite households in this sample might have varied in their opportunities and capabilities in wealth accumulation because of different focuses and investment in the productive activities. The moderate productive differentiation might still have enabled some exchange in society so that some non-elites could invest more energy in much more complex production like the bronze casting and turquoise item production to satisfy elites' demand.

7.5. Response to Research Question 5

Whatever differentiation is documented in answering the questions above, how much of it seems to differentiate households living in small on-the-ground structures as a group from those living in semi-subterranean structures?

Differentiation in wealth, prestige and production is detectable among the two household groups represented by two different housing structures in this household sample although such detectable differentiation is modest, while the ritual differentiation is not detectable. One may suppose that the households living in small on-the-ground structures would be wealthier, and more prestigious than those living in semi-subterranean structures, and that households living in semi-subterranean structures would participate more in production (Zhongguo 2003; Xu 2009 and 2022). Households living in small on-the-ground structures in this sample indeed are wealthier than those living in semi-subterranean structures and their standards of living were probably improved by their investment in productive activities, especially those activities with good economic returns. On the contrary, households living in small on-the-ground structures in this sample are actually less prestigious than those living in semi-subterranean structures. Such patterning suggests that investment in or participation in production was one effective way for the Erlitou non-elites in this sample to accumulate wealth and better their standards of living, but the labor mobilization or labor investment represented by housing structure did not effectively represent the non-elites' prestige or reputation in this household sample. Because of the small sample size, there is no clear patterning of the ritual differentiation between the two household groups.

However, definitive statements about any kind of differentiation between the two groups of household units remain inconclusive. In this sample, there are 27 household units whose residential structure nature cannot be determined (24 represented by household garbage without associated housing structures and 3 with very poorly preserved associated housing structures). Thus, the small data sample size makes it difficult to answer this question with much confidence.

7.6. Response to Research Question 6

Whatever differentiation is documented in answering the questions above, how much of it occurs among households living in small on-the-ground structures and how much among those living in semi-subterranean structures?

There is not much wealth-, prestige-, or productive-differentiation occurring among household units living in small on-the-ground structures, but some differentiation in wealth, prestige and production is detectable among those living in semi-subterranean structures in this sample, and no clear ritual differentiation is detectable among households living in either small on-the-ground structures or in semi-subterranean structures. The relatively close distance between household units living in small on-the-ground structures in the scaling space suggests little differentiation across any dimension; they shared similar levels of wealth, prestige, and production. Among households living in semi-subterranean structures in this sample, those slightly wealthier tend to be less prestigious, while those slightly more prestigious tend to be less wealthy; wealthier units focus more on productive activities, while slightly prestigious ones seem not to emphasize productive activities. There is only one household unit living in a semi-subterranean structure associated with scapulimancy. Such a small sample cannot lead to any conclusions about ritual differentiation among households living in small on-the-ground structures and among those living in semi-subterranean structures.

However, the answer to this question is still tentative and inconclusive. In this sample, there are only five households living in small on-the-ground structures and only two households living in semi-subterranean structures, and some household units are represented only by small household assemblages. Thus, the small data sample size makes it hard to answer this question with much confidence.

7.7. Summary

This research offers some new insights into the non-elites' lives in the Erlitou territorial state. Compared to the ruling elites of Erlitou, non-elites definitely were plain, less prestigious, mundane, but some were entrepreneurial. No kind of differentiation among non-elite families at the Erlitou site was pronounced, but it was only moderate. They probably occupied the low range of wealth accumulation across the whole spectrum of the Erlitou state. Compared to Erlitou elites, their houses were not

spacious. They lived in small housing structures, both on-the-ground and semi-subterranean structures, but they still could accumulate some wealth to improve their standards of living as evidenced by their capacity to store goods. Differences in the proportional consumption of storage ceramic vessels suggest disparities in wealth accumulation, although these disparities were moderate. Slightly wealthy non-elite families could also have more opportunities to consume pottery vessels decorated in complex patterns and personal ornaments, and to live in small on-the-ground housing structures rather than the cold, damp, and low semi-subterranean housing structures.

Archaeologists have found a specialized bronze casting workshop at the Erlitou site, and a specialized workshop enclosure including the known bronze-casting workshop and the turquoise workshop (Zhongguo 1999, 2003 and 2014). The complex specialized production, large-area specialized workshops, and palatial enclosure suggest that the Erlitou site was an ancient city composed of administrators and specialized elite-oriented craftworkers. Recently identified bone workshops and some crafting spots for pottery, lithic, and antler production seem to reinforce the opinion that the Erlitou site focused strongly on craft production (Chen and Li 2016; Zhao and Zhang 2021). According to the diachronic and site-section-based differences (the Erlitou site is divided into 15 sections by modern roads and village plans) in productive tools found in the 1959 – 1978 excavations, Liu (2006) argues that there was a mixed economy and that the Erlitou urban population includes not only elites and elite-oriented craftworkers but also independent craftworkers and farmers, although farmers constituted only a small portion of the population compared to craftworkers. Thus, because of the relatively low proportion of agricultural tools found in the 1959 – 1978 excavations and the large urban population at the Erlitou site (about 20,000 to 25,000, a considerable portion of which are supposed to have been craftworkers), the Erlitou site has been argued as non-self-sufficient and reliant on a large amount of food tribute from the hinterland (Liu 2006; Qiao 2010).

The palatial enclosure, the workshop enclosure (in which elite-oriented bronze casting workshop and turquoise workshop satisfied elites' demand for luxury goods), and some relatively large rammed earthen structures outside the palatial enclosure suggest that not only were there very exalted elites living luxurious lives in large, elaborate palaces and exercising considerable power, but also intermediate elites at a lower level enjoying relatively wealthy and prestigious lives. The elite economy, with attached specialists making elite goods in workshops, is one feature of Erlitou suggested by the complex elite-oriented bronze casting workshop and turquoise workshop (Zhongguo 1999, 2014, 2019; Liu and Chen 2012; Xu 2009, 2022). However, the small housing structures across the settlement and the large quantity of mundane, non-luxury daily life artifacts both suggest there were many less wealthy and less prestigious households living at Erlitou, and many of them may even have resided farther from the palace and workshop and even in rural areas centering on Erlitou. The large number of Erlitou non-elites presumably conducted various economic activities to feed themselves and the Erlitou elites, and some of them conducted specialized elite-oriented production to support the elites' luxurious and prestigious lifestyles. Therefore, Erlitou did not consist primarily of elites and elite-oriented craftsmen who produced luxury goods for elites. The vast majority of the Erlitou population was probably much more similar to the people of the 34 households examined in this study. Through entrepreneurial and industrious involvement in household-level production, some non-elite families like these 34 households, although not extremely wealthy or prestigious, were probably the "middle class" in Erlitou's hierarchical "social pyramid".

This research finds that, besides food tribute and specialized workshop production, Erlitou non-elites not only contributed to the whole community but also accumulated some wealth through household-level production. Differences in the proportional composition of practical tools and productive debris in household assemblages suggest that Erlitou non-elites emphasized different productive activities. Some of them produced daily subsistence on their own and some of them also spent some extra effort on other production. They could accumulate wealth through their investment in production, enough to provide for a slightly higher standard of living. By emphasizing more lucrative economic activities, some non-elites could also accumulate wealth more effectively than others. Furthermore, the moderate productive differentiation in the household sample, represented by different productive tools and different economic activities, suggests some degree of economic interdependence in which some households depended on others for certain kinds of goods, and those goods included not just crafts but also food. About half (although not all) of them participated in agricultural production. Non-food production suggests that the non-elite households in this sample were not completely self-sufficient. The "extra" food produced by some non-elite households at the Erlitou site could have helped to feed elites and other households who did not produce their own food in conjunction with crop tribute from the Erlitou hinterland. Granaries in the bronze age of China have been found at the Dongxiafeng 东下冯 site and the Yanshi Shang city 偃师商城 (both from the Erligang period) suggesting that Erligang (ruling) elites had the capacity of collecting, controlling, and storing large quantities of crop food (Zhongguo et al. 1988; Cheng and Zhou 1998; Shi and Jing 2018; Cao 2019). Although no granaries have been identified at the Erlitou site so far, Erlitou ruling elites should also have the capability to control and manage the collection of surplus food and crop tribute, as well as to oversee the redistribution of crops in order to maintain their authority and sovereignty and support Erlitou craftsmen, especially those engaged in elite-oriented production. Erlitou ruling elites, confronted with population increase, might also have enhanced their centralized control over natural resources, including both subsistence and exotic

raw materials for crafts, to preserve their authority and sovereignty. Such differentiated economic emphases among non-elite families suggest that some exchange in Erlitou society as well as wealth redistribution happen, to some extent, in the Erlitou state. Thus, the economy of the Erlitou state was composed not only of craft workshop-based production but also household-based production of daily necessities and crafts, as well as agricultural production for subsistence. Erlitou elites may have collected extra food produced by local households and those from the hinterland, and redistributed it to support themselves and non-elite craftworkers.

The extremely small number of ritual paraphernalia associated with non-elite household contexts suggests that they probably were excluded from most ritual activities and duties. An array of bronze, turquoise, jade, and lacquerware ritual paraphernalia exclusively seen in Erlitou elite tombs suggests that Erlitou (ruling) elites monopolized and professionalized worship, conducting ancestor venerations and the worship of and sacrifices to supernatural spirits and gods. A large worship and sacrificial area (extending 300 meters east to west and 200 meters north to south) is located 200 meters north of the palatial enclosure. Ritual facilities, several elite tombs accompanied by bronze and jade ritual paraphernalia, minimal daily garbage inside of this area, and its proximity to the palatial enclosure all suggest that this was an Erlitou elite ritual area (Zhongguo 2003; Li 2006; Du 2019). It includes three round rammed-earth altars (*tan* 坛) and some rectangular semi-subterranean pits (*shan* 墠), which are argued to have been for Erlitou's heavenly and earthly worship because of their forms similar to Neolithic ritual buildings of Hongshan culture, Liangzhu culture, and Xinzhai phase, as well as later Shang and Zhou ritual buildings (Li 2006; Du 2019; Zhongguo 2019; Xu 2009, 2022). The (ruling) elites might practice shaman dances and sacrifices with high-quality ritual paraphernalia, and carry out ritual activities in the hope of securing an auspicious future, happiness, and good harvest.

But Erlitou non-elites still had an even but moderate access to divination. In this non-elite household sample, 18 households had opportunities to practice scapulimancy. The lack of evidence that any of them had access to a storage of unused oracle bones, along with the small amount of used oracle bones, suggests that they still relied on professional diviners to help them conduct divination. In this case, non-elites probably did not serve in Erlitou's religious duties and only stayed in the low range of ritual-related social status. However, the factors that constrained non-elites' capacity to divine their own welfare are unknown; there is no clear detectable connection between scapulimancy and wealth or prestige among the non-elite households in this sample. Since the sample size is small, it cannot be completely ruled out that Erlitou non-elites' divinations were subject to their wealth or prestige. Collecting more ritual data from Erlitou non-elites in the future will enable us to better understand what principle(s) decided their opportunities to practice divination.

Erlitou non-elites also shared a similarly low level of prestige, possibly because of their low-level ritual status or low involvement in ritual activities. Some archaeologists argue that during the early phase of state formation in China, religious activities were monopolized by elites (Chang 1989; Feng 2013). By interpreting the lacquered wood stick found in a Taosi 陶寺 elite tomb as a gnomon (*Niebiao* 槷表) from late Neolithic China, Feng (2013) argues that Taosi elites were professionals in solstice surveying, through which they monopolized celestial observation and heavenly worship, connected with the gods and spirits, and, furthermore, legitimized their centrality and authority. Based on motifs on Yangshao pottery and an array of Longshan and Liangzhu ritual jades from late Neolithic China, Chang (1989) argues that ritual activities and religious duties have been long monopolized by elites, a pattern that lasted through the Three Dynasties. For example, Shang (ruling) elites consumed tons of oracle bones and bronze vessels during their ritual practices. Erlitou (ruling) elites were also likely to maintain their prestige, and by extension, their sovereignty through their monopoly on ritual duties, communications with ancestors and gods, and heavenly worship, represented by the greater quantity and diverse forms of ritual paraphernalia that they used. Because of the emergence of new forms of ritual paraphernalia, Erlitou elites had to find their way to secure raw materials and natural resources to support their ritual power, and bronze metallurgy represented by piece-mold techniques enabled Erlitou elites to consume new bronze ritual paraphernalia. Liu and Chen (2003, 2012) argue that the Erlitou state probably had the capacity to satisfy the (ruling) elites' demands for raw materials and natural resources from the Erlitou periphery, evidenced by the expanded Erlitou cultural sphere and outpost sites seen in the west and south from which Erlitou elites could obtain copper, tin, lead, and salt. Such procurement probably was to maintain the Erlitou (ruling) elites' high ritual-related status and high prestige-related status and, ultimately, their sovereignty and authority. In contrast, non-elites' prestige lacked a basis in ritual duties because of their limited involvement in ritual activities although they still could do some divination. Their lower prestige suggests Erlitou non-elites probably lacked the capacity to join various types of ceremonies or carry out ceremonial duties including ritual duties, so they seemed to be unlikely to consume prestigious artifacts. Although there was nuanced economic power among non-elite families represented by stored goods, feasting utensils and vessels, and standards of living (e.g., types of shelters), and some slightly wealthier families might have been more capable of sharing food and fermented beverages and living in better structures (small on-the-ground houses), their prestige probably was not based on such capacity.

Although this research does not find what the non-elites' prestige was based on, some slightly more prestigious non-elite families from the palatial enclosure and the workshop enclosure in the household sample suggest that non-elites' prestige may have been related to their relationship to the royal court. Some prestigious non-elites alongside other non-elites may have served the ruling elites and their family on a daily basis, forming a hierarchical system in the palatial enclosure, and some prestigious non-elites who may have specialized in elite-oriented production may have served in the hierarchical system of the workshop enclosure. Thus, access to the royal court and involvement in elite-oriented production suggest the non-elite families in this sample were not positioned at the very bottom of the Erlitou social hierarchy, but still enjoyed some degree of prestige. In order to figure out what was possibly behind the higher prestige-related status of these non-elites, future work should focus on Erlitou non-elites, especially on those from the palatial enclosure and the workshop enclosure where relatively prestigious non-elites are likely to be found. More comparative studies focusing on non-elite families in the palatial enclosure and the workshop enclosure will probably enable us to clarify how Erlitou non-elites negotiated their prestige and on what the prestige of Erlitou non-elites was based.

A person's reputation and respect may come from their professions or specific skills, not just from personal charisma and generosity (Brysbaert 2017). Also, both higher proficiency and a longer-time span engaging in one skill or profession can increase one's reputation and respect relative to others in one community or peer group. Drennan and his co-workers (2017) have found that Hongshan non-elites' prestige had a connection to involvement in production; households with higher prestige tended to be more focused on production. Filippini (2017) studies ancient blacksmiths from the western Hallstatt region of Europe between the First and Second Iron Ages and argues that blacksmiths, monopolizing advanced technical skills, enjoyed higher status because of consumers' dependence on their products. Although the 34 household units investigated in this study show no clear connections between prestige and the production of daily necessities among Erlitou non-elites, the subject is still worth exploring. The currently argued Erlitou elite-oriented productions are bronze casting and turquoise production. Recently, other workshops like bone workshops have been found in the palatial enclosure (Chen and Li 2016; Zhao 2022). Their proximity to ruling elites suggests that these workshops in the palatial enclosure may also be elite-oriented. The number of households involved in elite-oriented production in this sample is too small to reach any clear conclusion about this issue; there is only one household unit (W5) from the turquoise workshop that focused strongly on turquoise production, the three household units who were possibly involved in bronze-working not only participated minimally but also were not from the bronze-casting workshop, and no households in the palatial enclosure are from the workshops within it. Future excavations in the palatial enclosure and the workshop enclosure could collect more data on non-elite households, especially those who were involved in elite-oriented production. Compared with non-elite households who only focused on the production of daily necessities and subsistence goods, we can figure out whether involvement in elite-oriented production could promote non-elites' prestige.

A higher status non-elite, or a more prestigious non-elite, can also be represented by how they participate in the economic networks. By investigating the sources from which Hongshan households procured pottery, Li (2016) finds that higher-status households practiced in the economic networks in ways different from lower-status households; higher-status households could balance their social and economic ties to other households through their pottery procurement. As we have found that relatively prestigious non-elite households are likely to be found in the palatial enclosure and the workshop enclosure, and that prestigious non-elites seem not to emphasize productive activities, we can choose daily pottery from prestigious and less prestigious non-elite households in these enclosures to investigate how the two groups participated in Erlitou's economic networks according to the diversity in their pottery procurement sources. Based on the pottery sample from Section V and Section III (two of the 15 site sections divided by modern roads and village plans; Section V includes the palatial enclosure and the northern part of the workshop enclosure, and Section III includes the eastern end of the site), recent geochemical analysis on the Erlitou pottery suggests that there were probably multiple pottery procurement and production units at the Erlitou site (Zhongguo 2014). By comparing the pottery-procuring sources of prestigious non-elite households with those of less prestigious non-elite households, we can figure out whether and how differently prestigious non-elites participated in Erlitou's economic network from less prestigious non-elites; whether prestigious non-elites consistently had some specific sources while less prestigious non-elites used a random variety of sources suggesting that prestigious non-elites could balance their social and economic connections to other producing households better than less prestigious non-elites, just like higher-status Hongshan households. By comparing the pottery-procuring sources of prestigious non-elite households in the palatial enclosure with those of prestigious non-elite households in the workshop enclosure, we can find whether and how differently these two groups of prestigious non-elites participated in Erlitou's economic networks. Studying the participation of Erlitou non-elites in economic networks will help us understand how prestigious Erlitou non-elites maintained their prestige by their links and connections to other producing non-elites although they did not much participate in production.

Bibliography

Allan, Sarah 1991. *The Shape of the Turtle*. Albany: SUNY Press.

An, Jiayuan 安家瑗 1986. Leibo Xiaoyi 擂钵小议. *Kaogu* 考古. 1986(4): 344–347.

Blackmore, Chelsea 2016. *Constructing "Commoner" Identity in an Ancient Maya Village: Class, Status, and Ritual at the Northeast Group, Chan Belize*. Oxford: BAR Publishing.

Brysbaert, Ann 2017. Artisans Versus Nobility? Crafting in Context: Introduction. In *Artisans Versus Nobility? Multiple Identities of Elites and "Commoners" Viewed Through the Lens of Crafting from the Chalcolithic to the Iron Ages in Europe and the Mediterranean*, edited by Ann Brysaert and Alexis Gorgues, pp. 13–36. Leiden: Sidestone Press.

Cai, Yunzhang 蔡运章 2006. Lvsongshi Longtu'an Yu Xiabuzu De Tuteng Chongbai 绿松龙图案与夏部族的图腾崇拜. In *Erlitou Yizhi Yu Erlitou Wenhua Yanjiu* 二里头遗址与二里头文化研究, edited by Jingpen Du 杜金鹏 and Hong Xu 许宏, pp. 135–142. Beijing: Kexue Chubanshe.

Campbell, Roderick B. 2014. *Archaeology of the Chinese Bronze Age: From Erlitou to Anyang*. Los Angeles: The Cotsen Institute of Archaeology Press.

Campbell, Roderick 2018. *Violence, Kinship and the Early Chinese State: The Shang and Their World*. New York: Cambridge University Press.

Cao, Dazhi 曹大志 2019. Lun Shangdai De Liangchu Sheshi 论商代的粮储设施. In *Gudai Wenming* (vol.13) 古代文明(第 13 卷), edited by Beijing Daxue Zhongguo Kaoguxue Yanjiu Zhongxin 北京大学中国考古学研究中心 and Beijing Daxue Zhendan Gudai Wenming Yanjiu Zhongxin 北京大学震旦古代文明研究中心, pp. 169–200. Shanghai: Shanghai Guji Chubanshe.

Chang, Kwang-Chih 1983. *Art, Myth, and Ritual*. Cambridge: Harvard University Press.

Chang, Kwang-Chih 1989. Ancient China and Its anthropological Significance. In *Archaeological Thought in America*, edited by C. C. Lamberg-Karlovsky, pp. 155–166. Cambridge University Press.

Chen, Fangmei 陈芳妹 2006. Erlitou M3 – Shehui Yishushi Yanjiu De Xinxiansuo 二里头 M3——社会艺术史研究的新线索. In *Erlitou Yizhi Yu Erlitou Wenhua Yanjiu* 二里头遗址与二里头文化研究, edited by Jingpen Du 杜金鹏 and Hong Xu 许宏, pp. 241–269. Beijing: Kexue Chubanshe.

Chen, Guoliang 陈国梁 2008. Erlitou Tongqi Yanjiu 二里头文化铜器研究. In *Zhongguo Zaoqi Qingtong Wenhua: Erlitou Wenhua Zhuanti Yanjiu* 中国早期青铜文化：二里头文化专题研究, edited by Zhonguo Shehui Kexueyuan Kaogu Yanjiusuo中国社会科学院考古研究所, pp. 124–274. Beijing: Kexue Chubanshe.

Chen, Guoliang 陈国梁 2016. Erlitou Yizhi Zhutong Yicun Zaitantao 二里头遗址铸铜遗存再探讨. *Zhongyuan Wenwu*. 2016(3): 35–44.

Chen, Guoliang 陈国梁 and Zhipeng Li 李志鹏 2013. Erlitou Wenhua De Zhanbu Zhidu Chutan Yi Erlitou Yizhi Jinnian Chutu Bugu Weili 二里头文化的占卜制度初探——以二里头遗址近年出土卜骨为例. In *Sandai Kaogu* (Vol.5) 三代考古（五）, edited by Zhongguo Shehui Kexueyuan Kaogu Yanjiusuo 中国社会科学院考古研究所, pp 62–72. Beijing: Kexuechubanshe.

Chen, Guoliang 陈国梁 and Zhipeng Li 李志鹏 2016. Erlitou Yizhi Zhigu Yicun De Kaocha 二里头遗址制骨遗存的考察. *Kaogu* 考古, 2016(5): 59–70.

Chen, Xingcan 陈星灿 2006. Cong Huizui Fajue Kan Zhongguo Zaoqi Guojia De Shiqi Gongye 从灰嘴发掘看中国早期国家的石器工业. In *Zhongguo Kaoguxue Yu Ruidian Kaoguxue* 中国考古学与瑞典考古学, edited by Zhongguo Shehui Kexueyuan Kaogu Yanjiusuo 中国社会科学院考古研究所 and Ruidian Guojia Yichan Weiyuanhui Kaogu Yanjiusuo 瑞典国家遗产委员会考古研究所, pp. 51–61. Beijing: Kexue Chubanshe.

Chen, Xingcan 陈星灿, Li Liu 刘莉, Yun-Kuen Lee 李润权, Henry T. Wright 华翰维 and Arlene Miller Rosen 艾琳 2003. Zhongguo Wenming Fudi De Shehui Fuzahua Jincheng Yiluohe Diqu De Juluo Xingtai Yanjiu (Development of Social Complexity in the Central China: Research into the Settlement Pattern in the Yiluo River Valley) 中国文明腹地的社会复杂化进程——伊洛河地区的聚落形态研究. *Kaogu Xuebao* 考古学报, 2003(2): 161–218.

Cheng, Pingshan 程平山 and Jun Zhou 周军 1998. Dongxiafeng Shangcheng Nei Yuanxing Jianzhu Jizhi Xingzhi Lvexi 东下冯商城内圆形建筑基址性质略析. *Zhongyuan Wenwu* 中原文物, 1998(1): 73–76.

Clark, John E., and Michael Blake 1994. The Power of Prestige: Competitive Generosity and the Emergence of Rank Societies in Lowland Mesoamerica. In *Factional Competition and Political Development in the New World*, edited by Elizabeth M. Brumfiel and John W. Fox, pp. 17–30. Cambridge: Cambridge University Press.

Cook, Constance A. 2005. Moonshine and Millet: Feasting and Purification Rituals in Ancient China. In *Of Tripod and Palate: Food, Politics, and Religion in Traditional China*, edited by Roel Sterckx, pp. 9–33. New York: Palgrave Macmillan.

Costin, Cathy Lynne and Timothy Earle 1989. Status Distinction and Legitimation of Power as Reflected in Changing Patterns of Consumption in Late Prehispanic Peru. *American Antiquity*, 54(4), 1989, pp. 691–714.

Cowgill, George L. 1992. Social Differentiation at Teotihuacan. In *Mesoamerican Elites: An Archaeological Assessment*, edited by Diane Z. Chase and Arlen F. Chase, pp. 206–220. Norman and London: University of Oklahoma Press.

Dai, Xiangming 2006. *Pottery Production, Settlement Patterns and Development of Social Complexity in the Yuanqu Basin, North-Central China.* BAR International Series.

Dai, Xiangming 戴向明 2010. *Taoqi Shengchan Juluo Xingtai Yu Shehui Bianqian Xinshiqi Zhi Qingtong Shidai De Yuanqu Pendi* （陶器生产、聚落形态与社会变迁：新石器至早期青铜时代的垣曲盆地）. Beijing: Wenwu Chubanshe.

Deng, Shuping 邓淑苹 2017. Yuliqi Yu Yulizhi Chutan 玉礼器与玉礼制初探. *Nanfang Wenwu* 南方文物, 2017(1): 210–236.

Deng, Shuping 邓淑苹 2021. Yazhang Tansuo Dawenkou Wenhua Zhi Erlitouqi 牙璋探索——大汶口文化至二里头期. *Nanfang Wenwu* 南方文物. 2021(1): 201–222.

Dietler, Michael 2001. Theorizing the Feasts: Rituals of Consumption, Commensal Politics, and Power in African Contexts. in *Feasts: Archaeological and Ethnographic Perspectives on Food, Politics, and Power*, edited by Michael Dietler, & Brian Hayden, pp. 65–114. Tuscaloosa, Alabama: The University of Alabama Press.

Ding, Lanlan 丁兰兰. 2007. Shiqian Kecaopen Gongneng Kaocha 史前刻槽盆功能考察. *Wenbo* 文博. 2007(6): 45–51.

Drennan, Robert D. 2010. *Statistics for Archaeologists: A Common Sense Approach.* New York: Springer.

Drennan, Robert D., and Christian E. Peterson 2012. Challenges for Comparative Study of Early Complex Societies. In *The Comparative Archaeology of Complex Societies*, edited by Michael E. Smith, pp. 62–87. Cambridge: Cambridge University Press.

Drennan, Robert D., Christian E. Peterson, Xueming Lu and Tao Li 2017. Hongshan Hosueholds and Communities in Neolithic Northeastern China. *Journal of Anthropological Archaeology*, 47(2017): 50–71.

Du, Jinpeng 杜金鹏 2005. Erlitou Yizhi Gongdian Jianzhu Jizhi Chubu Yanjiu二里头遗址宫殿建筑基址初步研究. In *Kaoguxue Jikan* 考古学集刊 (Vol. 16), edited by Qingzhu Liu 刘庆柱 and Jing Zhang 张静, pp. 178–236. Beijing: Science Press.

Du, Jinpeng 杜金鹏 2006. Zhongguolong Huaxiahun Shilun Yanshi Erlitou Yizhi Longwenwu 中国龙, 华夏魂——试论偃师二里头遗址"龙文物". In *Erlitou Yizhi Yu Erlitou Wenhua Yanjiu* 二里头遗址与

二里头文化研究, edited by Jinpeng Du 杜金鹏 and Hong Xu 许宏, pp. 96–120. Beijing: Kexue Chubanshe.

Du, Jinpeng 杜金鹏 2007a. Yanshi Erlitou Yizhi Yihao Gongdian Jizhi Zairenshi 偃师二里头遗址一号宫殿基址再认识. In *Xiashangzhou Kaoguxue Yanjiu* 夏商周考古学研究, Jinpeng Du 杜金鹏 (auth.), pp. 86–94. Beijing: Science Press.

Du, Jinpeng 杜金鹏 2007b. Yanshi Erlitou Yizhi Sihao Gongdian Jizhi Yanjiu 偃师二里头遗址四号宫殿基址研究. In *Xiashangzhou Kaoguxue Yanjiu* 夏商周考古学研究, Jinpeng Du 杜金鹏 (auth.), pp. 95–106. Beijing: Science Press.

Du, Jinpeng 杜金鹏 2019. Yanshi Erlitou Yizhi Jisi Yicun De Faxian Yu Yanjiu 偃师二里头遗址祭祀遗存的发现与研究. *Zhongyuan Wenwu* (*Cultural Relics of Central China*) 中原文物. 2019(4): 56–70.

Elson, Christina M. 2006. Intermediate Elites and the Political Landscape of the Early Zapotec State. In *Intermediate Elites in Pre-Colombian States and Empires*, edited by Christina M. Elson and R. Alan Covey, pp. 44–67. Tucson: The University of Arizona Press.

Fang, Yousheng 方酉生 1995. Yanshi Erlitou Yizhi Disanqi Yicun Yu Jiedu Zhenxun 偃师二里头遗址第三期遗存与桀都斟鄩. *Kaogu* 考古, 1995(2): 160–169.

Feinman, G. M. 2016. Variation and Change in Archaic States: Ritual as a Mechanism of Sociopolitical Integration. In *Ritual and Archaic States*, edited by Joanne M. A. Murphy, pp. 1–22. Gainesville: University of Florida.

Feng, Shi 冯时 2013. Taosi Guibiao Ji Xianguan Wenti Yanjiu 陶寺圭表及相关问题研究. In *Kaoguxue Jikan* (vol. 19) 考古学集刊(19), edited by Qingzhu Liu 刘庆柱, pp. 27–58. Beijing: Kexue Chubanshe.

Filippini, Anne 2017. For Blacksmiths, are advanced technical skills the way to achieve elite status? The case of the western Hallstatt area during the transition between First and Second Iron Ages. In *Artisans Versus Nobility? Multiple Identities of Elites and "Commoners" Viewed Through the Lens of Crafting from the Chalcolithic to the Iron Ages in Europe and the Mediterranean*, edited by Ann Brysaert and Alexis Gorgues, pp. 191–208. Leiden: Sidestone Press.

Ford, Anne 2004. Ground Stone Tool Production at Huizui, China: An Analysis of a Manufacturing Site in the Yiluo River Basin. *Indo-Pacific Prehistory Association Bulletin.* 24(2004): 71–78.

Gao, Fanxiang 高范翔, and Yujue Wu 武钰娟 2022. Dao Yu Quanli Huan Songshan Diqu Henan Longshan Wenhua Zhi Erlitou Wenhua Shiqi Daode Liyong 稻与权力——环嵩山地区河南龙山文化至二里头文化时期稻的利用. *Nanfang Wenwu* 南方文物. 2022(2): 135–144.

Gao, Xisheng 高西省 2022. Erlitou Qingtong Yueqi Wuju Zuhe Zhuji Chutan Cong Xiangqian Lvsongshi

Longwen Tongpai Yu Tongling Zuhe Tanqi 二里头青铜乐器、舞具组合助祭初探——从镶嵌绿松石龙纹铜牌与铜铃组合谈起. *Wenwu* 文物, 2022(9): 36–45.

Ge, Yun 葛韵 2022. Kaogu Shiye Xia De Erlitou Wenhua Renxing Shehui Zhuanxing Yu Shehui Bengkui 考古视野下的二里头文化韧性、社会转型与社会崩溃. *Wenwu Chunqiu* 文物春秋, 2022(2): 3–15.

Hao, Yanfeng 郝炎峰 2008. Erlitou Wenhua Yuqi De Kaoguxue Yanjiu 二里头文化玉器的考古学研究. In *Zhongguo Zaoqi Qingtong Wenhua: Erlitou Wenhua Zhuanti Yanjiu* 中国早期青铜文化：二里头文化专题研究, edited by Zhonguo Shehui Kexueyuan Kaogu Yanjiusuo 中国社会科学院考古研究所, pp. 275–354. Beijing: Kexue Chubanshe.

He, Nu 何驽 2018. Erlitou Lvsongshi Longpai Tongpai Yu Xiayu Wanwu De Guanxi 二里头绿松石龙牌、铜牌与夏禹、萬舞的关系. *Zhongyuan Wenhua Yanjiu* 中原文化研究, 2018(4): 31–39.

Hu, Zhanghua 胡章华 2018. Shilun Nanning Diqu Beiqiu Yizhi Chutu De Bangqi 试论南宁地区贝丘遗址出土的蚌器. *Nanning Zhiye Jishu Xueyuan Xuebao* (Journal of Nanning Polytechnic) 南宁职业技术学院学报, 2018 vol.23 No.3: 89–95.

Hu, Xiaoqiang 胡晓强 2020. Erlitou Wenhua Taosanzupan Yanjiu 二里头文化陶三足盘研究. *Wenwu Chunqiu* 文物春秋, 2020(5): 30–37.

Inomata, Takeshi and Stephen D. Houston 2001. Opening the Royal Maya Court. In *Royal Courts of the Ancient Maya (Vol.1): Theory, Comparison, and Synthesis*, edited by Takeshi Inomata and Stephen D. Houston, pp. 3–23. Boulder: Westview Press.

Jaang, Li 2023. Erlitou: The Making of a Secondary State and a New Sociopolitical Order in Early Bronze Age China. *Journal of Archaeological Research.* (2023)31: 209–262.

Lee, Yun-Kuen 2004. Control Strategies and Polity Competition in the Lower Yi-Luo Valley, North China. *Journal of Anthropological Archaeology.* 23(2004)172–195. Doi:10.1016/j.jaa.2004.01.002

Li, Dong 李栋 2007. *Xiashangzhou Shiqi Fangwu Jianzhu Jishu Chubu Yanjiu* (*Preliminary Research on the House building Technology in Xia, Shang and Zhou Dynasties*) 夏商周时期房屋建筑技术初步研究. Unpublished Master's Thesis, Shandong University.

Li, Feng 2008. *Bureaucracy and the State in Early China: Governing the Western Zhou.* New York: Cambridge University Press.

Li, Feng 2013. *Early China: A Social and Cultural History.* Cambridge: Cambridge University Press.

Li, Feng 李峰 2022. *Zaoqi Zhongguo Shehui Yu Wenhuashi* 早期中国：社会与文化史. Beijing: SDX Joint Publishing Cmpany.

Li, Min 2018. *Social Memory and State Formation in Early China.* Cambridge: Cambridge University Press.

Li, Tao 2016. *Economic Differentiation in Hongshan Core Zone Communities (Northeastern China): A Geochemical Perspective.* Unpublished PhD Dissertation, Department of Anthropology, University of Pittsburgh.

Li, Yongqiang 李永强 2019. Zhoucheng Yu Huandishi Zhengyi Zaibianxi 轴承与环砥石争议再辨析. *Nanfang Wenwu* 南方文物. 2019(06): 108–116.

Li, Yongxian 李永宪, and Wei Huo 霍巍 1990. Woguo Shiqian Shiqi De Renti Zhuangshipin 我国史前时期的人体装饰品. *Kaogu* 考古. 1990(3): 255–267.

Li, Zhipeng 李志鹏 2006. Erlitou Wenhua Jisi Yiji Chutan 二里头文化祭祀遗迹初探. In *Sandai Kaogu* (Vol.2) 三代考古（二）, edited by Zhongguo Shehui Kexueyuan Kaogu Yanjiusuo 中国社会科学院考古研究所, pp. 170–182. Beijing: Kexue Chubanshe.

Li, Zhipeng 李志鹏 2008. Erlitou Wenhua Muzang Yanjiu 二里头文化墓葬研究. In *Zhongguo Zaoqi Qingtong Wenhua: Erlitou Wenhua Zhuanti Yanjiu* 中国早期青铜文化：二里头文化专题研究, edited by Zhonguo Shehui Kexueyuan Kaogu Yanjiusuo中国社会科学院考古研究所, pp. 1–123. Beijing: Kexue Chubanshe.

Liu, Li 2003. "The Products of Minds as well as of Hands": Production of Prestige Goods in the Neolithic and Early State Periods of China. *Asian Perspectives* 42(1): 1–35.

Liu, Li 2004. *The Chinese Neolithic: Trajectories to Early States.* New York: Cambridge University Press.

Liu, Li 2006. Urbanization in China: Erlitou and Its Hinterland. In *Urbanism in the Preindustrial World*, edited by Glenn R. Storey, pp. 161–189. Tuscaloosa: The University of Alabama Press.

Liu, Li 刘莉, Maureece J. Levin, Xingcan Chen 陈星灿, and Yongqiang Li 李永强 2018. Henan Yanshi Huizui Yizhi Xinshiqi Shidai He Erlitou Wenhua Shiqi Gongju Canliuwu Ji Weihen Fenxi 河南灰嘴遗址新石器时代和二里头文化时期工具残留物及微痕分析. *Zhongyuan Wenwu* 中原文物. 2018(6): 82–97.

Liu, Li. and Xingcan Chen 2003. *State Formation in Early China.* London: Duckworth.

Liu, Li. and Xingcan Chen 2012. *The Archaeology of China: From the Late Paleolithic to the Early Bronze Age.* Cambridge: Cambridge University Press.

Liu, Li., Xingcan Chen and Baoping Li 2007. Non-state Crafts in the Early Chinese State: An Archaeological View from the Erlitou Hinter land. *Bulletin of the Indo-pacific Prehistory Association.* 2007(27): 93–102.

Liu, L., X. Chen, Y. Lee, H. Wright and A. Rosen 2004. Settlement Patterns and Development of Social Complexity in the Yiluo Region, North China. *Journal of Field Archaeology.* 29: 75–100. https://doi.org/10.1179/jfa.2004.29.1–2.75

Liu, Wei 刘威 2021. Research on the Usage Tradition of Erlitou Culture Based on the Types of the Three-legged

Trays Unearthed (Cong Suizang Sanzupan Leixing Kan Erlitou Wenhua Qiyong Chuantong) 从随葬三足盘类型看二里头文化器用传统. *Beifang Wenwu* 北方文物, 2021(1): 38–57.

Lohse, Jon C., and Fred Valdez, JR. 2004. Examining Ancient Maya Commoners Anew. In *Ancient Maya Commoners*, edited by Jon C. Lohse and Fred Valdez, JR., pp. 1–21. Austin: University of Texas Press.

Lu, Liancheng and Wenming Yan 2005. Society during the Three Dynasties. In *The Formation of Chinese Civilization: An Archaeological Perspective*, edited by Kwang-chih Chang and Pingfang Xu, pp. 141–201. New Haven and London: Yale University Press.

Lv, Peng 吕鹏 and Xianguo Fu 傅宪国 2010. Dingsishan Yizhi Chutu Bangdao De Dongwu Kaoguxue Yanjiu 顶蛳山遗址出土蚌刀的动物考古学研究. *Nanfang wenwu* 南方文物, 2010(4): 48–54.

Marcus, Joyce 2004. Maya Commoners: Stereotype and Reality. In *Ancient Maya Commoners*, edited by Jon C. Lohse and Fred Valdez, Jr., pp. 255–283. Austin: The University of Texas Press.

Murakami, Tatsuya 2019. Labor Mobilization and Cooperation for Urban Construction: Building Apartment Compounds at Teotihuacan. *Latin American Antiquity* 30(4), 2019: 741–759. Doi:10.1017/laq.2019.78

Nishie, Kiyotaka 西江清高, and Daisuke Kuji 久慈大介 2006. Cong Diyujian Guanxi Kan Erlitou Wenhuaqi Zhongyuan Wangchao De Kongjian Jiegou 从地域间关系看二里头文化期中原王朝的空间结构. In *Erlitou Yizhi Yu Erlitou Wenhua Yanjiu* 二里头遗址与二里头文化研究, edited by Jingpen Du 杜金鹏 and Hong Xu 许宏, pp. 444–456. Beijing: Kexue Chubanshe. pp. 444–456.

Peng, Junchao 彭军超 2019. Hebei Shangdai Nongye Kaogu Gaishu Jiantan Youguan Gaidiqu Qingtong Nongju Fazhan De Wenti 河北商代农业考古概述——兼谈有关该地区青铜农具发展的问题. *Nongye Kaogu* 农业考古. 2019(4): 153–157.

Peterson, Christian E., and Gideon Shelach 2010. The Evolution of Early Yangshao Period Village Organization in the Middle Reaches of Northern China's Yellow River Valley. In *Becoming Villagers: Comparing Early Village Societies*, edited by Matthew S. Bandy and Jake R. Fox, pp. 246–275. Tucson: University of Arizona Press.

Peterson, Christian E., and Gideon Shelach 2012. Jiangzhai: Social and Economic Organization of a Middle Neolithic Chinese Village. *Journal of Anthropological Archaeology*. 31(2012): 265–301. Doi:10.1016/j.jaa.2012.01.007

Peterson, Christian E., Xueming Lu, Robert D. Drennan, and Da Zhu 2017. Upper Daling Region Hongshan Household and Community Dataset: An Introduction. Comparative Archaeological Database, University of Pittsburgh. Http: www.cadb.pitt.edu. Access date: September 27, 2025.

Peterson, Christian E., Robert D. Drennan, and Kate L. Bartel. 2016. Comparative Analysis of Neolithic Household Artifact Assemblage Data from Northern China. *Journal of Anthropological Research*, 72 (2016) 2: 200–225.

Pollock, Susan 2003. Feasts, Funeral, and Fast Food in Early Mesopotamian States. in *The Archaeology and Politics of Food and Feasting in Early States and Empires*, edited by Tamara L. Bray, pp. 17–38. New York: Kluwer Academic/Plenum Publisher.

Poo, Mu-chou 1998. *In Search of Personal Welfare: A view of Ancient Chinese Religion*. Albany: State University of New York Press.

Pu, Muzhou 蒲慕州 2007. *Zhuixun Yiji Zhi Fu Zhongguo Gudai De Xinyang Shijie* 追寻一己之福：中国古代的信仰世界. Shanghai: Shanghai Guji Chubanshe.

Qian, Yihui 钱益汇, Guoliang Chen 陈国梁, Haitao Zhao 赵海涛, Hong Xu 许宏, and Li Liu 刘莉 2014. Zhongguo Zaoqi Guojia Jieduan Shiliao Laiyuan Yu Ziyuan Xuanze Celve Jiyu Erlitou Yizhi De Shiliao Fenxi 中国早期国家阶段石料来源与资源选择策略——基于二里头遗址的石料分析. *Kaogu* 考古. 2014(7): 86–95.

Qiao, Yu 乔玉 2010. Yiluo Diqu Peiligang Zhi Erlitou Wenhua Shiqi Fuza Shehui De Yanbian Dili Xinxi Xitong Jichu Shangde Renkou He Nongye Kegengdi Fenxi (Development of Complex Societies in the Yiluo Region: A GIS Based Population and Agricultural Area Analysis) 伊洛地区裴李岗至二里头文化时期复杂社会的演变——地理信息系统基础上的人口和农业可耕地分析. *Kaogu Xuebao* 考古学报. 2010(4): 423–454.

Qin, Xiaoli 秦小丽 2014. Zhongguo Gudai Xiangqian Gongyi Yu Lvsongshi Zhuangshipin 中国古代镶嵌工艺与绿松石装饰品. In *Xiashang Duyi Yu Wenhua vol.2* 夏商都邑与文化（二）, edited by Zhongguo Shehui Kexueyuan Kaogu Yanjiusuo 中国社会科学院考古研究所, pp. 296–326. Beijing: Zhongguo Shehui Kexue Chubanshe.

Qin, Xiaoli 秦小丽 2022. Erlitou Wenhua Shiqi Lvsongshi Shipin De Shengchan Yu Liutong 二里头文化时期绿松石饰品的生产与流通. *Zhongyuan Wenwu* 中原文物. 2022(2): 64–74.

Ran, Weiyu 2022. *Sustaining Ritual: Provisioning a Hongshan Pilgrimage Center at Niuheliang*. Unpublished PhD Dissertation, Department of Anthropology, University of Pittsburgh.

Reinhart, Katrinka 2015. Ritual Feasting and Empowerment at Yanshi Shangcheng. *Journal of Anthropological Archaeology*. 39 (2015): 76–109.

Shelach, Gideon 2006. Economic Adaptation, Community Structure, and Sharing Strategies of Households at

Early Sedentary Communities in Northeast China. *Journal of Anthropological Archaeology*, 25(2006): 318–345.

Shelach-Lavi, Gideon 2015. *The Archaeology of China: From Prehistory to Han Dynasty*. Cambridge: Cambridge University Press.

Shelach, Gideon., Kate Raphael and Yitzhak Jaffe 2011. Sanzuodian: The Structure, Function and Social Significance of the Earliest Stone Fortified Sites in China. *Antiquity*, 85(2011): 11–26.

Shelach, Gideon and Yitzhak Jaffe 2014. The Earliest States in China: A Long-term Trajectory Approach. *J. Archaeol Res*. Doi 10.1007/s10814–014-9074–8

Shi, Xiqi 时西奇 and Zhongwei Jing 井中伟 2018. Shangzhou Shiqi Daxing Cangchu Jianzhu Yicun Chuyi 商周时期大型仓储建筑遗存刍议. *Zhongguo Guojia Bowuguan Guankan* 中国国家博物馆馆刊, 2018(7): 6–16.

Smith, Michael E. 1987. Household Possessions and Wealth in Agrarian States: Implications for Archaeology. *Journal of Anthropological Archaeology*. 6, 297–335.

Song, Zhaolin 宋兆麟 1997. Shiqian Shiwu De Jiagong Jishu Lun Moju Yu Chujiu De Qiyuan 史前食物的加工技术——论磨具与杵臼的起源. *Nongye Kaogu* 农业考古. 1997(3): 187–195.

Spencer, Charles S., and Elsa M. Redmond 2006. Resistance Strategies and Early State Formation in Oaxaca, Mexico. In *Intermediate Elites in Pre-Colombian States and Empires*, edited by Christina M. Elson and R. Alan Covey, pp. 21–43. Tucson: The University of Arizona Press.

Spielmann, Katherine A. 2002. Feasting, Craft Specialization, and the Ritual Mode of Production in Small-Scale Societies. *American Anthropologist* 104:195–207.

Sterckx, Roel 2005. Introduction. In *Of Tripod and Palate: Food, Politics, and Religion in Traditional China*, edited by Roel Sterckx, pp. 1–8. New York: Palgrave Macmillan.

Sun, Qingli 孙青丽, Zhi Shuo 朔知, Yan Wu 吴妍, and Yimin Yang 杨益民 2019. Starch Grain Analysis of the Grooved Basin from the Lingjiatan Site, Hanshan County, Anhui Province 安徽含山凌家滩遗址出土刻槽盆的淀粉粒分析. *Renleixue Xuebao (Acta Anthropologica Sinica)* 人类学学报. 2019, Vol. 38, No. 1: 132–147. DOI:10.16359/j.cnki. cn11–1963/q.2018.0036

Tang, Jigen 唐际根 1998. Yinxu Jiazu Mudi Chutan 殷墟家族墓地初探. In *Zhongguo Shangwenhua Guoji Xueshu Taolunhui Lunwenji* 中国商文化国际学术讨论会, edited by Zhongguo Shehui Kexueyuan Kaogu Yanjiusuo 中国社会科学院考古研究所, pp. 201–207. Beijing: Zhongguo Dabaikequanshu Chubanshe.

Tang, Jigen. 2004. *The Social Organization of Late Shang China – A Mortuary Perspective*. Unpublished Doctoral Thesis, The University of London.

Tao, Dawei 陶大卫, Yimin Yang 杨益民, Weidong Huang 黄卫东, Yan Wu 吴妍, Yaoli Wu 吴耀利, and Changsui Wang 王昌燧 2009. Diaolongbei Yizhi Chutu Qiwu Canliu Dianfenli Fenxi 雕龙碑遗址出土器物残留淀粉粒分析. *Kaogu* 考古. 2009(9): 92–96.

Tokudome, Daisuke 德留大辅 2015. Cong Liqi Kan Erlitou Wenhua Gediqu Zhijian De Guanxi 从礼器看二里头文化各地区之间的关系. In *Sandai Kaogu (vol. 6)* 三代考古（六）, edited by Zhongguo Shehui Kexueyuan Kaogu Yanjiusuo 中国社会科学院考古研究所, pp. 130–162. Beijing: Kexue Chubanshe.

Tu, Cheng-sheng 杜正胜 1987. An Examination of the Origins and Early Development of the Central Plains States of Ancient China Based on Archaeological Data 从考古资料论中原国家的起源及其早期发展. In *Bulletin of the Institute of History and Philology Academia Sinica (Vol. 58, Part 1)* 中央研究院历史语言研究所集刊. 58(1), 1–81.

Underhill, Anne P. 1994. Variation in Settlements during the Longshan Period of Northern China. *Asian Perspectives*. 1994, Vol.33, No.2, Special Issue: Regional Perspectives on States in Asia, pp. 197–228.

Underhill, Anne P., Geoffrey E. Cunnar, Fengshi Luan, Gary Crawford, Haiguang Yu, Hui Fang, Fen Wang, and Hao Wu 2021. Urbanization in the eastern seaboard (Haidai) area of northern China: Perspectives from the late Neolithic site of Liangchengzhen. *Journal of Anthropological Archaeology*, 62(2021)101288. https://doi.org/10.1016/j.jaa.2021.101288.

Wang, Jianfeng 王建峰 and Zhongwei Jing 井中伟 2020. Yinxu Xiaomintun Zumudi Fenqu Yanjiu 殷墟孝民屯"族墓地"分区研究. *Journal of National Museum of China* 中国国家博物馆馆刊. 2020(1): 35–43.

Wang, Lihua 王丽华 2018. Yunnan Jiangchuan Guangfentou Yizhi Chutu Gujiaoyabang Zhipin Ji Gubiao Henji Yanjiu (*Research on Bone, Horn, Teeth, Mussel Artifacts and Marks on Animal Bones from Guangfentou Site Jiangchuan, Yunnan Province*) 云南江川光坟头遗址出土骨角牙蚌制品及骨表痕迹研究. Unpublished master's thesis, Yunnan University.

Wang, Lixin 王立新 2006. Cong Songshan Nanbei De Wenhau Zhenghe Kan Xiawangchao De Chuxian 从嵩山南北的文化整合看夏王朝的出现. In *Erlitou Yizhi Yu Erlitou Wenhua Yanjiu* 二里头遗址与二里头文化研究, edited by Jingpen Du 杜金鹏 and Hong Xu 许宏, pp. 410–426. Beijing: Kexue Chubanshe.

Wang, Qing 王青 2019. Shilong (Pt.1) Erlitou Yizhi Chutu Diaokelei Shenling Xingxiang De Fuyuan 释龙——二里头遗址出土雕刻类神灵形象的复原, In *Yuanfang Tuwu* 远方图物, Qing Wang 王青 (auth.), pp. 234–261. Shanghai: Shanghai Guji Chubanshe.

Wang, Renxiang 王仁湘 1990. Zhongguo Gudai Jinshiju Bizhucha Yanjiu 中国古代进食具匕箸叉研究. *Kaogu Xuebao* 考古学报. 1990(3): 267–294.

Wang, Yongbo 王永波 2002. Sixing Duanrenqi De Qiyuan Dingming He Yongtu (The Origin, Nomination and Use of the Spade-shaped object) 耜形端刃器的起源、定名和用途. *Kaogu Xuebao* 考古学报, 2002(2): 125–156.

Wang, Zhijun 王志俊 2000. Zhongguo Xinshiqi Shidai Renlei De Shiwu Yu Jinshi Gongju 中国新石器时代的食物与进食工具. *Shiqian Yanjiu* 史前研究. 2000: 440–450.

Wang, Zijin 王子今 2006. *Quanli De Heiguang* 权力的黑光. Xi'an: Shanxi Renmin Chubanshe.

Winter, Marcus C. 1976. The Archaeological Household Cluster in the Valley of Oaxaca. In *The Early Mesoamerican Village*, edited by Kent V. Flannery, pp. 25–31. New York: Academic Press.

Xian, Yiheng 先怡衡, Yun Liang 梁云, Jingyi Fan 樊静怡, Yanxiang Li 李延祥, Chun Yu 于春, Weike Bao 包伟柯, Chaowei Duan 段朝玮, and Rui Wen 温睿 2021. Luonan Hekou Yizhi Chuchan Lvsongshi Chandi Tezheng Yanjiu 洛南河口遗址出产绿松石产地特征研究. *Disiji Yanjiu (Quaternary Sciences)* 第四纪研究. 2021, 41(1): 284–291. doi:10.11928/j.issn.1001-7410.2021.01.26

Xiao, Yu 肖宇 2020. Shiqian Shiben jiqi Jianzhu Yiyi Kaocha 史前石锛及其建筑意义考察. *Journal of National Museum of China (Zhongguo Guojia Guowuguan Guankan)* 中国国家博物馆馆刊. 2020(1): 45–55.

Xie, Liye 谢礼晔 2008. Erlitou Yizhi Shifu He Shidao De Weihen Fenxi Weihen Fenxi Zai Mozhi Shiqi Gongneng Yanjiu Zhongde Chubu Changshi 二里头遗址石斧和石刀的微痕分析——微痕分析在磨制石器功能研究中的初步尝试. In *Zhongguo Zaoqi Qingtong Wenhua Erlitou Wenhua Zhuanti Yanjiu* 中国早期青铜文化：二里头文化专题研究, edited by Zhongguo Shehui Kexueyuan Kaogu Yanjiusuo 中国社会科学院考古研究所, pp. 355–469. Beijing: Kexue Chubanshe.

Xu, Fei 徐飞, Chung Tang 邓聪, and Xiaohong Ye 叶晓红 2018. Shiqian Yuqi Daxing Zuankong Jishu Shiyan Yanjiu史前玉器大型钻孔技术实验研究. *Cultural Relics of Central China* 中原文物. 2018(02): 57–64.

Xu, Hong 许宏 2009. *Zuizao De Zhongguo* 最早的中国. Beijing: Kexue Chubanshe.

Xu, Hong 许宏 2012. Erlitou Wenhua Juluo Dongtai Saomiao 二里头文化聚落动态扫描. In *Zaoqi Xiawenhua Yu Xianshang Wenhua Yanjiu Lunwenji* 早期夏文化与先商文化研究论文集, edited by Aurora Center for the Study of Ancient Civilizations, Beijing University 北京大学震旦古代文明研究中心, Henansheng Wenwu Kaogu Yanjiu 河南省文物考古研究所, Hebeisheng Wenwu Yanjiusuo 河北省文物研究所, and Zhengzhoushi Wenwu Kaogu Yanjiusuo 郑州市文物考古研究所, pp. 31–44. Beijing: Kexue Chubanshe.

Xu, Hong 许宏 2014. *Heyi Zhongguo Gongyuanqian 2000 Niande Zhongyuan Tujing* 何以中国：公元前2000年的中原图景. Beijing: SDX Joint Publishing Company.

Xu, Hong 许宏 2016a. *Dadu Wucheng*大都无城. Beijing: SDX Joint Publishing.

Xu, Hong 许宏 2016b. Erlitou M3 Ji Suizang Lvsongshi Longxingqi De Kaogu Beijing Fenxi 二里头M3及随葬绿松石龙形器的考古背景分析. In *Gudai Wenming*, vol. 10 古代文明(第 10 卷), edited by Beijing Daxue Zhongguo Kaoguxue Yanjiu Zhongxin 北京大学中国考古研究中心 and Beijing Daxue Zhendan Gudai Wenming Yanjiu Zhongxin 北京大学震旦古代文明研究中心, pp. 39–53. Shanghai: Shanghai Guji Chubanshe.

Xu, Hong 2018. Erlitou: The origin of the tradition of non-fortified primary capitals in early China. *Archaeological Research in Asia*. 14(2018): 71–79.

Xu, Hong 2022. *The Earliest China*. Singapore: Springer.

Xu, Hong 许宏, Guoliang Chen 陈国梁, and Haitao Zhao 赵海涛 2004. Erlitou Yizhi Juluo Xingtai De Chubu Kaocha 二里头遗址聚落形态的初步考察. *Kaogu* 考古, 2004(11): 23–31.

Xu, Jingjing 许晶晶, Jinbo Zhou 周金波, and Hailin Yi 乙海琳 2021. Jiangsu Dongtai Kaizhuang Yizhi Zhigu Shougongye Shixi (A Study of Bone Making Handicraft at the Kaizhuang Site in Dongtai, Jiangsu Province) 江苏东台开庄遗址制骨手工业试析. *Southeast Culture (Dongnan Wenhua)* 东南文化. 2021(3): 92–101.

Xu, Yongjie 许永杰 2017. Shiqian Sanzhong Liangshi Jiagong Gongju 史前三种粮食加工工具. *Dazhong Kaogu* 大众考古. 2017(9): 44–51.

Yan, Zhibin 严志斌 2020 Lacquer Gu, Round Pottery Sheets and Handle-Like Objects 漆觚、圆陶片与柄形器. *Journal of National Museum of China*. 2020(1): 6–22.

Yang, Hongxun 杨鸿勋 1982. Shifu Shixie Bian Jianji Shiben Yu Shibianchan 石斧石楔辨——兼及石锛与石扁铲. *Kaogu Yu Wenwu* 考古与文物. 1982(1): 66–68

Yang, Hongxun 杨鸿勋 2008. Yangshao Wenhua Juzhu Jianzhu Fazhan Wenti De Tantao 仰韶文化居住建筑发展问题的探讨, in *Yanghongxun Jianzhu Kaogu Lunwenji* 杨鸿勋建筑考古学论文集, Hongxun Yang 杨鸿勋 (auth.), pp. 15–48. Beijing: Qinghua Daxue Chubanshe.

Yang, Zhuhui 杨筑慧 2021. Quanyue Shikong De Shouge Gongju Hejian 穿越时空的收割工具——禾剪. *Nongye Kaogu* 农业考古. 2021(3): 121–129.

Ye, Wansong 叶万松 and Defang Li 李德方 2001. Yanshi Erlitou Yizhi Shouwen Tongpaishi Kaoshi 偃师二里头遗址兽纹铜牌考识. *Kaogu Yu Wenwu* 考古与文物, 2001(5): 40–48.

Ye, Wenkuan 叶文宽 1989. Leibo Yuanliu Kao 擂钵源流考. *Kaogu* 考古. 1989(5): 456–462.

Yin, Zhiqiang 殷志强 1986. Zhongguo Gudai Shifu Chulun 中国古代石斧初论. *Nongye Kaogu* 农业考古. 1986(1): 137–143.

Yu, Jinling 余金玲 2016. Luotuodun Yizhi Chutu Lujiao De Henji Guancha Yu Yanjiu Henji Shengcheng Fangshi De Moni Shiyan (*The Analytical Observations on The Patterns on Antlers Excavated from Luotuodun Site --- The Simulation Experiment of The Patterns' Generation*) 骆驼墩遗址出土鹿角的痕迹观察与研究——痕迹生成方式的模拟实验. Unpublished Master's Thesis, Nanjing University.

Zhang, Sulin 张素琳 2003. Yuanqu Gucheng Dongguan Miaodigou Erqi Wenhua Zhuangshipin He Yueqi De Chubu Yanjiu 垣曲古城东关庙底沟二期文化装饰品和乐器的初步研究. In *Zhongguo Shiqian Kaoguxue Yanjiu* 中国史前考古学研究, edited by Shaanxisheng Wenwuju 陕西省文物局, Shaanxisheng Kaogu Yanjiusuo 陕西省考古研究所, and Xi'an Banpo Bowuguan 西安半坡博物馆, pp. 296–307. Xi'an: Sanqin Chubanshe.

Zhao, Haitao 赵海涛 2020. Erlitou Duyi Juluo Xingtai Xinshi 二里头都邑聚落形态新识. *Kaogu* 考古. 2020(8): 109–120.

Zhao, Haitao 赵海涛 2022. Erlitou Duyi Buju He Shougongye Kaogu De Xinshouhuo 二里头都邑布局和手工业考古的新收获. *Huaxia Kaogu* 华夏考古. 2022(6): 62–67.

Zhao, Haitao 赵海涛 and Fei Zhang 张飞 2021. Erlitou Duyi De Shougongye Kaogu 二里头都邑的手工业考古. *Nanfang Wenwu* 南方文物. 2021(2): 126–131.

Zhao, Zhijun 赵志军, and Chang Liu 刘昶 2019. Yanshi Erlitou Yizhi Fuxuan Jieguo De Fenxi He Taolun (Analysis and Discussion on Flotation Results from the Erlitou Site in Yanshi City) 偃师二里头遗址浮选结果的分析和讨论. *Nongye Kaogu* 农业考古. 2019(6): 7–20.

Zheng, Ruokui 郑若葵 1995. YInxu Dayishang Zuyi Buju Chutan 殷墟"大邑商"族邑布局初探. *Zhongyuan Wenwu* 中原文物. 1995(3): 84–93.

Zhongguo Shehui Kexueyuan Kaogu Yanjiusuo 中国社会科学院考古研究所, Zhongguo Lishi Bowuguan 中国历史博物馆, and Shanxisheng Kaogu Yanjiusuo 山西省考古研究所 1988. *Xiaxian Dongxiafeng* 夏县东下冯. Beijing: Wenwu Chubanshe.

Zhongguo Shehui Kexueyuan Kaogu Yanjiusuo 中国社会科学院考古研究所 1995. *Cream of the Pottery Erlitou* 二里头陶器集萃. Beijing: China Social Sciences Publishing House.

Zhongguo Shehui Kexueyuan Kaogu Yanjiusuo 中国社会科学院考古研究所 1999. *Yanshi Erlitou* 偃师二里头. Beijing: The Encyclopedia of China Publishing House.

Zhongguo Shehui Kexueyuan Kaogu Yanjiusuo 中国社会科学院考古研究所 2003. *Zhongguo Kaoguxue: Xiashang Juan* 中国考古学·夏商卷. Beijing: Zhongguo shehui Kexue Chubanshe.

Zhongguo Shehui Kexueyuan Kaogu Yanjiusuo 中国社会科学院考古研究所 2014. *Erlitou: 1999–2006* 二里头：1999–2006. Beijing: Wenwu Chubanshe.

Zhongguo Shehui Kexueyuan Kaogu Yanjiusuo 中国社会科学院考古研究所 2019. *Erlitou Kaogu Liushi Nian* 二里头考古六十年. Beijing: Zhongguo Shehui Kexue Chubanshe.

Zhongguo Shehui Kexueyuan Kaogu Yanjiusuo 中国社会科学院考古研究所, and Zhongaomei Yiluohe Liuyu Lianhe Kaogudui 中澳美伊洛河流域联合考古队 (eds.). 2019. *Luoyang Pendi Zhongdongbu Xianqin Shiqi Yizhi 1997–2007 Nian Quyu Xitong Diaocha Baogao* 洛阳盆地中东部先秦时期遗址：1997–2007年区域系统调查报告. Beijing: Kexue Chubanshe.

Zhongguo Shehui Kexueyuan Kaogu Yanjiusuo Erlitoudui 中国社会科学院考古研究所二里头队 1983. 1980 Nian Qiu Henan Yanshi Erlitou Yizhi Fajue Jianbao 1980年秋河南偃师二里头遗址发掘简报. *Kaogu* 考古, 1983(3): 199–205.

Zhongguo Shehui Kexueyuan Kaogu Yanjiusuo Erlitoudui 中国社会科学院考古研究所二里头队 1985. 1982 Nian Qiu Yanshi Erlitou Yizhi Jiuqu Fajue Jianbao 1982年秋偃师二里头遗址九区发掘简报. *Kaogu* 考古, 1985(12): 1085–1194.

Zhongguo Shehui Kexueyuan Kaogu Yanjiusuo Erlitou Gongzuodui 中国社会科学院考古研究所二里头工作队. 2005. Henan Luoyang Pendi 2001–2003 Nian Kaogu Diaocha Jianbao 河南洛阳盆地 2001–2003年考古调查简报. *Kaogu* 考古. 2005(5), 18–37.

Zhongguo Shehui Kexueyuan Kaogu Yanjiusuo Henan Diyi Gongzuodui 中国社会科学院考古研究所河南第一工作队 2010. Henan Yanshishi Huizui Yizhi Xizhi 2004 Nian Fajue Jianbao 河南偃师市灰嘴遗址西址2004年发掘简报. *Kaogu* 考古, 2010(2): 36–46.

Zhu, Fenghan 朱凤瀚 2004. *Shangzhou Jiazu Xingtai Yanjiu* 商周家族形态研究. Tianjin: Tianjin Guji Chubanshe.

Zou, Heng邹衡 1980. *Xiashangzhou Kaoguxue Lunwenji* 夏商周考古学论文集. Beijing: Wenwu Chubanshe.